THE HIGHEST STAGE OF
WHITE SUPREMACY

THE HIGHEST
STAGE OF
WHITE SUPREMACY

THE ORIGINS OF SEGREGATION IN SOUTH AFRICA AND THE AMERICAN SOUTH

JOHN W. CELL
DEPARTMENT OF HISTORY, DUKE UNIVERSITY

CAMBRIDGE UNIVERSITY PRESS

CAMBRIDGE
LONDON NEW YORK NEW ROCHELLE
MELBOURNE SYDNEY

1982

Published by the Press Syndicate of the University of Cambridge
The Pitt Building, Trumpington Street, Cambridge CB2 1RP
32 East 57th Street, New York, NY 10022, USA
296 Beaconsfield Parade, Middle Park, Melbourne 3206, Australia

First published 1982

Printed in the United States of America

Library of Congress Cataloging in Publication Data
Cell, John Whitson,
The highest stage of white supremacy.
Includes bibliographical references and
index.
1. South Africa – Race relations.
2. Segregation – South Africa. 3. Segregation –
Southern States. 4. Southern States – Race
relations. 5. Afro-Americans – Southern States –
Segregation. I. Title.
DT763.C36   305.8′00968   82–4312
ISBN 0 521 24096 4 hard covers   AACR2
ISBN 0 521 27061 8 paperback

For GERALD W. HARTWIG   1935–1980

Contents

Preface

In this book I compare the evolving matrix of race and class relations in two societies that are widely regarded as being the most
pervasively racist in the world, South Africa and the Southern
United States. My particular concern is the origins of the system
and ideology called segregation, which emerged in mature form
in the American South after about 1890 and in South Africa
around the time of the Union of 1910. Segregation in my view
should be distinguished from the broader ethos of white supremacy, of which segregation is a distinct form. Unlike slavery or
serfdom, which are characterized by vertical forms of domination – white over black – the lines of authority in segregation are
primarily horizontal, depending not only on the direct exercise
of force and personal intimidation but on some degree of accommodation and tacit acceptance on the part of those whom it is
designed to control.

Although it owed much to the white supremacist past of slavery and the frontier, segregation was not merely a direct continuation of previous forms of social relations and control. As a
system, if not in all of its particular parts, it was essentially new.
As I explain in the first chapter, the histories of South Africa and
the American South, and in particular the white supremacist cultures that were the products of those histories, would account
for all sorts of "solutions" other than the path that was taken.
The study of the origins of segregation therefore involves not so
much the search for harbingers and precedents as it does the
analysis of the particular circumstances and forces to which
the new system was a response. My book centers on the period
1890–1925.

Segregation has often been interpreted as the stubborn persistence into the capitalist era of the "irrational" legacy of the past. On the contrary, I argue, segregation was closely associated with what we commonly regard as indexes of modernization: with cities and towns, with the early stages of industrialization, with class and state (or party) formation. Its ideology was created on the whole by well-educated and comparatively moderate men as an apparently attractive alternative to more extreme forms of white supremacy. The subtlety and sophistication of these founding fathers should not be underestimated. As an ideology and system of race and class relations, segregation has demonstrated – and continues to demonstrate in South Africa – an impressive capacity for absorption, flexibility, and mystification. It was, to paraphrase the title of a famous book by Lenin, the highest stage of white supremacy.

As the reader will discover, this book is not based on extensive archival research but on a combination of secondary and contemporary published sources. Among other things it is a comparison of how historians of South Africa and the American South have analyzed the origins and evolution of segregation. I hope that, by examining historiography, I have contributed something to history.

My own background is that of a student of British imperialism, and I happened onto this subject in the course of work on a longer and still unfinished project on British thought about Africa between the two world wars. One of the main currents in the British discourse was segregation, which intertwined confusingly with indirect rule; and the effort to understand that interaction led me more deeply than I had expected into South African sources. At that point I had done very little systematic reading of American history. In the South African materials, however, I found not only many interesting comparisons with the racially discriminatory society in which I had lived for more than forty years but also a clear and important, though certainly not determinative, link between the two evolving systems of segregation. I first tried to bring the two cases together in a paper at St. Antony's College, Oxford, where I was a visiting fellow in 1978. I then tried to write an article. But the subject had already gone far beyond that, and it would not go away.

When this book was accepted for publication nearly a year ago, there had been virtually no systematic comparison of American and South African history since Maurice Evans's *Black and White in the Southern States* (1915). Since then, while I was working on revisions, three important books have appeared. For obvious reasons, I avoided reading them thoroughly until my own work was completed. Also for obvious reasons, I did not overload my footnotes with detailed references to our many points of agreement or our occasional disagreements.

George Fredrickson's *White Supremacy: A Comparative Study on American and South African History* (New York: Oxford University Press, 1981) strikes me as a wise, imaginative, and very sound work whose extremely warm critical reception is fully justified. I particularly admire Fredrickson's grasp of the broad contours of South African and American frontier history, his perceptive analysis of the very important differences between the cases of blacks in America and Africans in South Africa, and his emphasis on the high degree of mixing that went on between Afrikaners and Khoikhoi in the Cape Colony until well into the nineteenth century. I am reassured to find that we have not only a great many points of agreement but that we have relatively little overlap. The reason is our one important disagreement: the relative degree of emphasis that we place on the slave and frontier past in explaining the evolution of race relations in the twentieth century.

Fredrickson's canvas is much broader than mine, and to me that is his book's greatest strength. His concern is with white supremacy in general, not with the specific system of segregation. He believes that in South Africa segregation was present in reasonably clear outline in the minds and in much of the practice of "trekking" Afrikaners as early as the 1830s, and that it grew organically and rather spontaneously out of previous forms of domination. For America as well his emphasis is on evolution rather than revolution. I believe instead that, in both societies, segregation *as a system* was essentially new and that it was an act of *creation*. Fredrickson devotes several chapters to the long span before the late nineteenth century. I deal with that period in a few pages, not because I regard it as unimportant or uninteresting but because I believe it has relatively little to do with the origins of segregation. Both American and South African historians, of course, have been arguing just this question for some time. Our two books are unlikely to settle it.

Stanley Greenberg's *Race and State in Capitalist Development: Comparative Perspectives* (New Haven: Yale University Press, 1980) is the second work with which my book will inevitably be compared. A political scientist, Greenberg provides an incisive theoretical critique of the literature on modernization (including traditional Marxism), plural societies, and what he calls primordialism, concluding that none of the prevailing approaches satisfactorily accounts for the persistence of discrimination in societies that experience rapid growth and change. This critique he supports with detailed case studies of South Africa and Alabama, along with shorter examinations of Israel and Northern Ireland. Capitalism, he argues, did not act as a solvent, as much of the literature had predicted. Instead it intensified race relations. For the same class actors who controlled the building and shaping of capitalism – large farmers, businessmen (particularly those in extractive industries), and white workers who were both organized and "bounded" from their black competitors – had vested class interests in maintaining and reinforcing racial discrimination. To me the book's most valuable contribution is the extensive documentation on these particular class actors. Greenberg proves, for instance, what I have only suggested: that large farmers' demands for cheap, plentiful black labor close at hand – the very opposite of the proclaimed program of territorial segregation or apartheid – persisted into the 1950s in Alabama and even later in South Africa.

Although Greenberg's general thesis is in some ways very close to my own argument, our books have important differences in emphasis and coverage. First, although Greenberg does have a good deal of important material on who or what was urging segregation, he does not pay much attention to segregation as an ideological umbrella that enabled whites to agree while continuing to conflict. Second, he does not identify segregation as a program first proposed by moderates, rather than by the extremists with whom it eventually came to be associated. Third, the selection of his two primary case studies – Alabama, a state; South Africa, a country (why not Alabama and the Transvaal?) – means that Greenberg has avoided many of the very difficult problems of the history and historiography of "the South." Fourth, like Fredrickson, and perhaps very wisely, Greenberg does not deal with the impact of segregation on the segregated. Dissatisfied as I am with how far I myself have been able to pursue that theme, I understand the reticence. But, it seems, I could not or would not avoid the problem.

The third book, a symposium volume edited by Howard Lamar and Leonard Thompson, *The Frontier in History: North America and Southern Africa Compared* (New Haven: Yale University Press, 1981), has a great deal of overlap with Fredrickson's work but virtually none with mine. The reason for this is the editors' judgment that to a large degree the histories of race relations on the frontier and in the post-frontier era are separate and distinct. "The termination of the process [of struggle for control of the frontier contact zone]," write the editors,

> is most clearly indicated by political events – that is to say, when one group establishes political control over the other. Once that has been done, the frontier ceases to exist. This does not mean that the relations between the inhabitants then become static, but rather that *a new structural situation has been created* and that the ongoing historical process is no longer a frontier process. Subsequent relationships are relations of ethnicity and class within a single society, not frontier relationships between different societies. [p. 10; my italics]

With this view, which stresses discontinuity, I strongly concur. The same judgment would also apply, I believe, to the histories of slavery and segregation.

Whereas only a few years ago I felt myself being pulled into a historiographical vacuum, there are now four systematic comparisons of white supremacy in South Africa and the American South. After a great deal of methodological discussion, as well as some outstanding pioneering ventures, comparative history is apparently becoming routine.

I have to acknowledge with gratitude the financial support I have received over the years from the Social Science Research Council, the National Endowment for the Humanities, St. Antony's College, Oxford, and Duke University. The readers for

Cambridge University Press provided me with penetrating and valuable criticisms, which I hope I have met. I am particularly grateful to colleagues in American history: William Chafe, Raymond Gavins, Lawrence Goodwyn, Donald and Jane Mathews, Sydney Nathans, John Salmond, Anne Scott, Donald Scott, Richard Watson, and Peter Wood. I have profited much from criticisms and help from present and former Duke students, notably Carolyn Conley, Elizabeth Lunbeck, Mary Rayner, and Kenneth Vickery. Sherman and Jackie James gave me extremely helpful reactions. At a very taxing period in her own professional life, my wife Gillian discussed the work with me extensively and shared the frustrations. So did our children: Thomas, Katherine, and John. I am dedicating the book to the memory of my colleague in African history and my very close friend, Gerald W. Hartwig.

September 1981   J. W. C.

1. The problem of segregation

According to Webster's *Intercollegiate Dictionary,* segregation is "the separation of a race, class, or ethnic group by enforced or voluntary residence in a restricted area, by barriers to social intercourse, by separate educational facilities, or by other discriminatory means." And a segregationist is one who favors such separation. Although the separation may be voluntary, the compilers assume that it is ordinarily not. The words "enforced," "barriers," and "other discriminatory means" all imply inequality and deprivation imposed and maintained by force. Moreover, according to common usage, a segregated society is one whose institutions, mores, and beliefs are literally permeated by wholesale discrimination. An American reader, at least, would recognize this definition as useful and accurate. Embodied in those few words is the tortured experience of the reader's own country.

In the *Oxford English Dictionary,* the relevant "S" volume of which was compiled between 1908 and 1914, we find that this definition of segregation is comparatively recent. Several citations are given, some going back as far as the seventeenth century. But they refer mainly to religion or to the natural sciences. Even in the case of a reference to the *British Medical Journal* of 1904 – "Manson has also declared segregation to be the first law of hygiene for the European in the tropics" – the reader must supply the missing social and historical context. One must know that the "sanitation syndrome" was frequently used as a pretext for creating exclusive living and recreational facilities for Europeans throughout the colonial empires, even in countries such as

1

Nigeria or Malaya, where the European presence was proportionately minuscule.[1]

In the history of race relations segregation is what Raymond Williams calls a key word.[2] It is a term like those – state, nation, sovereignty – that evolved in the three centuries after 1500 to embody dominant European political trends: absolutism, the rise of the nation-state, the bourgeois and democratic revolutions. It is a word like those – factory, industry, class, capitalism – that were either invented or greatly modified so that nineteenth-century Britons and Americans might discuss the far-reaching and disturbing consequences of the rapid alteration of the mode of production and of social relations in their societies. Clusters of key words reflect the emergence of new social forces or the acceleration of older ones. More precisely, they reveal the conscious recognition and identification of those forces. Together they define the boundaries of a terrain of discourse and controversy.

Segregation is an even more overriding term. It is a word like "culture" in Williams's seminal book, *Culture and Society:* a term not easily defined, ambiguous and self-contradictory. Culture is both the maintenance of high standards of excellence (as in literature) and the way of life of a whole society (as in anthropology). Yet, as Matthew Arnold in the nineteenth century and T. S. Eliot in the twentieth argued forcefully, those definitions and the social aims they imply are in conflict. High standards are essentially elitist. The gradual enlightenment or improvement of the whole society must therefore necessarily result in cultural deterioration. Culture, then, is not merely a key word. It is the centerpiece of a long and unfinished debate, a clue to what Carl Becker and other intellectual historians have called climates of opinion and to what Marxists call mystification and ideology.

Like culture, the term "segregation" is profoundly ambiguous and self-contradictory. It is many things. Simultaneously it is a conscious policy, a process (by definition never completed), a system, and an ideology. It is both discrimination imposed by force and – or so its proponents have often declared – a positive, humane approach to one of mankind's most intractable problems, enabling each group to develop to its highest potential, at its own pace, in its own way, maintaining its distinctive cultural values. I shall argue that this state of ambiguity and contradiction was skillfully and very deliberately created. Confusion has been one of segregation's greatest strengths and achievements.

The *OED*'s surprising omission therefore provides an important clue to the problem of the origins, dynamics, and course of segregation in South Africa and the American South. The present usage *is* comparatively recent, having become current in the United States only after 1890 and in South Africa about a decade later.

I do not intend to imply that before those two dates these two societies had not discriminated against people of color. Both of them had done so, in extremely systematic fashion, ever since their founding as settlement colonies in the seventeenth century. Nor does the omission imply that either society had ever been integrated in any sense. In practice, in both societies, the races had always been largely separated. What I do mean to argue is that before the turn of the century, "segregation" in its modern sense had not entered the English language and that rapid adoption of the word in the decade or so after 1900 signals that race relations in both societies had entered an important new phase.

The novelty of segregation must therefore be sharply qualified. Obviously, the construction of discriminatory systems that were so pervasive and totalitarian that they call to mind Marc Bloch's definition of European feudalism as a "state of society"[3] could not have been accomplished with wholly new materials. Segregation was a phase, the highest stage, in the evolution of white supremacy. The forces that created it had developed mainly in the past. Only in the twentieth century, however, did the conception of segregation as something more than the mere physical separation of peoples enter the English language and hence become conscious thought. The coining of such an ambiguous, contradictory key word is a clue not so much to new conditions or practices as it is to growing consciousness, synthesis, and ideological crystallization.

The driving force, the ultimate cause, behind segregation was white racism. In both South Africa and the American South color prejudice was very old. It had been imported in the minds and psyches of the earliest European settlers, who could hardly have escaped it. The association of blackness with all things evil, ugly, and satanic and of whiteness with all things pure, beautiful, and godly was fundamental to their psychology, to the way medieval and early-modern Europeans (especially northern Europeans) perceived and organized the world.[4] In the conditions of southern Africa and northern America this color syndrome acquired immediacy and relevance. Unconscious associations could be projected upon groups of people who were at the same time different, exploitable, and dangerously competitive. It was in the settlers' interest to attack and dominate them. In these circumstances color prejudice was transformed into racism, which permeated thought, mores, institutions, and social relations.

In both countries, ever since the seventeenth century, racism had been eminently functional. It had legitimized slavery. It had supported long assaults against antagonists on the opposite sides of moving frontiers. Servitude and the Darwinian struggle for existence both became more acceptable to conscience when the victims could be identified as subhuman.[5] Virtually essential for the creation and survival of "white man's countries" in regions that were already inhabited, racism had been a fundamental component in the evolution of both societies.

Racism would have made difficult or even impossible the establishment around the turn of the century of truly democratic, nondiscriminatory systems of good race relations in either South Africa or the American South. Yet racism would account for a wide range of conceivable alternatives – extermination, the reimposition of slavery, deportation – that were not in fact undertaken. It follows that racism alone cannot be a necessary and sufficient explanation of any particular form of discrimination. The explanation of how and why segregation developed must therefore lie in a conjunction of racism with other forces and processes, which ruled out some alternatives and which made segregation appear to be the natural and even inevitable solution to what was called in America the Negro Problem and in South Africa the Native Question.

In the 1930s liberal commentators in both societies regarded segregation as a temporary phenomenon, an anachronistic survival from earlier, more primitive stages of evolution, the product of rural, preindustrial, economically backward conditions that were being left behind. Fundamentally incompatible with the imperatives of a modern, urban, industrial economy, both segregation and the race prejudice that fed it would be doomed to comparatively rapid obsolescence. "The race relations cycle," concluded Robert E. Park, one of the founders of the Chicago school of American sociology, "– contact, competition, accommodation, and eventual assimilation – is apparently irreversible." As it had proved to be throughout history, the city would once more become the irresistible vehicle of social change and political evolution. Prejudice, that still potent survival from rural exploitation and dominance, would be dissolved in the urban melting pot. Race would be superseded by class. For American blacks the "great migration" after 1915 to the Northern cities would be decisive: "America and, perhaps, the rest of the world, can be divided between two classes: those who reached the city, and those who have not yet arrived."[6]

Gunnar Myrdal, the great Swedish economist whom the Carnegie Corporation chose in the 1930s to direct a massive survey of the Negro Problem – a work that was to play such a significant role in preparing the intellectual climate for the Supreme Court's historic *Brown* decision of 1954 – also predicted that segregation would be a temporary phenomenon. Although not without trauma and violence, Myrdal concluded, the structure of systematic discrimination that had been built up over the centuries would be dismantled. In this process, however, the primary role would be played not by economic or demographic forces but by those that lay within the American value system. Segregation, the insidious nature of which Myrdal analyzed in such exhaustive detail, blatantly contradicted the highest ideals of the world's largest and greatest democracy. Particularly as the United States attempted to assert its support for the struggle of the colored peoples of the world against colonialism, its exclusion of over one-tenth of its citizens from full civil and political rights would prove increasingly embarrassing. Segregation must and would be eliminated because it contradicted the American Dream.[7]

South Africa's white liberal historians – notably W. M. Macmillan, Eric Walker, C. W. De Kiewiet, the Australian Sir Keith Hancock, and more recently Leonard Thompson – were much more cautious. With a significant watershed occurring in 1936, when the Cape Province's African voters were disfranchised, segregation was obviously still on the rise. So was its apparent primary cause, the insurgent and as yet far-from-satiated force of Afrikaner nationalism.

For liberal historians the most significant fact, and the central problem, of South African history was the remarkable persistence of the Afrikaner mentality and national character. In accounting for it they weighed inheritance and environment. They stressed the rigid Calvinism that the Dutch and French Huguenot settlers had brought with them in the seventeenth century; their almost total isolation from the liberalizing currents of European thought in the eighteenth and early nineteenth centuries; their development of the habit of dominance over colored slaves; their defiant rejection of British liberal humanitarianism in their Great Trek of the 1830s; their constitutions in the Orange Free State and the Transvaal Republic, bluntly specifying "no equality in church and state"; their long struggle against both the harsh physical environment and the fierce resistance of Bantu-speaking Africans; the unification of all these strands into nationalism under the pressure of the British "imperial factor"; and the final hardening of Afrikaner reaction in the crucible of the Boer War. The history of the Afrikaner people was thus a succession of powerfully formative experiences. None of them, perhaps, was inevitable. But each made the outcome of the next more predictable. As Afrikaner nationalism gained impetus, so South Africa's Native Policy became ever more extreme. Segregation was thus the logical conclusion of the Afrikaner people's peculiar history.[8]

To be sure, liberal historians agreed, English-speaking whites shared the Afrikaner ethos. Natalian sugar planters had exploited and discriminated against Indians. Johannesburg's mining magnates had done the same, and on a larger scale, against Africans. Sir Keith Hancock reserved some of his most biting irony for the English-speaking labor unions, whose notable contribution of the industrial color bar must not be overlooked when patriotic white South African historians came to record the heroic struggle through which an alien egalitarian influence had been driven from their beloved land.[9]

The prejudices of Britons overseas were unattractive. Because they had not been formed by the same process that had shaped

Afrikaner attitudes, they were even less excusable. But English-speaking whites had remained in touch with the liberalizing currents of British and world opinion. Culturally they were on the defensive. By the 1930s they were no longer in political control.

The correlation between segregation and the insurgence of the Afrikaners was apparently clear and direct. To many observers it still is. In Afrikaner nationalism, white supremacy had become a positive ideology, unapologetic and unblushing. This force gave South African race relations their unique character. It accounted for the remarkably persistent power of anachronism. In the series of formative experiences since 1652 a solid base of discriminatory attitudes and practices had been built up, institutionalized in slavery over Malays and Khoikhoi, and then applied to relations with Bantu-speaking Africans. Thereafter, as African participation in the European market and industrial economy had increased, the policy of segregation had been extended: layer upon layer, dimension after dimension.

Like contemporary Americans, liberal South Africans perceived segregation as a legacy of prejudice that had survived from an isolated, rural, frontier past. First formed in a simple, undifferentiated, unindustrialized economy, segregation would become increasingly anachronistic as the society developed. The forces that were breaking down the lines of caste and class elsewhere in the world would, it might be hoped, gradually dissolve them even in South Africa. Ultimately segregation would be – and would be seen to be – fundamentally incompatible with the needs of modern industrial capitalism. Then, in time, it might disappear.

As Keynesian economists argued in the 1930s, the most important factor in the healthy development of any economy was an expanding home market. South Africa's had scarcely been tapped. Increasing consumption by the African majority would stimulate secondary industries and services. Improving African living standards would raise the prosperity of all. As industry became more sophisticated the color bar would become increasingly inconvenient, inefficient, and expensive. Presumably, at some point, anything that stood in the way of the "rational" development of capitalism would dissolve. In particular, as Afrikaners moved into cities and into industrial jobs, as they became more prosperous and better educated, it might be supposed that they would become more tolerant.

We are less sanguine now. In the United States the legal edifice of segregation has indeed been largely dismantled, and partially for reasons that Myrdal, Park, and other liberals predicted: the changing climate of American (especially Northern) opinion, the embarrassment of blatant domestic discrimination for American foreign policy, the large increase of black voters in the North during and after World War II, and, most important, the struggle of blacks themselves for civil liberties and political rights. Driven by these forces, desegregation developed momentum, often going far beyond the wishes of individual presidents or heads of the Department of Justice. Federal intervention overcame the campaign for states' rights. Disproving countless predictions that desegregation would fail unless it were voluntary, the power of the national state changed folkways.

Few, however, now conceive that the Negro Problem, especially its socioeconomic aspects, is close to being resolved. The problem, we now realize, depends comparatively little on individual attitudes and much more on the racism that is ingrained in institutions. Successive efforts to break the cycle of poverty, poor education, low expectations, and low achievement have so far largely failed. The most significant change has been a widening of geographical focus. Racism is now a national and not merely Southern problem. Particularly in the large cities, North and South, there is more residential segregation now than there was in the 1950s. Some blacks are moving into the middle class, but then some so-called exceptions always did. In aggregate statistics the gaps between white and black in education, salaries, unemployment, and standards of living are being reduced very slowly even in times of prosperity. In periods of recession the gaps widen perceptibly again.

In South Africa the long run to which liberals of the 1930s looked with hope has become increasingly remote. The modernization of the economy, which they counted on so heavily, has happened. The country is no longer backward, no longer dependent on European industrial production. Although it remains very significant as an earner of foreign exchange, the mining sector is not the single great engine from which secondary industries spin off. Except for oil, in which South Africa as a nonproducer is in company with such industrial giants as Japan and West Germany, the economy is largely self-sufficient. The white population is overwhelmingly urban, with less than ten percent employed in agriculture. Even the vast majority of Afrikaners live in town. The "last trek" has been completed. The poor-white problem has been solved.

Yet only the white half of the cycle of development has taken place. The living standards of the large majority of Africans have improved only slightly, if at all. In the 1930s their population was six million. It has since more than trebled. But the portion of territory that is demarcated as Bantu homelands remains precisely what it was under the Natives Land Act of 1913: less than thirteen percent.[10] Even before World War II, according to the Native Economic Commission of 1932, the African reserves were hopelessly eroded and overcrowded. Increasingly, as liberals predicted, Africans have perforce taken jobs in so-called white areas. Most of them remain in unskilled positions at very low pay. But there are increasing exceptions: individual Africans in skilled positions, breaches of the job color bar. The consequences that were presumed to follow from industrialization, however, have not occurred. What is impressive is the South African economy's ability to incorporate growing numbers of skilled African workers while continuing to maintain a persistent pattern of discrimination.

Still less has the "rational" development of industrial capitalism produced the anticipated liberalization of South African politics. Indeed, political and economic trends seem to have been running in opposite directions. After 1948, when the Nationalist Party began its uninterrupted ascendancy in power, segregation hardened into apartheid. In a long series of acts – the Group Areas Act, the Bantu Education Act, the Natives (Abolition of Passes and Co-ordination of Documents) Act, the latter being a bill that emphatically did not abolish passes – what nationalist politicians called the laxity of mere segregation has been tightened with unprecedented thoroughness. Under the Suppression of Communism Act of 1950, all effective African political organizations (including the Pan African Congress, the African National Congress, and most recently the black consciousness movement) have been banned as statutory Communists, their leaders placed under house arrest, incarcerated, or (in hundreds of "suicides" or deaths under interrogation for which no responsibility could be determined) worse. Until the mid-1960s, at least, apartheid steadily became more thorough, more efficient, and more severe.

Since then, the system has in some ways softened again, into what is now called separate development. Beginning with the Transkei, some homelands (which still remain less than thirteen percent of the land) have become "independent." Even in white areas there have been indications or promises of some relaxation, principally in sport, and perhaps some recognition of African trade unions. On the whole, however, Leonard Thompson's masterful survey, completed in 1965, remains depressingly current.[11] The millions of Africans who live and work permanently in white areas continue to be regarded and treated as transient aliens, as are Turks or Italians in Germany: They must carry identity passes, they can be returned to the homelands if they become "redundant" (or for no reason at all), and they lack the votes and rights of citizens.

Because the Nationalist Party did emerge as the spearhead of right-wing Afrikaners, with heavy reliance on rural votes in its early victories, many students have maintained the liberal interpretation in much the same terms as had their predecessors of the 1930s. There are good reasons for their doing so. Only since South Africa's departure from the Commonwealth in 1962 have large numbers of English-speaking whites supported nationalist candidates. Most of the leading politicians, most of the police, and of course all of the members of the influential secret society called the Broederbond continue to be Afrikaners. But in the face of the continuing ability of the economy to modernize while persisting in discrimination, both the argument that segregation runs against the economic grain and the hope that it is therefore doomed to collapse someday from internal causes have become increasingly less credible.

Thus the course of South African history since World War II has strongly favored structural interpretations, which place less emphasis on the remote frontier past and stress instead the integral, organic, perhaps even essential role of racial exploitation in the country's modernization. If these analyses are correct, then the prediction that segregation will eventually fade away like some quaint museum piece is dangerously mistaken.

As Pierre Van den Berghe has reminded us in an excellent if necessarily outdated survey, the mixing of white and black (or brown, red, or yellow) in the same society has by no means always produced the same results. Comparing race relations across a broad spectrum – from societies like Mexico that apparently are successfully integrated; through those like Cuba, Jamaica, or Brazil, where, in his opinion, race relations over the last century have been comparatively tolerant; to those of South Africa and the American South, in which extreme racial hostility exists – Van den Berghe argues that all systems fall between two poles or ideal types. These he calls the paternalist and the competitive.[12]

Of the two the paternalist has been much more prevalent. It is, or used to be, found in most of the settlement colonies of Africa – Kenya and Rhodesia until the 1950s, the Portuguese colonies of Angola and Mozambique until the 1960s – in the Caribbean, and in South America. It is characterized by a preindustrial economy, which concentrates on one or two cash crops for export, such as sugar, tobacco, or coffee. Social mobility, both horizontal and vertical, is limited. The white ruling class is small, indeed numerically insignificant. The large subordinate caste is typically composed of slaves, indigenous forced labor, serfs, or subsistence peasants. In standards of living, in social status, and in law, extremely wide gaps separate the two castes. In part for that very reason – because the superior caste's hegemony appears to be secure – concubinage, miscegenation, and other forms of interracial contact are frequent. In such a society an aristocratic government aims to maintain the status quo. Among the dominant group there is a constant but not necessarily aggressive racist ideology, which stresses the innate, childlike inferiority of the subordinate caste and its need for guidance and protection.

In such paternalist societies violence is usually initiated from below in the form of peasant risings or slave revolts. On such occasions the ruling class, who typically feel themselves betrayed by ungrateful servants for whom they have done so much, may retaliate savagely. If their repression succeeds, the storm passes and the paternalist regime is reestablished. If the revolution is accomplished, however, its triumph is swift and conclusive. The white ruling class undergoes a sudden, traumatic transformation. Because the ideology of dominance no longer fits the facts, it evaporates, leaving salty traces such as the wry jokes old Kenya hands used to tell about having the Kaffirs be prime minister. Within a short time most whites leave. Those who remain adjust with remarkable ease to their new status as marginal, politically powerless, but still probably comfortable members of a black society. For most of the subordinate caste, however, for those whom Frantz Fanon called "the wretched of the earth," the revolution changes little. They continue to be the deprived, powerless citizens of an underdeveloped country.

At the other end of the spectrum of race relations is what Van den Berghe calls the competitive model, found in South Africa, in the American South, and (until the revolution of the 1950s) in Algeria. It is characterized by a comparatively sophisticated, industrializing economy, a relatively complex division of labor, and a high level of social mobility. The dominant race is either a majority or a proportionately significant minority. Between the two races the gap in economic position and social status is wide, but not so wide as in the paternalist model. However, the range and degree of personal contact across racial lines are also much less frequent. There is segregation, both de facto and de jure. Such a society possesses not an aristocratic government but a "democracy" restricted to members of the dominant race: a "pigmentocracy" or a Herrenvolk.[13] The tone of race relations is especially virulent, volatile, and explosive. Aggression is initiated not only from below but from above, in the form of lynchings, police riots, or waves of blatantly discriminatory legislation. The prevailing ideology of the dominant race is a curious and contradictory mixture. The subordinate group is portrayed not only as naturally inferior, childlike, and servile but also as innately aggressive, dangerous, and uppity.

Van den Berghe's typology contains several important suggestions for the student of segregation. First, segregation is typical of modern, complex, industrializing, and therefore increasingly urban societies. We should not expect to find it prevailing in simple, undifferentiated countries. In the case of a plantation economy we expect some variety of forced labor: slavery, an indentured immigrant population, or an indigenous labor supply that is "encouraged" by a quota system or a labor tax. But segregation is essentially a horizontal organization of society: on the plantation, in rural areas generally, the relationship of master and servant is typically vertical. On the moving frontier, on the other hand, we expect incessant competition for living space and resources between members of economic systems that are not only separate but fundamentally incompatible. We expect warfare to be more or less permanent, very likely ending in the extermination or physical removal of the weaker people.

Unlike the frontier, segregation is a settled system, in which all sections of society participate, albeit unequally, in a single economic whole. The plantation and the frontier may well have contributed to segregation; but they are quite different situations.

Second, many societies, those with histories of "good race relations," have maintained themselves for long periods somewhere near the paternalist pole of the spectrum. For a society to gravitate from one typology to the other is therefore not automatic. At some point in their histories, however, South Africa and the American South, both of them examples of bad race relations, moved from the paternalist to the competitive model. In both societies slavery was abolished by outside authority: by act of the British parliament in 1834 in the case of South Africa, by the Thirteenth Amendment after the Civil War in the case of the American South. Yet slavery was also abolished in the Caribbean and in Brazil, neither of which developed either competitive race relations or segregation. One must therefore explain not only why segregation developed but why some other form of paternalism did not replace slavery.

Third, it can be inferred from Van den Berghe's analysis, as well as from the definitions from the OED with which this chapter began, that segregation is a comparatively recent phenomenon. Historically both South Africa and the American South have been backward parts of the Western world, where the various indexes that have been associated with the core areas of Western Europe and the northeastern United States – high standards of living, large cities, factories – have appeared only within the past half-century or so. Precisely in those periods, race relations left the paternalist and entered the competitive phase.

It is possible – but not probable – that one system of race relations could phase into another by easy, gradual stages. More likely, the transition would be achieved by powerful forces, by a huge release of organized and concentrated energy, by the same causes that were bringing about the systemic transformation of the larger society.

By segregation, then, I understand far more than mere physical separation. Segregation is at the same time an interlocking system of economic institutions, social practices and customs, political power, law, and ideology, all of which function both as means and as ends in one group's efforts to keep another (or others) in their place within a society that is actually becoming unified. Both the structure and the dynamics of segregation are thus profoundly paradoxical. Social patterns and economic trends appear to run in opposite directions. To its members such a society may appear to be normal, logically and permanently divided. But if the groups that compose it were truly separate, if they really lived their lives apart, if economy and society were indeed plural or dual, there would be no need for segregation.

Ordinarily segregation is taken to be synonymous with specific discriminatory practices. These cover the whole range of opportunities, facilities, and rights. In a segregated society we expect job restrictions and unequal wages; inferior housing, education, transportation, health, and social services; prejudiced courts and police forces; reduced or nonexistent political rights. Some of these practices are de facto, some de jure. Between the two levels there is constant interaction: Custom becomes law; law creates custom. The process is circular: Segregation maintains discriminatory distinctions, which persist in order to maintain segregation. But the essence of the system is not the particular forms of deprivation, discrimination, and inequality, no one of which is absolutely essential to its survival. Instead, the crux of segregation is the monopoly by the dominant group over the political institutions of the state.

From "inferiors," segregation demands deference and at least the outward etiquette of humble submission. At every turn, unrelentingly, backed by sufficient power to enforce the rules, the subordinate caste are reminded of their place. To survive they must conform; to conform they must accommodate. Stanley Elkins's use of the analogy of the Nazi concentration camp to suggest how the closed-behavior system of the plantation may have produced a stunted personality that approximated the Sambo stereotype has been hotly disputed.[14] On the contrary, argue his critics, slaves had a good deal of leverage on the plantation. They were able to maintain some psychological autonomy, particularly in their religion.

Even less than the plantation can a large-scale society, however totalitarian, actually control the minds of the victims. Significant-other role models cannot be eliminated. Nonetheless, the subordinate caste must have two faces, two styles, two manners, to some extent two personalities, which are hard to keep completely separate. Outward accommodation becomes inward self-deprecation. From W. E. B. Du Bois to Steve Biko, the foremost freedom fighters have always stressed that the first and most crucial stage in the struggle must therefore be the liberation of the victims from the oppression that exists within their own minds and souls.[15]

With much less thoroughness and severity segregation also shapes the mentality and controls the behavior of the dominant caste. Its members, too, know and keep in their places. Where self-interest is insufficient, peer pressure goes to work; if that fails, there is law. Few whites, for instance, will want to break the code by moving into a black neighborhood where housing is inferior. White owners may want to sell to blacks, but if they do, they are ostracized; if they persist, law intervenes. The attitudes of individuals may affect personal relations across caste lines, but the effects of eccentric nonconformers upon the system are minimal.

As I shall show, Marxist historians of South Africa have identified segregation as a system and ideology peculiarly appropriate to a specific stage of capitalist productive relations. Segregation, in their view, has functioned (as it was consciously intended) to mystify the real, structural line of class by means of fictitious, irrational, superstructural categories of race. As I shall try to demonstrate in this book, this identification of segregation with capitalism, industrialization, urbanization, and modern state formation contributes much to an understanding of race relations not only in South Africa, where the Marxist perspective has been applied with some precision, but also in the American South after the Civil War, where this approach is only now beginning to be employed.

But the Marxists have gone too far. By identifying class as real and structural while insisting that race is fictitious, mystifying, and superstructural, they have oversimplified a complex problem. Marxism, it has often been conceded, has never satisfactorily accounted for nationalism. The same is true of racism. These forces are not merely superstructural. They exist! In the colonial situation, as Frantz Fanon has argued, in societies that are in fact racially stratified, "Marxist analysis should always be slightly stretched."[16] The consciousness, consolidation, power, and hegemony of class are always developed and exercised in the context of specific historical circumstances. Throughout much of the world, race is an important part of that context.

Race is more than a passive factor manipulated in the interests of class. Problems in race relations demand the spirit of Marxist analysis more than the letter. As E. P. Thompson has vividly explained, by "class" Marx intended not a static thing or category but the consciousness of a developing relationship.[17] Class is a concept made in history by the confused, ambiguous experience of real individuals in specific situations. Base and superstructure are not therefore discrete, separate entities. They are constantly entangled.

Precisely the same sort of comments should be made about race. To physical anthropologists the races of mankind may have some validity as a system of classification based on scientifically established investigation. But the problem that confronts the student of race relations in the modern world has nothing to do with physical anthropology. All attempts, from Count Gobineau on, to bring the disciplines of sociology, or social anthropology, and physical anthropology together have resulted in a great deal of confusion as well as in immense amounts of suffering.

For the student of society race is a historical phenomenon. It is rooted in the specific power relations of the particular societies where peoples meet, live, work, fight, and propagate the (usually mixed) species. More generally, the concept of race reflects the interaction of dominant and subjected groups throughout history. "For this reason," wrote a brilliant Afro-American student of the subject, "much false race theory is orthodox history, as well as the apologia of prevailing practice."[18]

As with class relations there must be enemies as well as allies: As Thompson says, there is no love without lovers. Where only one race exists (as in pre-Columbian America or in most parts of Africa before conquest), there is no race consciousness. People are organized instead into clans, tribes, or nations: For all practical and historical purposes race does not exist. Only when racially conscious groups collide, with the one rationalizing its dominance while the other strives to maintain its identity and integrity, does race become a social and historical factor. Only then does it become a problem for the student of society.[19]

Neither class nor race can be held constant. Both are historical phenomena. Both powerfully influence the direction of the societies in which they are situated. Both reflect social structure. Whether in paternalist or competitive systems, the prevailing organization of society at any particular time is an intersection of race and class. As Fanon put it, "the economic substructure is also a superstructure."[20]

In modern, capitalist, competitive societies that become or remain racially stratified, as in South Africa or (at least until yesterday) in the American South, the two phenomena of race and class intersect in particularly confusing, complex ways. Most of the victims are poorer than most of the dominant caste, although there are bankers, professionals, members of the labor aristocracy, and peasants as well as proletarians. They are not a simple horizontal class.

This baffling intersection of race and class did not simply happen. It was made to happen. To those whose lives it regulates, segregation may appear to be normal and natural. It is neither. It is a state not of social equilibrium but of chronic tension and imbalance. Such apparent stability can be achieved and maintained only by well-organized and well-mobilized forces. Segregation is created and enforced by power. It is a political phenomenon. Its immediate causes are therefore also political. But its true origins are far broader. An entire system is being pervaded, molded, and reorganized. The largest, most powerful of social forces are at work.

Segregation is usually associated with the ignorant and the unenlightened. It is sometimes associated with mental illness.[21] It has been made synonymous with reactionary racism. To an American who has lived through the second reconstruction of the 1950s and 1960s the word calls up images of hooded Klansmen, fire hoses, vicious dogs, and tear gas; of governors standing in the schoolhouse door. The argument of this book is that in its early phases segregation has instead been closely associated with forces that we usually regard as progressive: cities, factories, advanced communications, and modern politics.

Segregation was not the crude and rigid system that much of the historical literature has presumed. Those who believed in it were by no means abnormal or mentally ill. Segregation triumphed for the very reason that it *was* flexible and sophisticated. Mystifying, rationalizing, and legitimizing a particular configuration of caste and class, it enabled white supremacy to survive in an increasingly threatening, hostile world. As a result of segregation, white supremacy remained at least superficially compatible not only with the needs of industrial capitalism but with a Christian if paternalist conscience, and even with an advancing democratic or progessive creed.

This was no small achievement. Far from being the crude, irrational prejudice of ignorant "rednecks," segregation must be recognized as one of the most successful political ideologies of the past century. It was, indeed, the highest stage of white supremacy.

The intellectual history of segregation is a tale of toughness and resilience. Easily compressed into the simplest, most manipulable of campaign slogans, it has been expanded and refined into subtle treatises. It has absorbed some ideologies and allied itself with others. In its classic form, in the late nineteenth and early twentieth centuries, segregation became so intertwined with racism that the two words have been used interchangeably. Yet, demonstrating its amazing flexibility, segregation has survived racism's gradual decline (even in South Africa) from intellectual respectability.[22] Never without its critics, even at the height of its success, its premises and its internal logic were skillfully exposed. Time and again segregation was demystified. Time and again the ideology rebounded, continuing to cloud realities, contriving to turn natural opponents into effective, convinced supporters.

The most impressive characteristic of segregation was a complex fabric of structural ambiguity. Although the dominant caste's monopoly of political power might be applied through extralegal or even explicitly illegal means (it being well to remind inferiors from time to time that the exercise of power was essentially unrestrained), segregation was ordinarily carried out under a façade of constitutionality. Courts, legislatures, elections, investigating commissions, perhaps even opposition parties had the appearance and to some extent the reality of impartiality. Both the morale and what the Italian Communist Antonio Gramsci called the hegemony of the dominant caste were thereby strengthened.[23] The education and organized opposition of the powerless were made the more difficult. The victim feared the loss of what seemed to be, and to some extent were, means of protection within the system. Riots, police brutality, threats, and (in the South) lynchings were all frequent enough reminders that the alternative to legal segregation was the uncontrolled violence of anarchy.

This structural ambivalence extended deeply into the ranks of the oppressed. To the emerging (and in South Africa the traditional) black elite, segregation offered a basis for collaboration that the harder, more inflexible forms of white supremacy could never have permitted or achieved. Although they were still confined within the boundaries of caste, a small minority might overcome the barriers of class. In their limited success lay hope, not only for themselves but ultimately for their people. Whatever their own feelings were, the position of the much maligned black bourgeoisie was structurally ambiguous. Under a less sophisticated system it would not have been. The elite of the subjugated caste had a stake in the system.

Here was a basis for collaboration, for acquiescence, accommodation, and consent. Force lay behind segregation. It was omnipresent: In the horrifying poetry of the South African Dennis Brutus, searchlights play upon the bedroom walls. Yet most of the time segregation was largely self-enforcing. One day in 1960 some black college students in Greensboro, North Carolina, sat-in at a lunch counter and launched a wave of protest and non-cooperation that exposed the hegemony of segregation, demystified it, and ultimately swept it away.[24] This incident prompted surprise that sit-ins had not been conducted in any systematic, well-organized way before. But the times were right, and so was the place. That same year, in a place called Sharpeville in South Africa, Africans who tried noncooperation by handing in their passes met with a more rigorous response, to say the least, which left scores dead.

Like other pervasive social systems, like feudalism or capitalism in Marx's grand scheme of the epochs of history, segregation neither began nor ended. It overlapped substantially with the phases that preceded and, in the United States, to some extent replaced it. Tracing such a phenomenon to its chronological roots, looking for harbingers or precedents within previous systems of race relations, may thus become what Marc Bloch called the historian's "idol of origins" – a psychologically satisfying but ultimately fruitless search for the beginning of an infinite series.[25]

The process that created it began long before segregation became the dominant system of racial regulation and control. Yet segregation came into full flower only after previous modes of stratification had broken down or been abolished. At that critical point of *crystallization* segregation became not merely a de facto tendency or practice. Instead it emerged as both a de jure system and a coherent, articulate ideology. It is at that point, not before, that its true origins can be studied most effectively. For, as Bloch explained so persuasively, origins are not the same as precedents or harbingers; they are the conjunction of historical forces that control society at the particular time when the new formulation becomes dominant. In Bloch's view, for example, the origins of feudalism were not in Roman law or Germanic custom but in the European crisis of the ninth and tenth centuries.[26] Similarly, the primary origins of segregation are not in slavery or on the frontier but in the modern conditions of the 1890s and after.

In this book, then, I shall analyze cooperatively the origins of the system and ideology of segregation in South Africa and the American South. How was segregation achieved? In whose or in what interests? In what specific circumstances? What, if any, linkage existed between the two cases? I shall begin by examining how these two societies appeared to some contemporary observers around the turn of the twentieth century.

2. Contemporary perspectives

Like patterns based on class or caste, race relations are mainly shaped and altered by the internal dynamics of the particular societies in whose institutions color distinctions, once having been imposed by power, have taken root. Racist societies, however, are not isolated, self-contained islands. They participate in an international dialogue, sharing information, attitudes, stereotypes, moral standards, and attempts to resolve problems that they perceive to be common.

For Europeans and their descendants overseas, large numbers of whom were both literate and conscious of world politics, this dialogue had gone on since the beginning of modern history. They continually discussed such questions as policies toward aboriginal inhabitants of settlement colonies; the justification, regulation, and eventually the abolition of slavery; and relations between "civilized" or "advanced" and "uncivilized" or "backward" countries. In some cases, for instance, the establishment of slavery in the New World in the sixteenth and seventeenth centuries, when the recognition that servitude was a *problem* lagged behind the rapid spread of the system from colony to colony in response to a compelling need for labor, this dialogue was of secondary importance. In other cases, the international climate of opinion forced the pace.

In the late nineteenth and early twentieth centuries this international dialogue on comparative race relations dramatically accelerated toward a shrill climax. Historians have analyzed the debate under familiar headings: Social Darwinism, manifest destiny, the new imperialism, segregation. Both white Americans and white (especially English-speaking) South Africans participated in this discussion. As I shall show in Chapter 8, the American debate on segregation was an important though by no means a determining influence on the South African dialogue.

Although its pace increased, the international white discussion built on earlier foundations. What was essentially new in this period was the emergence of a *black* dialogue. In the United States and in the Caribbean, in West and South Africa, small but gradually increasing numbers of black people also exchanged information, attitudes, stereotypes, and strategies. Pan Africanism was already an idea. By the end of World War I it would become both an organization and a force, from which the oppressed black peoples of diaspora and the fatherland alike could draw intellectual and psychological sustenance. The pattern of influence, again, ran mainly from America to South Africa.

In this chapter I set the scene for the rest of the book by analyzing the efforts of four contemporary observers to compare race relations in South Africa and the American South around the turn of the twentieth century. These men wrote from very different perspectives. Sir James Bryce was an aristocratic English diplomat and historian. Maurice Evans was an Englishman who lived most of his adult life in Natal, where he served on several commissions investigating the Native Question. Henry M. Turner and Levi J. Coppin were both Afro-American bishops of the African Methodist Episcopal Church. From their very different perspectives these observers agreed, first, that the two societies were traveling the same road toward a much more competitive and troubled racial system and, second, that the American South was miles ahead.

In 1888 the sometime British ambassador to the United States, Sir James Bryce, published the first edition of *The American Commonwealth*. Almost at once it became a classic analysis of the American political system by a foreigner, a work outranked only by Alexis de Tocqueville's *Democracy in America*. Bryce's remarks on federalism, for example, would be quoted and requoted by the founding fathers of Australia, in British debates about the Irish Question, and by the builders of the Commonwealth of Nations. For Englishmen generally, including English-speaking white South Africans, Bryce became the accepted authority on American race relations.

The first edition, however, provides no basis for such a reputation. Although "the relations of the advanced and backward races of mankind" would later become one of the author's favorite lecture topics, in 1888 Bryce included only a few superficial pages on the Negro Question. And the Question was not how a race of former slaves was managing to survive in a cruelly discriminatory society, but the troubles white Americans were facing in trying to deal with them. In the North, he found, where blacks were frequently denied the chance to seek a livelihood, they were grudgingly accepted in politics. In the South, where they were excluded politically, they were the backbone of the largely agricultural economy. On no other subject were the acute regional differences that still remained in the American body politic two decades after the Civil War so clearly revealed.

In the third edition (1894), which he revised again in 1910, Bryce took the subject more seriously, adding new chapters on "The South since the War" and "The Present and Future of the Negro." The problem of the previous decade, he wrote, had grown increasingly severe. He now perceived a cancerous, perhaps incurable contradiction: Legally and economically this backward race was an integral part of the nation; socially and politically it was both "unabsorbed and unabsorbable."[1] The attempt during Reconstruction to apply the full logic of American democracy had been nobly idealistic, but it had failed disastrously. Ignorant and untrained, the freedmen had been totally unprepared for the franchise. Inevitably the result had been a feast of corruption and misgovernment. To be sure, most of the violence had been committed by Southern whites, who were even more embittered by Reconstruction than by the war itself. After the mid-1870s, however, the North had wisely abandoned its misconceived policy. Theoretically, blacks were still participants in Southern politics. In practice, by means of corruption and intimidation that were poisoning the atmosphere, they were being systematically excluded.

Throughout America, Bryce reported, race relations were rapidly getting worse. In the North they had never been good. The antebellum South, however, had once known close personal relations between masters and slaves: "The legal inequality was so immense that familiarity was not felt to involve any disturbance of the attitude of command." To some extent these bonds of sympathetic understanding between older members of the planter class and their former slaves remained, but they were weakening. The prevailing tone was bitter and competitive.

Like other observers before and since, Bryce blamed the deterioration on the "mean whites." They had always hated blacks, and Reconstruction had angered them further. Between white and black there was now astonishingly little social intercourse. The races had separate railway carriages, separate washroom facilities, separate education, and separate churches. Lynching was on the rise: "In some parts of the South a white man would run little more risk of being hanged for the murder of a negro than a Mussulman in Turkey for the murder of a Christian." In place of the close and sometimes friendly relations that once had existed between the races, the South had evolved a "complete . . . system of separation."[2]

Of the prewar Southern way of life, wrote Bryce, only the approach to the Negro Question remained fundamentally unaltered. In all else the South was now much like the North. Its "mean whites" no longer despised manual labor. Its leaders welcomed Northern capital and tourists. Southerners were avidly building railways and factories. Economic links between the regions were being forged ever more strongly. Stubborn and vexing, the Negro Question kept the nation divided. By the latest census there were some nine million blacks. What was to be done with them?

To some extent, Bryce thought, the problem seemed to be resolving itself. The natural habitat of the African race was tropical. Now that they were free, blacks might be expected to gravitate toward the more climatically suitable regions. There were signs that they were doing so. But there was no indication that this territorial separation could ever be complete. The possibility of setting aside a state or two for blacks was theoretically attractive, but it found little support. Back to Africa? There were too many blacks, and few wanted to go; white Southerners recognized that without black labor their economy would collapse. Blacks, it seemed, would remain in North America.

It was no aim of Bryce, an Englishman who knew well enough how his own countrymen sometimes treated Asians, to blame white Americans. The problem defied solution. Clearly, legislation had done more harm than good. Without enthusiasm Bryce recommended the limited franchise, based on high property and educational qualifications, which was then in vogue in the Cape Colony of South Africa. For the few blacks who were rising into the middle class, it would create a useful safety valve. (In fact, although the color-blind franchise of the Cape is usually regarded as a liberal measure, the South's solution was very comparable, not only in methods but in the token number of black voters. Not even Mississippi disfranchised *all* black voters.) In the long run, the friend of America must hope, the "mean whites" would gradually improve their attitudes. But it might take centuries.

In 1910 Bryce added still another chapter: "Further Observations on the Negro Problem." Here he described the consolidation of a racial system based on segregation. In 1894 the South, like the rest of the nation and indeed the whole Western world, had been in the throes of an economic depression. By 1910 the South had resumed its development. Cities, railways, and education had all progressed. So had the Negro Question. Whereas in 1888 the black voter had been very largely excluded by informal means that corrupted the whites, by 1910 he was effectively disfranchised throughout the South. Recognizing its former error, the North had wisely acquiesced. There were still lynchings, but they seemed to be decreasing. Violent riots had occurred, notably in Wilmington, North Carolina, in 1898 and in Atlanta in 1906. Oddly enough, given the concentration of "mean whites" in rural areas, much of the violence seemed to take place in towns. On the whole, however, the elimination of black political competition had created a calmer, saner atmosphere. It was easy to denounce the hypocritical evasion of the Fifteenth Amendment. But things had been far worse between 1873 and 1890, the era before the new state constitutions had begun to appear. The black vote had "demoralized . . . the whites; it exacerbated feelings between the races; and as the negroes were gaining nothing in those years by their nominal right to the suffrage, they have lost little by its curtailment."[3]

Northerners now understood this. So, apparently, did most

blacks. At least those whom whites considered the best of their leaders did. Although Booker T. Washington, Bryce was careful to indicate, had not renounced political rights for all time, he had sensibly put economic progress and self-sufficiency first. He had accepted fully the social separateness of the races. To be sure, Afro-Americans were divided, with W. E. B. Du Bois representing the more militant position. Washington, however, seemed to have more influence, and one might hope that his patiently sane approach could be maintained. But an outsider like Bryce perceived what Americans sometimes ignored: Wide as were their differences, Washington and Du Bois agreed on the need for greater race consciousness.

The most encouraging trend was the South's economic progress. Blacks would share in the rising prosperity, and they would be increasingly needed. White attitudes should also improve: "Men are more kindly when they are more comfortable." On the other hand the growing Afro-American race consciousness could be expected to increase rivalry and therefore white insecurity. That would be unfortunate, "but the African cannot be prevented from seeking to improve his situation merely because his competition will displease the whites." On the whole, however, Bryce was optimistic. At bottom the problem was a moral one. Not long ago slavery had been defended by biblical citation. Now no one defended it. Might not a moral revolution one day make race friction passé? "It is at any rate in that direction that the stream of change is running."[4]

In 1897, midway between the Jameson Raid of 1895 and the outbreak of the Boer War, Bryce recorded his *Impressions of South Africa*. His timing was impeccable; once more he had a bestseller. This travel book shows little evidence of the wide reading and close observation of *The American Commonwealth*. The chapter on "Blacks and Whites," in particular, is little more than a collection of stereotypes, some of which had already been exploded.

Within the British Empire, thought Bryce, South Africa was an anomaly, fitting neither the model of self-governing white settlement colonies in the temperate zone nor that of dependent, crown colonies in the tropics. In Australia, New Zealand, and Canada the aborigines had been dying out; in South Africa the Natives were increasing. Thus "the general difficulty of adjusting the relations of a higher and lower race, serious under any kind of government, here presents itself in the special form of the construction of a political system which, while democratic as regards one of the races, cannot safely be made democratic as regards the other."[5] In that respect the problem was the same that he had studied in the American South.

Certainly there were important differences. Because they had the advantage of having been schooled in slavery, Bryce pointed out, Afro-Americans were far ahead of South African Natives in work habits and education. They were Christian; Africans were mainly pagan. On the whole, however, the Bantu-speaking peoples were considered of superior racial stock – with larger heads and therefore greater intelligence – compared with the West Africans from whom American blacks were mostly descended. There was therefore no reason to think that the Natives would not progress.

As they did progress – and this the American analogy seemed to demonstrate conclusively – the Native Question would intensify. As in America, there was little discourse or understanding. "Complete social separation" was the rule: "Each race goes its own way and lives its own life." Although it was not yet so bitter, in South Africa one met the same kind of racial hostility, especially among poor whites. The trend of the future was obvious: Increasingly whites would be threatened; increasingly they would retaliate.

The South African cycle of competition, hostility, and violent reaction, thought Bryce, was running behind the American. How far behind remained to be seen. The atmosphere was much quieter – no lynchings or riots. As yet the rule of the superior race went unchallenged. But in the long run, Bryce sadly concluded, the demographic facts were against a white man's country that was becoming increasingly dependent on black labor. The day would arrive, perhaps by the twenty-first century, when the gold mines would presumably be exhausted: "South Africa will see itself filled by a large coloured population, tolerably homogeneous," poor and culturally backward, pathetically degenerating like a colony of the Portuguese.[6]

Like Bryce, a Natalian expert on the Native Question named Maurice Evans (whom C. Vann Woodward has aptly called "the man on the cliff")[7] analyzed the explosive Negro Question in the United States. Like Bryce, he thought the American problem more advanced; he too saw there the mirror of South Africa's troubled future. In both countries, he concluded, the only hope lay in some system of segregation. In neither, despite much discussion, had segregation ever been seriously attempted.

In two well-researched volumes – *Black and White in South East Africa* (1911) and *Black and White in the Southern States* (1915) – Evans made the first systematic comparison of race relations in the two societies. Considering his time, place, and subject, he was surprisingly objective. His reading of the American literature was impressive; he interviewed widely; he traveled beyond the usual showplaces of American Negro education; he conscientiously tried to report all points of view.

Like any good scholar, Evans identified his own bias. He profoundly disagreed with most of the participants at the London Inter-Racial Congress (1911), who had overwhelmingly argued that environment rather than heredity determined racial characteristics.[8] To be sure, he conceded, no satisfactory scientific data existed. Perhaps no other subject so abounded in shallow stereotypes. Evans pointedly refused to discuss the still popular measurement of skulls, generally used to conclude that African brains were smaller and less "convoluted." Nor did he engage, as such authorities as Lord Bryce and Sir Harry Johnston had done, in the fascinating but pointless exercise of reasoning by analogy.[9] For Evans, the degeneration of Haiti and Liberia under African self-rule apparently proved nothing about the black man's innate capacities and shed no light on his future in the very different situations of South Africa or the American South. With remarkable restraint Evans tried to restrict himself to what he saw, heard, and read. Still, the question of race was one on which every person, especially one who had lived long among Africans, was entitled to a subjective opinion. "Race," he quoted approvingly from the West Indian (and Liberian) black nationalist Edward Blyden, "is deeper than culture."[10]

Black and white, then, were profoundly different. On that basis an equitable system of segregation could justifiably be developed. Difference, however, did not necessarily mean innate, permanent inferiority. That, from the whites' point of view, was a dangerous illusion. In Evans's view, the problem was not the Africans' racial backwardness but rather their demonstrated and perhaps unlimited capacity.

In his first book, Evans projected for his own country a troubled, divided future: "A white oligarchy, every member of the race an aristocrat; a black proletariat, every member of the race a server; the line of cleavage as clear and deep as the colours."[11] South Africa's fundamental problem was black labor. Cheap, ubiquitous, and increasingly efficient, it was the taproot of the Native Question. The white working man simply could not compete with it. Immigrants passed by on the way to Australia, and indigenous Afrikaners became poor whites. Was it conceivable that a white minority, with no working class of its own, growing increasingly dependent on the labor of the black majority, could survive economically? How could such a society hope to remain a white man's country?

According to Evans, Africans legitimately aspired to higher living standards. Most of the race remained backward. But that condition was only temporary. Africans had already demonstrated their potential: They could be educated; they could perform skilled as well as unskilled labor; they could become successful farmers. How could they be held down? The tax revolt of 1906–8 in Natal, led by the minor Zulu chief Bambatha, had shown the danger.[12] Ordinary Africans were reasonable people demanding sufficient land on which to maintain an independent existence, on which to keep their family and tribal system intact. They wished the freedom to work for wages that would reflect the fair market value of their labor. Above all, they wanted to be left alone. The small, educated, detribalized elite, of course, were demanding far more than that. They wanted political and perhaps even social equality. If the legitimate economic demands of the masses remained unfulfilled, how in good conscience could even the premature claims of the few be rejected?

What had to be minimized was competition – in the labor market, for land, above all in politics. By threatening the white working class, rivalry would poison race relations. It might even end the paternalist altruism of those considered the "better sort" of whites.

Two priorities, Evans maintained, must be recognized. First, in the interest of both races, the bulwark of European civilization, which Africans had already shown themselves capable of absorbing, must be maintained. Second, fundamental differences among the races must be preserved. The world would be poorer for the loss of separate racial identities and distinctive cultures. South Africa's policy must be fair. It must not burden Africans with repressive restrictions. No inflexible color line should be laid down. Africans must be given room to maneuver and to live their lives. But the only conceivable solution, the only means of maintaining both civilization and racial distinctiveness, was segregation.

All of the necessary elements for segregation, Evans thought, were already present. From the Transvaal came "the great principle that the white man must rule"; from Natal, in the example of the mid-nineteenth-century administrator Sir Theophilus Shepstone, the idea that European rule "should be personal, fatherly, sympathetic, and not rigid and impersonal"; from the Glen Grey district in the Cape, the argument that Africans, under white guidance, could successfully manage many of their local affairs; from Basutoland, the example of orderly, gradual progress and contentment among a people who maintained traditional customs and tribal rule; from both the Cape and Basutoland, the recognition of the missionary's important contribution to African education and regeneration; and from the many "recent voices advocating segregation" within the past decade, "a support for the great truth that if the races are to develop along lines which will give each its full and true ethnic value, the points of contact must be as few as possible, the races must live their home and race lives apart."[13]

All these strands had been spun separately in the various districts of South Africa. As yet, in Evans's opinion, the cloth of segregation had not been woven. There was, of course, a Native Policy. But, let his readers candidly admit the truth, it was merely repression. It was unconscionable. Perhaps worse, it was inexpedient. In the short run repression might seem to succeed. In the long run the Africans' inevitable progress would doom it to disastrous failure.

Segregation, in Evans's view, was different from mere repression. A positive policy, based on mutual respect and sympathy, it would give to each race the opportunity to preserve its unique culture. It was the only conceivable solution. But as of 1911 Evans saw few signs that his white countrymen yet appreciated the true significance of the Native Question. They had little sympathy and even less knowledge of the African. Above all, they had not yet resolved to make the necessary sacrifice. If segregation were to have a chance of success, there was one absolutely essential condition. Africans must have more land. Whites had taken over most of it. Apparently they meant to keep it. And that would be their downfall.

Thus Maurice Evans went to America with his thesis already firmly in his head. Whereas Bryce and de Tocqueville had regarded the Afro-American as a threatening complication in the context of the larger problem of democracy, the color question was Evans's primary concern. Like W. E. B. Du Bois, whom he quoted, Evans thought the most crucial problem of the twentieth century would be the color line.

In many ways Evans was struck by similarities between the two racially stratified societies. In the black-belt regions of South Carolina, Alabama, or Mississippi, where the huge black majorities in some counties sometimes compared with the 10:1 ratio of Natal, he felt quite at home. In the cities, however, he saw the troubled future of his own country and of the world.

On the basis of the American analogy, Evans argued in his second book (1915), certain fondly held premises of the South African debate must be abandoned.[14] Was the African race, apart from a few exceptions, incapable of education "beyond a certain stage"? On the contrary, a people who had been kept almost entirely ignorant under the slave codes was now perhaps fifty percent literate. Were Africans innately improvident, unsuited either for skilled industrial work or for farming their own land? The Afro-Americans' astonishing economic progress – and as Booker T. Washington observed, it needed to be compared with the living standards of the peasants of southern or eastern Europe – clearly proved otherwise. Was South Africa's poor-white problem the result of the white working man's apathetic response to competition with a black majority? The South's black minority had apparently caused a deterioration no less acute.

Whether on its home continent or in the New World, Evans continued to believe, the African race was fundamentally distinctive in ways a changing environment would only modify. Time would tell whether the race was inferior: It was profoundly different. And the main conclusion from America seemed unarguable. The black man was on the make. The Afro-Americans' amazingly successful struggle up from slavery should destroy forever the white South Africans' comforting illusion that Bantu-speaking peoples would remain a supine, servile, unassertive race. On the contrary, everything suggested that they would be increasingly aggressive, dangerous competitors.

South Africa's race relations were in an earlier, less explosive phase. What were only tendencies in Evans's country were accomplished facts and themes when reflected in the American glass. Religious separatism – for example, the Ethiopian movement, which had so alarmed white South Africans in recent years – was so common that, strangely enough, Americans took it for granted. The advanced ideas that appeared occasionally in the African vernacular press back home, Evans noted, were present in all their strident, articulate militance in the black newspapers of New York or Washington. Miscegenation was so common in America that one rarely saw a full-blooded African. The aggressiveness of Afro-Americans was matched, indeed far more than matched, by the violent white reaction. Fortunately, South Africa had so far managed to preserve law and order; lynching remained a peculiarly American disease. Even a South African found the bitter tone of race relations shocking!

Would all this conflict, which would ultimately be made incalculably worse by the structure of South Africa's demography, be its future? It would be unless white South Africans acted in time. Some Americans were doing their best. On both sides of the South's color line the "saner elements," the Edgar Gardner Murphys and the Booker T. Washingtons, were rejecting the radical extremism of the Ben Tillmans or that of Du Bois's National Association for the Advancement of Colored People. The moderates were agreed: Competition must be removed as much as possible from American life. In facilities, opportunities, and services the rule supposedly was "separate but equal." That rule should be enforced. Here and there interracial conciliation committees were trying to make segregation work fairly and justly.

For America, it seemed to Evans, it was already too late. The prevailing hope was that by remaining on the land, performing the agricultural occupations in which their history had placed them and to which their racial temperament was perhaps suited, Afro-Americans would avoid competing with whites. But that hope was based on a cruel fiction. The agrarian land shortage was already acute. Both blacks and whites were being pushed into the towns. Everywhere, in rural as well as in urban areas, competition was increasing. Inevitably, therefore, American race relations would continue to deteriorate.

South Africa's clock was ticking. Would its statesmen act courageously and in time? America's tragic mistakes must be avoided. Perhaps its most disastrous experiment, according to Evans, had been to confer universal male suffrage upon a people educationally and temperamentally unsuited to exercise it. That error, at least, South Africa would apparently not repeat. Economic rivalry, however, was still more fundamental. In America the causes of competition for land and jobs could not conceivably be removed. In South Africa sufficient space still remained for a viable, equitable system of territorial segregation. The Natives Land Act of 1913, which had promised that, in time and after proper surveys, Africans would be guaranteed some thirteen percent of the land, had been an encouraging beginning. But the process must not stop there. There had been much superficial talk of segregation. As of 1915, in Maurice Evans's considered opinion, it was far from being achieved.

In 1898 Bishop Henry M. Turner of the African Methodist Episcopal Church (AME), the "Black Moses" who inspired the most significant back-to-Africa movement among Afro-Americans before Marcus Garvey's militant campaign after World War I, visited South Africa.[15] His immediate purpose was to add to his church's flock some sixty ministers and ten thousand members of the Ethiopian Church. Secondarily, he intended to expand the

AME's field of operations from West Africa into the southern and central regions of the continent. His aims beyond that? Who can tell?

Since its recent secession from the (English) Wesleyan Methodist Church, the all-black Ethiopian Church had been unsupported and unsupervised.[16] No one was staffing its schools or training or ordaining its ministers, which meant the marriages performed in the church could not be lawfully recognized. By both the Boer and the British authorities, the Ethiopians were suspected (not without reason) of preaching the seditious doctrine usually associated with that wild renegade English missionary, Joseph Booth: "Africa for the Africans."[17] For these reasons the Ethiopian Bishop James Dwane led a delegation to America in 1896 to request union with the AME. A special conference had approved. Thus, in February 1898, despite his wife's recent death, Bishop Turner set out by steamer with his son David for Liverpool. He survived a severe storm to arrive by March in Cape Town. It was the start of a triumphant and, for the subsequent development of African political consciousness, an important procession, a fascinating example of the interaction of ideas between the African diaspora and the fatherland.

On the eve of his departure, in an interview published in the AME's missionary journal, *The Voice of Missions,* of which he was also the editor, Bishop Turner specified the prospects. His information about South Africa was not terribly accurate. No, he was not going to what the headline called the Dark Continent for any ulterior motive – not as an agent for any colonization scheme – but solely to do God's work. As a field for missions, South Africa's potential was enormous and rapidly expanding: "The influx of Europeans into the country will prove of incalculable advantage to the natives by bringing them into contact with schools, churches, beneficial forms of government, better modes of life and the other civilizing influences which European colonization produces wherever it goes."[18] Schools and churches were the Afro-American missionaries' opportunity. Why should they not share the white man's burden?

To be sure, because all of the colonies were under white control, South Africa was "not as desirable for a home to the American Negro as Liberia, where he has a government of his own laws and runs things after his own notions." Even so, "in any of the South African colonies the condition of the educated colored man is a thousand-fold better than in America." Africa – and here the bishop began to speak generally – was the black people's natural home. Individually, Afro-Americans might succeed among whites. But as Turner had said in his important essay of 1895 on "The American Negro and the Fatherland": *"There is no manhood future in the United States for the Negro . . . He can never be a man – full, symmetrical, and undwarfed."*[19] Only by raising a strong, modern black nation could the Afro-American become a force in the world. Only in Africa could that conceivably be achieved.

A bit impatiently the better-informed reporter brought the enthusiastic old bishop back to the point: "But will not the young negro encounter in the white provinces of South Africa about the same obstacles he finds here?" "No, indeed," replied Turner, still speaking generally. "Color is no bar in Africa. The negro is eligible to any office in the gift of any of the colonial governments and he can do anything or be anything he chooses and has the ability to carry out." "But, bishop," the reporter protested, "society there is yet young and crude. Don't you think that racial differences will appear in the future?" Had there not, already, been some trouble with the Germans over the color line? "Yes," Bishop Turner admitted, "that is to some extent true." If peoples of Teutonic blood should ever settle densely there, then the color line would certainly develop. But there were important physical reasons, which Turner left unexplained, why this was unlikely. "It is unfortunately for us true that the territory is held largely by Teutonic peoples, the English and Germans, or Boers, who," unlike other European peoples among whom Turner had traveled, "are the most susceptible of race prejudice."

"I believe," Turner concluded, returning to the idea that was the keystone of his ministry, his life, and the movement he inspired, "that God permitted the black man to be brought here and to serve a term of bondage to the white man for the black man's good." Just as Jehovah had once allowed the Hebrews to remain in Egypt, so God had permitted a "manual laboring school" where His people might come in "direct contact with the mightiest race that ever trod the face of the globe." In their painful captivity the poor blacks had suffered grievously. But they had learned of God. His purposes unfathomable, His ways mysterious, God at length had removed the curse of slavery and bade His people make ready. Their destiny was not in America. As long as they remained there they would suffer: "We are now receiving knocks and buffetings until God in His wisdom shall see it is time for us to move, and then I think the American nation will aid us in getting to Africa."

With this simple, touchingly naïve faith, which inspired leaders like Booker T. Washington or Du Bois even as it drove them to distraction, Bishop Turner went to South Africa. "The race has not had a greater man within church and state," *The Voice of Missions* called after him. "He may well be styled the Moses of the race. May He that kept Israel, keep him in this far away land."[20]

The bishop declared himself much impressed with Cape Town. Its climate was magnificent, its polyglot population fascinating. There were all varieties of whites – English, French, Italians, Spanish, Germans (he still apparently thought the Boers were German – not, after all, a very serious mistake) – as well as Malays, Hottentots, Chinese, Fingoes, Kaffirs, Basutoes, and other African nationalities: "all colors, shades, hues, dress, languages, habits, and modes," all jostling together. The Hottentots, "an old defunct race" who, "like our American Indians, will soon be extinct," were clayish yellow, and the Africans were not so black as the Negroes of the tropics. The Africans, he observed later with some relief, though certainly "raw" and "wild," had satisfactorily "large heads" and perhaps more common sense than American blacks. In Cape Town, except for white women, everybody seemed to marry and intermarry indiscriminately, as they pleased: "Here is mongrelization to the heart's content."

Turner observed that among whites there was race prejudice, but it was not confined to the African. All colored peoples "come in for a share" – except for Turner. To his amazement he and his son were not considered Negroes but Americans. Even in his European travels, when he had not found a color line, he had never been denied the "high honor" of being a Negro: "But we learn that we will get Negro to our heart's content when we reach the Transvaal Republic." And with that Turner concluded his first letter from South Africa. The messenger had just come in with the Atlanta *Journal*. He must see what was happening with the *Maine*. In South Africa they were saying it must end in war between America and Spain.

From Cape Town the bishop went quickly by train to the world's largest ten-year-old city, Johannesburg. Along the route he noticed all-black section crews, foremen as well as hands: "Negroes have charge of the entire railway, naked as many of them are." As they neared Johannesburg, he began to see the difference between this settlement colony and West Africa. The concentration of machinery impressed him. Some of the gold mines, he was told, already extended to a depth of 1,800 feet, which took a cruel toll in lives: "But the men who lose their lives are chiefly Kaffir Africans, who, it appears, do the principal part of the hard work." Turner did not mention, and presumably did not see, that recent marvel of social engineering, the closed compound, the long distances African laborers often traveled on foot, or the wage structure of the industry. He did notice that Africans were forbidden to buy land in the city or walk on the sidewalks. But again, he himself, as well as the Fisk University Jubliee Singers, who happened to be there at the time, were treated as Americans and were permitted to stay at the best hotel. He was told of the franchise restrictions under which "outlander" Europeans suffered (and which became the pretext for the Boer War a year later). Naturally enough, in view of the hardships facing Africans, these did not depress him unduly.

In Pretoria Turner presided over a conference, where he appointed Dwane a Vicar Bishop and, after only the most perfunctory inspection of credentials, ordained large numbers of Ethiopian ministers. Perhaps, he admitted, he had somewhat exceeded the technical limits of his powers. (All appointments were supposedly subject to review by the general conference; his actions would be severely criticized at home.) But the iron was hot; he had been sent to effect a union with the Ethiopians and he had done so. Moreover, the Ethiopians had had the stronger bargaining position. Within a few years Dwane would become dissatisfied and secede again, this time from the AME. For the moment, however, the picture looked bright: "As God lives there is a prospect for the African."

Also while in Pretoria the bishop interviewed President Paul Kruger of the Transvaal, "a genial man, very large, with a deep guttural voice," rather more like an emperor than a president. (Since no translator was present the exchange of views was somewhat limited.) On the whole, Turner's impressions of the Boers – and somewhere along the line he had grasped that they are Dutch, not German – was not unfavorable. Like his own people they were extremely religious; at any rate they were no worse than the English and Americans in the Transvaal. "We were never treated better," Turner reported. "They treated us to everything but whiskey, and that was offered forty times."

Next Turner moved quickly through the Orange Free State, stopping briefly at Bloemfontein, then on to Queenstown in the Eastern Cape. There, he was told, Africans were being given home rule. They enacted their own laws, held their own councils, collected their own taxes, decided what improvements were needed: "This is good, we grant, more than any other country is granting the negro, but the question is, will it last? We very much doubt it."

Turner's whirlwind tour had confirmed his impression of South Africa's vast potential for Afro-American missionaries. The expansion of European civilization would be their opportunity, the African's apparently insatiable thirst for education their toehold. (One of the direct results of Turner's visit was an acceleration in the number of African students going to Wilberforce and other American Negro colleges, further speeding up the interchange between diaspora and fatherland.) But the prospects for anything grander, he admitted, were severely limited. The country's resources were boundless: "But the white races have got control of it and will keep it." No longer was he convinced that physical reasons would prevent South Africa's becoming a white man's country:

> The cities they are building, the spacious churches they are erecting, the public houses and private residences they are putting up and the crowded ships coming to every harbor, prove that the white man is here to stay, and he intends to boss the country. The only hope, then, left the negro to become a manager of a nation is in Liberia or Central Africa.[21]

South Africa, Turner concluded sadly, would not be the Afro-American's Zion. In the future, as the white population increased, as the white man's state became more powerful, the problem of the color line would become more severe. Bishop Turner's perspective was limited: He identified only slightly with the "raw natives"; he knew nothing of their long history of resistance to European rule. There was much in the South Africa of 1898 that he neither saw nor understood. The point is nonetheless worth stressing: As far as Turner was concerned, Cape Town, Pretoria, and even Johannesburg seemed a long way from (and behind) Atlanta.

In 1900 a younger, more sophisticated bishop, Levi J. Coppin, came out to take charge of the AME's operations in South Africa, which had been disrupted first by Dwane's secession and then by the Boer War. Coppin stayed until 1904, his work constantly hampered by the war, by martial law in the defeated Boer republics, and by the mounting white suspicion and hostility against all-black churches. Like Turner, Coppin sent back to *The Voice of Missions* periodic reports, which were published separately.[22] Like Turner's, they reveal something of an Afro-American perspective on comparative race relations in South Africa and the American South.

Bishop Coppin arrived to find Cape Town gripped by crisis: bubonic plague. He noted the incidence of the disease, which spread fairly evenly according to the size of each group in the population: More Europeans than Africans were infected, and still more Cape Coloureds. Yet the blame was being placed not on the spread of a world pandemic from Asia to this port at the southern crossroads, where traffic had increased enormously during wartime, but on the filthy living conditions of newly arrived Africans. By way of remedy the city and the colonial legislature were establishing what they called Native locations.

As a recent student has argued, the sanitation syndrome was an important factor in the origins of urban segregation in South Africa.[23] In Durban, Cape Town, Port Elizabeth, Johannesburg, eventually throughout South Africa, and, indeed, in tropical Africa as well, European authorities used disease as a rationalization for fixing the Africans' place in town. Their real motives were political. By putting Natives in separate locations they could police them more effectively, regulate the flow of labor, and send "excess" Africans back to the reserves. They could "protect" Africans from the vices and "advanced ideas" of the city. They could restrict the effects of African poverty on Europeans and minimize its logical results: disease and crime. Their model was the closed compound that had been developed, partly in response to smuggling, in the diamond mines of Kimberley. According to Coppin, the ideal would never be completely realized: Individual African servants would continue to live in the European homes where they worked. But the bulk of Africans, who had come to work on the docks and the railways of Cape Town, would soon be living in the Native locations as temporary residents.

Bishop Coppin may have followed closely the reports of city council commissions and colonial legislative debates in the *Cape Times*. If so, he would certainly have understood all this. As it was, he appreciated much of the significance of the sanitation syndrome. The Coloured People, who had thought of themselves as white, far above the Natives in status, were sometimes being treated like Africans. It was just as well, thought Coppin, that they were being stripped of the illusion that white people would really consider mulattoes to be their equals. When Coppin visited Cape Town's new Native location, he was shocked. In one place he found eight Africans living in a single room: two dressed in cotton shirts and trousers, four in blankets, two entirely nude.

> If they are as children they should be dealt with as such. They
> were not asked whether they wished their lands taken from
> them or not, and why should they be asked whether they
> wish to wear some sort of clothes or not? If civilization
> means to rob the native of all that is worth his having, and
> then leave him to do as he wishes, it is not a blessing to
> him. [24]

The locations, it seemed, were means by which whites might hide Africans from their consciences and evade their obligations. Africans would be herded into the locations. A railroad would perhaps be run out to them. At low wages that would give them no chance for improvement, Africans would be left to fend for themselves. "Once they owned all the land by inheritance." Now they were being permitted to live only where the white man dictated. "When we are told that a man in America is denied civil and political rights on account of being a descendant of Africa," Coppin concluded, "we are content to call it unjust, ungodly; but when we are told that an African in Africa is denied civil privileges because he is an African, we feel that besides being unrighteous and unworthy our Christian civilization, it is ridiculous in the extreme." Not that Coppin was opposed to European colonization. In the bush, here and there, one sometimes met an educated, Christian African. But there was so little light, and so much darkness:

> I do not say that civilization should not advance to those who are trampling upon the hidden treasures of the earth without making an effort to obtain them, or without having a proper conception of their value; to those whose broad acres are lying without cultivation and improvement; nor should it be expected that those who go to their relief, and that, too, at great sacrifice, should not have ample remuneration; but the least to be expected of those who come and take their inheritance is that they should give them kindness and civilization in return.[25]

The perspective of Afro-American missionaries was limited and ambiguous. Even while suffering under American racism, they partly accepted its premises: Whereas Turner spoke of the large heads of Africans, Coppin praised them as long-headed. To both of them, Africans were heathen, ignorant, superstitious, and wild. They were all those things of which Afro-Americans were so often accused and which they were desperately trying to escape. There is nothing strange about these attitudes. How could it have been otherwise? Moreover, the doctrine that Coppin mainly preached (at least where white men could hear him) was that of cooperation and loyalty, of diligent manual labor that would make the African a useful, dignified, and ultimately an accepted member of society, that of "the threefold power of cultivating the head, the heart and the hand."[26]

The foremost authority on the subject has distinguished three types of Afro-American influence on African political consciousness in South Africa.[27] The first, associated with the missionaries, was imitation of whites, acceptance of their values, and dutiful submission to their authority. The second, associated with Booker T. Washington and with such important South African disciples as John Dube and D. D. T. Jabavu, was like the first, except that it also stressed the accumulation of capital and property as a basis for economic self-sufficiency and race advancement. The third, associated with the great intellectual W. E. B. Du Bois, stressed the Congress and Pan African ideas: Africans should organize in permanent groups, such as the West African Congress or the NAACP, for the purposes of militant agitation and resistance; they should understand their problems in the perspective of a world history in which the fundamental conditions, the historical forces that created them, and the proper strategies for opposing them in all countries were essentially the same.

Although there is value in such a tripartite analysis, it is an oversimplification. For the intentions of missionaries and other accommodationists were by no means the same as the effects of what they symbolized. Colonial officials were strongly suspicious of the unsettling influence of all-black churches. Undoubtedly, the authorities created imaginary conspiracies. Undoubtedly, on the whole, they were right.

In fact, even the missionaries' intentions were not entirely clear. In August 1901, for instance, Bishop Coppin called together some twenty-five African chiefs who were gathered in Cape Town on the occasion of a visit from members of the British imperial royal family. He reminded them that August was the very month, long ago in 1619, when twenty slaves had landed in Jamestown, Virginia. God in His mysterious wisdom had "permitted a branch of the parent tree to be broken off and planted in America. This branch has grown into a great tree, spreading forth its branches until they reached Africa, the Fatherland." Now a new century had begun: Let the dead past bury the dead. Africans must lift themselves up, becoming educated, economically prosperous, and Christian. They must overcome tribal differences: "Let Ethiopia stretch forth her hand to God and become a people."[28]

One interested witness to this convocation, a fascinating Afro-American sea captain named Harry Dean, hints at the undercurrents that rippled out from meetings like this.[29] Even if we discount Dean's story that Coppin persuaded him to go as his agent to Pondoland, to find out whether Portuguese East Africa might be secured as a Zion for American Negroes (though the first part at least may very well be true), we can credit his impression of the meeting's electric atmosphere. It was indeed an unsettling influence: this idea of the essential unity of diaspora and fatherland, this idea of African nationalism.

In May 1903 Bishop Coppin addressed a gathering of a different kind when, along with the principal of the AME's Bethel Institute in Cape Town, Reverend Allen H. Attaway, he was asked to appear before the South African Native Affairs Commission.[30] As Coppin knew very well, the future of his mission hung in the balance. At first there was some sparring: When had the AME been founded? Why was it called African? Methodist? Episcopal? Was it all black in America? What were their objectives? Patiently Coppin answered. Preaching, teaching, and (with some emphasis) industrial education: "We think people in the lowest stage of civilization should have the industrial idea emphasized" to cure their poverty and to make them self-supporting, valuable members of the state. Poverty? Did Coppin mean that the Native, on four shillings a day, was poor? Hastily Coppin retreated. He had not meant to say that; he had meant poor in the scale of civilization. Wherever he had gone, he had been impressed with how quickly Natives had advanced, with just how much white people had done for them. What syllabus did the AME's school teach? Why, the syllabus of the Cape Colony's education department.

The cross-examination became more direct. What was the connection between the AME and the Ethiopian Church? Since Dwane's secession, none whatever. What was the connection with Joseph Booth, who preached "Africa for the Africans"? No connection. Did he know Booth? Well, yes. In fact, realizing that Booth's movements had probably been traced, Coppin admitted to having seen him in February – or was it March? He tried to recall the conversation. Something about some ridiculous commercial venture in Central Africa. Coppin's church lacked the money and had no interest in that sort of thing.

Well, why was he here? Wasn't there enough work to be done among his own people in the South? Had he come to promote some scheme of migration to South or Central Africa? Coppin agreed that some Afro-Americans were looking for an asylum. In America, however, he was usually thought to be on the other side. How about race relations in the South? "I should not say they were dead in love with each other," he replied wryly. (Asked the same question, Attaway responded that some of his best friends were Southern white people.) Had Coppin perhaps read that "credit to his race," Booker T. Washington? Coppin knew him well, as a man: His ideas summed up perfectly what the AME was trying to do.

Was Coppin aware that Native ministers, purporting to represent the AME, had recently been accused of sedition in the Orange River Colony? That was indeed unfortunate, but Coppin knew nothing about it. The authorities had refused him permission to travel in the former republics, and unsupervised Native preachers might well do anything. Hadn't Bishop Turner been too quick in ordaining ministers? Yes, agreed Coppin, he thought he had. And finally: "Is your aim out here loyalty to the Government of the Colonies and friendly relations with the white races?" To that there could be but one response:

> I trust all the gentlemen present, and . . . everybody else in the civilized world for that matter, are prepared to believe that I am frank, truthful, and unevasive: and I answer emphatically "Yes." It seems to me that a course other than that would mean purposed and presumptuous and premeditated self-murder. I do not see what object I could have other than that.[31]

From the initial sparring to the loyalty oath, Bishop Coppin had made only one slip – the one about poverty. Throughout his life, beginning with his boyhood on the Eastern Shore of Maryland, he had learned to give apparently truthful answers to the probing questions of suspicious white men. It is unlikely that Coppin revealed to the commission the full range of his aims, activities, and associations. At the interview he was asked if the AME had an official publication. Yes, he said, *The Voice of Missions*. He did not volunteer to provide a complete file. It is not clear whether the Native Affairs Commission or the South African police ever acquired the journal. If they did, they would have found a rather interesting letter from Horatio Scott, an AME missionary in Port Elizabeth, who painted a glowing picture of vacant land and rising economic prospects: "Come on, my brave brothers and sisters, and help to reclaim the true Christian virtues of the sons and daughters of Ham."[32] In South Africa, it seemed, there was room for millions of American Negroes.

3. Recent interpretations of the origins of segregation in South Africa

In 1903 the widely recognized leader of the defeated but still un-bowed Afrikaner people, Louis Botha – general during the Boer War, future prime minister of the Union, and South Africa's Robert E. Lee – appeared before the Transvaal Labour Commission. That body had been convened by the British high commissioner, Sir Alfred Milner, to investigate the causes and consequences of a widespread, prolonged labor shortage that was seriously undermining the postwar rebuilding of the region's economy. Africans were staying at home in large numbers, somehow contriving to support their families on their small plots, unwilling to come out to work for the reduced level of wages that mining magnates, industrialists, large farmers, and government officials all agreed "the country" in such straitened circumstances could afford to pay. In effect – and Afro-Americans from afar envied their ability to assert their economic independence – Africans were mounting a successful general strike.[1] The Labour Commission was charged with deciding whether southern Africa's supply of labor was or could be equal to the demand and with determining whether, after all, some extraordinary measure, such as the importation of indentured Chinese coolies, might not be essential.

A large Afrikaner farmer himself, General Botha spoke for his class as well as for his people. Like mining and railroad men, he said, farmers were crying out desperately for labor, at wages they could afford to pay. Without it they must go under. But, he believed, there was no need to go outside for it. Southern Africa had available a huge, practically unlimited reservoir of African

46

labor. Wisely managed by an administration astute enough to heed the experience of Afrikaners, who had behind them several centuries of close contact with the Native mind, that resource would prove to be the region's greatest strength, enabling agriculture and industry alike to grow and prosper. Fortunately the resource was infinitely renewable. It could and should be tapped.

General Botha was a thoroughgoing, unapologetic white supremacist. He hated the Cape Colony's color-blind franchise, that hypocritical and dangerous experiment the British Colonial Office, in utter disregard for southern African realities, had forced upon his Afrikaner brothers to the south. The very thought of Africans voting, or of white politicians courting them, was anathema to him. Having won the war, he agreed, the British now had the power. But, he hinted none too subtly, any hopes of fundamental reconciliation, trust, and cooperation between Boer and Briton depended on the maintenance of white supremacy. On that question no compromise was possible. White must be on top.

At least as significant, however, is what Botha did not say. He expressed no desire to maintain the distinctive racial identity of Africans who were comfortably developing on their own lines, under their own traditional tribal institutions and customary law, on locations safely removed from white areas. This, as the knowledgeable reader will recognize at once, is the language of what would come to be called, in turn, segregation, apartheid, and separate development.

Botha was for the opposite of all that. He did not use the word "segregation." What he demanded was cheap, plentiful African labor. He wanted it close at hand and evenly distributed. He was not concerned that African family and tribal life might thereby be disrupted. Indeed, he urged that all of the large concentrations of Africans who were under British imperial control – including Basutoland, Zululand, Swaziland, and Bechuanaland – should be broken up at once. In their tribal reserves, he charged, Africans merely stagnated, doing little enough for themselves and even less for the country. Tribal homelands should no longer be protected. Whites should be able to buy land there, and Africans who lived in them should pay rent to the state. Outside the reserves, under a squatters' law like the one the Transvaal Republic had placed on its statute books in 1895, what Botha called Kaffir farming – that is, the renting of white-owned land to African peasants for cash or for a share of the crop – should be prohibited.

In the heyday of segregation zealots such as George Heaton Nicholls would proclaim the matchless virtues of the tribe. An authentic creation of the African tradition, the tribe would enable the race's distinctive "genius" to be nurtured and preserved. General Botha's testimony was strikingly devoid of such mystification. His objectives were clear and forthright. He wanted all Africans to be turned into detribalized proletarians, as soon as possible and by any means necessary. He wanted these landless people to be distributed evenly throughout the Transvaal's so-called white areas. Once they were there, economic necessity, taxation, "moral persuasion," and perhaps even force would "encourage" them to work in the industries and especially on the farms where their labor was so desperately "required."[2]

Botha's statement was typical of the testimony that was being given by numerous Afrikaans-speaking witnesses to various government commissions in the first decade of the twentieth century. They all demanded white supremacy. But the notion that tribal reserves could be used both as a dormitory for redundant Africans and as a regulative device, that from them millions of Africans would ebb and flow as the basis of South Africa's economy, that on the preservation of the homelands depended the health of white society, had apparently not occurred to them. These Afrikaner witnesses did not call for segregation. Nor had they learned to speak its mystifying language. Why, after all, would a farming people choose to be permanently separated from their most valuable asset, from the indispensable supply of African laborers on whom they counted to do the work?

In fact, of course, large farmers in South Africa's white areas have never been separated from African laborers. Under segregation what was really a system of labor control would be disguised by the language of physical distance and removal. But that mental transition was still in the future. Botha, at least, was unaware of it. For such a gyration to occur, and then for it to be made to appear the logical and perhaps even inevitable conclusion of this farming people's own history, would require both imagination and finesse. About 1910 General J. B. M. Hertzog of the Orange Free State, the future leader of the Nationalist Party, began to use the word "segregation" in his speeches. He borrowed the slogan, however, from English-speaking whites. Afrikaners for the most part were racists, fervent white supremacists. The language and the details of segregation would represent not a direct continuation of the prevailing Afrikaner ideas about how economy and society should be regulated, however, but a distinct departure from them.

In what, for want of a better term, is called the liberal interpretation of South African history, the formative experiences of slavery and the frontier are central. In the often persuasive and sometimes brilliantly distinguished prose of W. M. Macmillan, C. W. De Kiewiet, Sir Keith Hancock, and Leonard Thompson, the attitudes, practices, and mores of the twentieth century have been explained primarily on the basis of inheritance. There can surely be no quarrel with the general proposition that modern discrimination owes much to the racism of the past. Indeed, the argument that past and present are related is a truism. The question is not whether the experiences of the frontier and slavery have been important forces in South African history. Rather, it is the problem of linkage. How, under what specific circumstances, did the language and institutions of the particular system of race relations called segregation emerge?

General Louis Botha's testimony before the Transvaal Labour Commission of 1903 helps clarify the theoretical gap that many recent scholars have detected in the liberal interpretation of modern South African history. Botha did not use the word "segregation." And he fundamentally opposed many of the details that would be closely associated with it. Did segregation grow directly out of the Afrikaner past? If so, how?

Despite the great weight that has been placed upon it, the structure of frontier society – that is, the precise forms of social relations that existed in the Orange Free State, the Transvaal, and the northern Cape Colony during the late nineteenth century among large Afrikaner landowners, bywoner poor whites, and African peasant squatters, laborers, and tribesmen – is an immensely complicated subject that still awaits detailed analysis.[3] What we can be confident about is that those relations were not based on anything like modern segregation. Some Africans lived apart in tribes. Others lived and worked on white farms, which indeed had often been their own homes. But there were no Native locations or white areas from which Africans were excluded. Whites depended on African labor. And, as Botha explained, they wanted it nearby, under their direct personal control.

Nor, in the period before the 1830s, was slavery (another underinvestigated subject) much like segregation. Typically, as such liberal historians as Macmillan and De Kiewiet had observed themselves, masters and servants were joined in a system that combined direct exploitation with close (and often cruel) affective relations. The strength and sincerity of Afrikaner paternalism, like that of slaveowners in other parts of the world, varied considerably according to individual personalities and circumstances. We may well believe that many whites, especially the women on whose virtue racial purity depended, tried to maintain their distance, and that slaves were kept in their place.

The social relations of slavery were certainly based on white supremacy. But the vertical relationship of white over black, carried on within the close confines of comparatively isolated, largely self-contained units, is very different from the horizontal demarcations that are typical of segregation. The institutions and language of segregation, then, were not inherited directly from slavery. Nor could they have grown automatically out of the Afrikaners' own frontier past. They had to be invented.

Undoubtedly the uncompromising racial attitudes of Afrikaners, some of which had been formed as early as the seventeenth century, have been an important force in building and maintaining segregation. At the least they were a significant limiting factor. They would have made difficult or even impossible the development or imposition of any racial order in which white supremacy did not appear to be secure. But, as I argued in the first chapter, segregation should be distinguished from white supremacy. Racism alone cannot explain the development of any particular system and ideology of race relations. Instead we must emphasize secondary causes, the particular circumstances in which specific social formulations took shape.

Afrikaners adapted readily enough to segregation and soon became some of its most fervent advocates. Their past helped them to do so. There is, to repeat, no question that Afrikaner history has been a powerful force in the evolution of South Africa's racist society in the twentieth century. But the assumption that the specific institutions and ideology of segregation grew in any direct way out of the organization of the Afrikaners' own political economy as late as the 1890s must apparently be abandoned.

In recent years many historians have shifted the search for the origins of segregation to the only other available candidates, South Africa's English-speaking whites. Some students have emphasized the discriminatory policies that were being formulated with respect to Africans and Indians in Natal, where the white settlers were overwhelmingly English-speaking. Others have focused on the regulations that were being developed toward African peasants by English-speaking administrators in the eastern Cape. Still others have stressed what unquestionably was the center of South Africa's political economy, the mining–industrial complex that was exploding so rapidly on the Rand in the southern Transvaal. In all these areas, especially in the crucial period after the Boer War culminating in the formation of the Union in 1910, English-speaking whites were largely in control.

THE NATALIAN INTERPRETATION

In a well-researched, well-argued, but in my view ultimately unpersuasive book, David Welsh has traced what he calls *The Roots of Segregation* to nineteenth-century Natal.[4] As early as the 1850s, he writes, the Native policies of Natal and the Cape Colony were already diverging sharply. In the Cape, under the constitutional settlements of 1852 and 1872, when the colony received first representative and then responsible government, Coloured and African males who met high property and educational qualifications could vote. Enough of them did vote to make a significant difference in some electoral districts. The Cape could therefore claim to have evolved a workable safety valve. In Natal, although the conditions for responsible government in 1890 were formally similar, virtually no Africans and only a few Indians voted. In practice Natal's franchise was as racially exclusive as the regulations of the Orange Free State or the Transvaal.

The Cape's official Native policy, as articulated by the contro-

versial mid-Victorian governor Sir George Grey, was amalgam-
ationist. In Grey's opinion the British Empire's "weaker races,"
such as the aborigines of Australia, the Maoris of New Zealand,
or the Africans of South Africa, were in a race for survival. Backward peoples must adapt themselves, they must become economically indispensable to Europeans, or they must suffer the
fate of the American Indians. The European cultural frontier –
law, hospitals, jobs, education, Christianity – should therefore
be extended as rapidly as possible. At every opportunity, such as
the strange and tragic cattle-killing of 1857 – when a "revitaliza-
tionist" prophet persuaded large numbers of Xhosa to destroy
their crops and kill their herds, after which their ancestors would
join in an attack that would drive the white people into the sea –
African political institutions should be undermined and replaced.
Left in isolation, Grey believed, barbarous peoples were doomed.
Only if they became "part of ourselves" could they survive.

Meanwhile, the principal Native administrator of Natal, Sir
Theophilus Shepstone, was evolving a different approach. He
called it separation. Facts, he believed, must be faced. Africans
were a distinct people and should be treated as such. They should
be governed indirectly through their own chiefs and laws, which
should be protected as much as possible from erosion caused by
European influence. The fundamental bases of African society,
especially their rules of land tenure and marriage, should be
maintained. Shepstone's objective, he insisted, was not to keep
Africans in their backward, barbarous state. Too rapid a process
of Westernization, however, would be destructive to them, as
well as dangerous for the whites who were such a tiny minority
among them. Africans, Shepstone believed, should advance not
as individuals but as groups, whose identity and integrity were
preserved.

In many ways, Welsh continues, Shepstone's doctrine of separation was out of step with the dominant mid-Victorian motif
of environmentalism. Even most white Natalians opposed him.
Like the contemporary Afrikaner farmers of the northern Cape,
the Orange Free State, or the Transvaal, they wanted land that
belonged to Africans. They also wanted labor. And the tribal
system, in their view, prevented potential laborers from coming
out to work. If it could have been stripped of its liberal rhetoric,

which they did not admire, the Natalian colonists would have preferred Sir George Grey's policy of turning Africans into consumers and producers in the European-controlled economy. Shepstone, however, argued that aggressive detribalization would be disastrous for the small, vulnerable colony of Natal. And he prevailed.

By the 1890s Shepstone, and more significantly his followers, had begun to mold his pragmatic and sometimes inconsistent views into a coherent doctrine. By then the severe labor shortage of the mid-nineteenth century, which had driven Natal's sugar planters to import thousands of Indian coolies, had become less acute. At once pushed and pulled into a closer, more constant relationship with the white economy, Africans were coming out to work in larger numbers. Meanwhile, Natal was being spared the frontier conflicts that were threatening neighboring colonies. On its own borders the British army in the early 1880s fought a fierce, protracted war against the Zulu. Inside the colony proper, where Shepstone still ruled, law and order were preserved.

The conviction that Shepstone's program had saved them gradually gained ground among white Natalians. "Shepstonism" became a doctrine: The tribe might progress, but it should advance as a cohesive group, that is, very slowly. Africans must be governed indirectly: through their own chiefs, according to their own laws, on their own lines. Later events seemed to confirm the soundness of the formula. Shepstone left office with the coming of responsible government in 1890. The African tax revolt of 1906–8 could therefore be blamed on a mistaken departure from his principles.[5] In the testimony and conclusions of the Natal Native Affairs Commission, which investigated the causes of this "reluctant rebellion," the Shepstone doctrine was strongly reinforced. During the era of national unification, Welsh concludes, Natalians were among the foremost advocates of segregation.

Indeed, they were. For example, Natal's permanent undersecretary for Native affairs, S. O. Samuelson, had learned the lesson well. Europeans and Africans must inevitably conflict, he testified before the South African Native Affairs Commission of 1903–5, as long as their "progress and advance . . . followed the same lines." In the interests of both white and black "the nationalities and characteristics of our natives" should therefore be preserved. Before the same body J. C. Stuart urged that Africans be controlled through their own chiefs and laws. "To manage in this way," he explained helpfully, "means *to keep the Native in his place.*"[6] In the 1920s the historian Edgar Brookes found in Shepstone's policies what at the time he believed to be a positive, humane solution to South Africa's Native Problem. Later he recanted. The educationist Charles Loram maintained that Africans should be given distinctive training, appropriate to a realistic assessment of their likely future as manual workers in agriculture and industry, in institutions patterned after Hampton and Tuskegee in the American South. Still later, George Heaton Nicholls elevated the Zulu royal family to a largely mythological but extremely functional cornerstone of separate development.[7]

Welsh's analysis of Natal's very substantial contribution to the theory and practice of segregation is valuable. Yet the linkage between precedents and development seems weak. Like the more common attribution of segregation to traditional Afrikaner racism, the Natalian interpretation is anachronistic. From Welsh's own evidence it is clear that Shepstone himself was not diametrically opposed to amalgamation. "Segregation" was a word he used infrequently. He was no doctrinaire. In his view the separate administration of Africans, employing their own institutions wherever possible, was a practical necessity. They were different, and they had to be dealt with on that basis. But separation was not to him an end in itself. It was not, he insisted, a policy of perpetual stagnation. It was fully "capable of being modified [so] as to advance their [Africans'] progress to a higher and better civilization."

The policies of Shepstone and Sir George Grey certainly conflicted. Whereas Grey thought the structure of tribal authority should be weakened whenever possible, Shepstone believed that it should be preserved. The argument between them, however, was not about ends but means. As late as 1892, in an exchange of public letters with President F. W. Reitz of the Orange Free State, Shepstone (who by then was out of office, and was addressing a local audience rather than superiors in Cape Town or Whitehall) condemned repression. "The human intellect," he maintained, in language that even Grey could hardly have improved upon, "cannot be fettered: when aided by education it will rise to the level that is due to it, whether covered by a coloured skin or a white."[8] Shepstone's basic philosophical assumptions, after all, were environmentalist. Evidently the mantle of "father of segregation" rests uneasily on Sir Theophilus Shepstone's mid-Victorian shoulders.

This is not to discount Welsh's close analysis of how white Natalians developed and fabricated Shepstone's pragmatic program into an important component of the emerging ideology of segregation. On that point the evidence is solid and persuasive. The trouble is that by this stage in his argument, Welsh is no longer tracing the roots of segregation in the nineteenth century. He is talking about the *making* of a twentieth-century ideology in the twentieth century. One of the ways ideologies are constructed is to search the past for harbingers, superficial similarities, and fictitious lineages. What in reality is new or discontinuous can then be presented as merely the logical, natural extension of the wisdom and experience of history. In the early twentieth century many South Africans, including Natalians, were engaged in this enterprise. The tendency endures.

MARXIST REVISIONISM

Unlike the Natalian interpretation, those who have stressed unfolding policies toward African peasants, beginning in the eastern Cape, and the impact of the economic revolution that centered on the gold-mining region of the southern Transvaal have not been concerned with tracing the origins of segregation to precedents or harbingers within any particular colony. They have emphasized the relationship of segregation not to place but to process. Or, rather, to interrelated processes: to state formation, to changes in the mode of production, to the formation of capitalist and proletarian classes among whites, to the development and subsequent underdevelopment of African peasants. In the main the revisionists are Marxists or neo-Marxists. Their emergence in the last decade or so has been largely responsible for the most significant reinterpretation of South African history since the rise of the liberal school in the era between the two world wars.[9]

The very term "race relations," the revisionists insist, belongs within quotation marks. Most South African historians have held that attitudes are primary, that inherited racism has molded social, economic, and political institutions into strangely contorted shapes. The revisionists emphasize instead the controlling role of class. They do not of course deny that the cultural legacy of the past has contributed to the attitudes and practices of the present. They do deny that it has been a determining force. The true origins of segregation, they maintain, are to be sought not in the Calvinist religion or the frontier tradition of the Afrikaners but in the massive structural changes that have transformed the country during the last century into a modern, industrial, urban, and above all capitalist society. In no sense, the revisionists conclude, are South African race relations a dinosaur, an anachronistic museum piece doomed to spontaneous internal decay as capitalism develops and matures.

On the contrary, the revisionists argue, segregation should be understood as a distinctly twentieth-century phenomenon, which developed to fit the specific circumstances of the twentieth century. Between about 1890 and, say, the victory of General J. B. M. Hertzog's Nationalist–Labour coalition in the election of 1924, rapid, fundamental, and closely interrelated changes took place in South African society. On the Rand the gold industry was consolidated and rationalized as the essential basis for capital accumulation and for the construction of an infrastructure in transportation and manufacturing. An autonomous, unitary state, the Union of South Africa, was created. Agriculture was decisively transformed. Rooted in the rapidly altering productive relations, classes formed and came into fundamental antagonism. The political climax of the period was the so-called Rand Revolution of 1922, a violent confrontation between white labor and the capitalist state that helped to bring about the Nationalist–Labour coalition the following year.

Closely and structurally related to all these developments, the system and ideology of segregation took shape during the same period. Although it was perforce built out of historical materials, the revisionists maintain, segregation was no mere extension of the discriminatory attitudes and practices of the past. Created to resolve unprecedented problems, it was essentially new. It was an order of race relations. Its primary function, however, was to mystify and legitimize a new system of class relationships. Segregation was thus an integral part of the complex process by which industrial capitalism developed in the specific circumstances of South Africa. (Some go further and use the word "essential.") During this critical, pivotal period the country – or rather the white part of it – began to escape from its former position as a backward economy on the periphery of the world system, a supplier of agricultural materials heavily dependent on European and especially British manufacturers. It was then that a decisive intersection took place between class and race. Of that union segregation was born.

Some revisionists pinpoint the critical turning point still more narrowly to the Milner era of reconstruction in the Transvaal following the British occupation of Johannesburg in 1901.[10] Until Britain's Liberal government under Sir Henry Campbell-Bannerman conceded responsible government to the former republic in 1907, Sir Alfred Milner's regime in the Transvaal exercised what appeared to be dictatorial powers. This period must indeed rank high on the list of occasions when things might have gone differently, when South Africa might conceivably have taken an alternative road toward a more liberal society. Instead, the Milner regime established a close alliance with the mining magnates and made the crucial decision to consolidate and defend a cheap-labor policy. Simultaneously, Martin Legassick and others conclude, more than any other single group, men high in the largely English-speaking power elite of the Transvaal were implanting segregation into the region's institutional patterns.

As the Transvaal goes, so goes South Africa. In many ways the location of the origins of segregation at the center of the developing economy, rather than on the periphery in Natal, is persuasive. Segregation has been built and maintained by power. And since the 1890s the nexus of economic and political power has been on the Rand. Nevertheless, the stress on the Milner era seems a little too specific. By 1907 processes that were crucial to the simultaneous development of capitalism and segregation were still far from complete. The autonomous Union of South Africa was created by act of the British Parliament only in 1909. The Mines and Works Act consolidated the job-reservation system in industry in 1911. The Natives Land Act, the single most important piece of the segregationist program, was passed in 1913, the Native Affairs Act for the administration of the reserves in 1920, and the Native (Urban Areas) Act in 1923. In 1922 the crucial confrontation took place between an autonomous, capitalist state and an urban Afrikaner working class. In 1907, when Milner left South Africa, neither of those two crucial forces had existed.

The revisionists all agree, however, that by the election of 1924 the essential institutions, framework, and ideology of modern South African class and race relations had been created. Contrary to the perceptions of many contemporaries, they conclude, General Hertzog's subsequent campaign for segregation was not a significant departure from the program of the South African Party, which had held power under Generals Botha and Smuts since 1911. The central thesis of the revisionists is stark and clear. A system of race relations that is not only compatible with capitalism but that, in the specific conditions of South Africa, has enabled capitalism to develop there is no mere anachronism. Segregation has its roots in the most vital, the most central processes of modern South African society. It is therefore unlikely to wither away.

As the reader may have gathered, I largely agree with the main conclusions of the Marxist or neo-Marxist revisionist interpretation. I also believe, as I shall show in later chapters, that these conclusions can be fruitfully applied to the somewhat different case of the emergence of segregation as a new order of race relations in the American South. Primarily for the benefit of readers who may be unfamiliar with recent analyses of South African history, I shall summarize the Marxist explanation of the origins of segregation in the period 1890–1924 in some detail. The political and economic processes to which segregation was integrally related occurred together. In the hope of being intelligible, however, I shall consider them separately.

STATE FORMATION

From the Great Trek of the 1830s until the Boer War of 1899–1902, except for Britain's abortive occupation of the Transvaal in the late 1870s, the political power of South Africa's whites had been decentralized into four small competing units. Natal and the Cape Colony had remained subject to some degree of control from the British Colonial Office, which accounts for the language of racial equality in their constitutions. Despite large numbers of Afrikaners in the northern Cape, in both colonies the economic and political power had been concentrated in English-speaking hands.

The two northern republics, the Orange Free State and the Transvaal, had been formed by "trekking" Boers – partly in reaction against Britain's policies of the 1830s, when slavery had been abolished, and partly in continuation of a pastoral people's quest for land, grass, and water. In a virtually unceasing struggle – fought, as De Kiewiet explained, not because Boers and Africans were different but because, since both were cattle people, their economic objectives were fundamentally the same – Afrikaner commando had met the impi of Zulu and Sotho.[11]

Throughout the mid-nineteenth century Britain's frontier policy had alternated confusingly between intervention and passive withdrawal. In 1852, for instance, citing the experience of successive governors-general under the East India Company, who time and again had found that occupying "just the next piece" was essential for preserving order in the territory they already controlled, Sir Harry Smith had annexed the Orange River Territory. Two years later the action had been reversed. Britain would remain neutral, a British colonial secretary had written, and if "the natives should choose to slaughter each other and the Boers & Missionaries choose to assist them, we can't prevent their doing so."[12] Yet even the expansionist urge of what John S. Galbraith has called reluctant imperialists was hard to stop.[13] In the late 1850s Sir George Grey had proposed the federation of all four white units; the Colonial Office had turned him down. In 1877 the Conservatives, whose colonial secretary was the earl of Carnarvon, had annexed the Transvaal. In what is often called the First Anglo–Boer War, Afrikaners had resisted. By 1881 Gladstone's Liberal government had again withdrawn.

In 1899, when the young Cambridge graduate Jan Christian Smuts, the attorney general of the South African (Transvaal) Republic, called his fellow Afrikaners to arms with his fiery pamphlet *A Century of Wrong,* he described the tangle of Anglo–Boer relations since the Great Trek as "a strange pursuit."[14] For the mid-nineteenth century, at least, that description is accurate. From the British perspective the interior of southern Africa had been a vexing frontier problem, but little more. In the Afrikaners' view the British imperial factor, however bumbling and inconsistent it might be, had been a source of constant anxiety and irritation. Resisting it had become the raison d'être of the two republics.

All of that changed with the opening of the gold industry on the Witwatersrand in the late 1880s. Suddenly the formerly despised interior of southern Africa became the richest prize of all in the scramble of the so-called new imperialism. Both capital, much of it accumulated from the diamond fields around Kimberley in the eastern Cape, and the international community of mining men whom the Afrikaners called Uitlanders swarmed into the instant city of Johannesburg. Already insecure, the Afrikaners felt embattled. The South African Republic under President Paul Krüger excluded Uitlanders from the franchise, providing a case for an aggressive British "forward policy." In a plot hatched by Cecil Rhodes, a fabulously rich mining magnate and the conquering founder of Rhodesia who at the time was prime minister of the Cape, and with the complicity of the Conservative colonial secretary Joseph Chamberlain, the celebrated putsch called the Jameson Raid tried in 1895 to overthrow Krüger's regime. From the British perspective it failed disastrously.

Four years later, after an exchange of ultimata between Krüger and the British high commissioner Sir Alfred Milner, the Boer War began. The British were overconfident; the Boers' skill and tenacity surprised them; the war was difficult and protracted. Not until 1902, and in the late stages only by systematically occupying the country district by district, building blockhouses at regular intervals, and rounding up the people into a new invention called concentration camps, did the British manage to finish this small war. Even then, with results that were to be significant for the later political history of the country and for the African majority, the peace of Vereeniging had to be negotiated.

Virtually all historians of South Africa would probably agree on the general outline of this political narrative. The most controversial point remains the degree to which, as the radical English economist John A. Hobson and other pro-Boers claimed at

the time, British economic imperialism in general and the Randlords in particular provoked the war as a means of protecting
vital fields of investment. The crucial role of one Randlord, Cecil
Rhodes, seems clear enough. Recent research on such magnates
as Julius Werhner and Alfred Beit, who were more directly involved than Rhodes was in the mining industry itself, however,
has cast doubt on this apparently obvious case of the economic
causes of imperialism.[15] In general, the big men of the Rand seem
to have been reasonably content with the Krüger regime. Little
evidence connects them directly to conspiracy; what capitalists
wanted primarily was stability. As usual the economic and political factors that led to this particular event are tangled. It is, however, difficult to avoid the conclusion that the Boer War was the
violent climax of a general crisis that had been created by the
rapid invasion of capital and capitalists into the Transvaal's agrarian society.

The most significant point for the Marxist revisionist interpretation concerns not the causes of the war but its results. During
the reconstruction of the defeated Afrikaner republics under the
British high commissioner Sir Alfred Milner, white political
power was centralized for the first time in South African history.[16] An era of state formation followed, the most important
events of which were the Liberal government's dramatic conces-
sion of responsible government to the Transvaal and the Orange
Free State in 1907, a constitutional convention, the passage
through the British Parliament of the Act of Union, and the
transfer of power to an autonomous Union of South Africa in
1910.[17] The first prime minister was an Afrikaner, General Louis
Botha. From the perspective of Milner, as well as from that of
educated Africans and their white supporters, this appeasement
of the Afrikaners was at least premature. They protested vigorously, but without result.

Whose, or what, interests would this new state serve? How
would it reflect, and how would it alter, the balance of class
power, the basic institutions and structure of society? For all except "crude" Marxists – and this point bears stressing because it
is still frequently misunderstood – economic forces do not determine political behavior in any direct, automatic, mechanical way.
The crucial factor in any situation is the relationship to the organs

of power of more or less organized, more or less conscious groups called classes. These classes do have their roots in changing productive relations, so that contradictions inherent in the mode of production *ultimately* become decisive. But that is in the long run, measured by the glacial passage of the great epochs of history. Real people live in the short run. And they fight it out in terms of political power. In that sense Marx might more accurately be described as a political than an economic determinist.

For Marxist revisionists the era of state formation after the Boer War is therefore intensely significant. As we have seen, the narrower argument has been made that the period 1901–7 was pivotal, the one occasion when the course of South African history might have been turned in a radically different direction. In fact, however, Milner's dictatorship was far from absolute. The high commissioner was hemmed in by severe budgetary constraints, by the swift resurgence of Afrikaner political organization, by sharp class divisions within the English-speaking community, and by the imperial government's inability and, after the Liberal victory of 1906, its refusal to support his policies.

All of Milner's objectives – rebuilding the war-damaged economy, reconstructing the Afrikaners, attracting large numbers of British immigrants, creating a great dominion called the United States of South Africa – depended on getting the gold mines back into full, profitable production. They were the only available source of rapid capital accumulation, the indispensable basis for railroads, harbors, roads, agricultural subsidies, and the costs of bureaucracy.

The mining magnates may or may not have needed Milner's small war to guarantee their profits. If Milner were going to achieve *his* plans, however, he certainly needed them.[18] The most difficult problem for the mining magnates, and thus for Milner, was how to attract sufficient Africans at wages about one-third below the prewar rate. In order to break the African strike, the Milner regime helped the Chamber of Mines extend its recruitment far afield into East and Central Africa. In a controversial decision, which united South Africa's white labor advocates and British humanitarians into an unlikely alliance, he agreed to import Chinese coolies. Milner's motives were political. But his policies had enormous repercussions for the concentration and exercise of economic power.

With the Act of Union of 1909 – the new government actually took office in 1910 – white power became still more concentrated. The last effective imperial restraints on local initiative were removed. As General Kitchener had agreed in the Treaty of Vereeniging in 1902, the question of an African franchise had not been discussed until after responsible self-government had been conceded to the two northern territories. During the constitutional convention the Native Question was once more postponed, leaving the existing arrangements undisturbed. Otherwise, neither Natal nor the former Afrikaner republics would have joined the Union. The next half-century would show, as General Smuts explained at the time, that the supposedly entrenched position of African and Coloured voters in the Cape was but "a slight check, perhaps no check at all."[19]

In the United States the "great migration" of blacks that began in 1915 gradually affected the balance of political power in several key Northern cities – but only because they had the vote in the North. In South Africa not only was the franchise not extended but, after 1936, it was lost in the Cape itself. The decision to leave to the future what Smuts called the sphinx problem of the vote for Africans, Coloureds, and Asians was therefore more than "a detail."[20] The most significant trend of this early period of state formation, however, was the consolidation of large landowners, industrialists, and mining magnates in the South African (later the United) Party under Botha and Smuts. In an apt description borrowed from German history, this power elite has been called "the alliance of gold and maize."[21]

During the ascendancy of the Botha–Smuts regime, that is, until 1924, the overall objective of Britain's policy of appeasement appeared to have succeeded. The South African Party proved to be a willing group of collaborators, favorable to the Empire's commercial and strategic interests.[22] In 1914 South Africa's rulers suppressed an Afrikaner rebellion. A South African force defeated the Germans in South-West Africa. Joining both the King's African Rifles and volunteers from British East Africa, South Africans chased the Germans around Tanganyika. Smuts joined the Imperial War Cabinet and helped to organize the Royal Air Force. In the shape of a Class C mandate over South-West Africa, which in effect made the territory part of the Union, collaboration bore fruit. South Africa's role as a loyal member of the Commonwealth seemed to be secure.

This apparent long-term complementarity of interests between Britain and South Africa's "natural rulers" was illusory. Botha died in 1919. Smuts, who was much less popular or trusted, replaced him. In 1922 Smuts clashed violently with white workers, many of them Afrikaners, in the Rand Revolution. The following year the "small men" of both white "races" formed an opposition: the Nationalist–Labour pact under General Hertzog, which swept Smuts from power in 1924. These political alignments lasted until the national government of 1931, which was formed in response to the crisis of the Depression, when Smuts agreed to serve under Hertzog. In the late thirties the Purified Nationalists under D. F. Malan splintered off to the right. Hertzog resigned in 1939, and Smuts took the country once more into a British war. Malan's Nationalists came to power in the watershed election of 1948 and have never since relinquished it. In that year a new phase in the career of segregation – apartheid – began.[23]

In the constitutional deliberations leading to the Act of Union, the Native Question had frequently been cited as a pressing reason to choose the unitary over the federal model.[24] The problem involved the whole country. It therefore needed to be confronted as a whole by a centralized state capable of pooling all available ideas and implementing them rapidly. The threads of Native policy, the laws and practices that had evolved for more than half a century in the four units, were gathered together by the South African Native Affairs Commission (1903–5), under the chairmanship of Sir Godfrey Lagden. After union white power was brought to bear on the Native Question as never before.

All of the basic decisions that were to affect Africans so seriously – fixing the limits of the reserves and protecting them against white intrusion, routing railways so they served white agriculture and industry, enforcing low average wages that "the country" could afford, regulating African settlement in white areas and especially in towns – had deep economic roots and enormous economic impact. But they were by no means the automatic, determined results of economic laws. Indeed, they were often made precisely in order to prevent the predictable effects of supply and demand. They were political decisions, made for political reasons and enforced by political power. For Marxist revisionists, as well as for other historians, the crucial mechanism in the development of the persistent pattern of race and class relations called segregation was the centralized power of the South African state.

THE MINERAL REVOLUTION AND EARLY INDUSTRIAL CAPITALISM

During the last hundred years the South African state has intervened powerfully in the economy, distorting its shape in ways that could not have been predicted in the 1860s. In that decade, despite the importance of the harbor at Table Bay in the western Cape as a halfway house between Europe and Asia, South Africa had still not been brought effectively into the world economy. From the interior came agricultural exports: a few hides, a little grain, some inferior wine. Communications were primitive; the accumulation of capital was low. South Africa lagged far behind Australia.[25]

In the 1880s the mineral revolution began to change these conditions dramatically. Within a generation the world economy took hold and bit deep. Employing technology and techniques invented in earlier gold rushes in California, Victoria, and western Canada, an international mining community invaded the Transvaal. So did thousands of Africans, tribesmen miraculously transformed into miners, who were soon working at depths of 2,000 feet or more. The city of Johannesburg sprang forth almost instantly.

The central importance of the mineral revolution in South African economic history is obvious. For at least the half-century after the 1880s, mining was absolutely crucial for the accumulation of capital and for the support of transportation, agriculture, and secondary industry. More recently, relative to the expanding industries that it helped to generate and nurture, mining has declined. It still looms large, however, in any government's calculations of revenue and foreign exchange. In the decade after the Boer War, when the economy had to be rebuilt as a basis for a new nation, mining was especially pivotal.

First the diamond fields of Kimberley in the eastern Cape, then the gold and coal mines on the Witwatersrand river in the southern Transvaal: Both were pacesetters as well as models in the formation of South African industrial capitalism. Much of the early transportation system connected these centers of extraction in the interior with the ports of Durban, Port Elizabeth, and Cape Town. Revenue from gold subsidized what at first were uneconomic railway branches into white agricultural areas. Mining directly stimulated local engineering and manufacturing. The rapidly expanding urban–industrial complex on the Rand was a primary market for domestic agricultural and industrial production. The low wages paid African mine laborers, the majority of whom have been foreign migrants until very recently, helped to reduce wage levels throughout the economy. The organization of the African work force in the closed–compound system, which had first been developed at Kimberley, partly in response to diamond smuggling, and which had then been transmitted to the Rand as a means of social control, was widely imitated.[26] The mineral revolution is thus a code name for a complex, interacting, and ultimately self-sustaining process of economic, social, and urban growth.

All historians trace the origins of modern South African economic history to these complex changes. Marxist revisionists have concentrated on the gold industry – some charge unduly. But they can hardly claim to have discovered its central importance.

One revisionist work, Frederick Johnstone's *Class, Race, and Gold,* emphasizes two basic facts that do seem absolutely crucial. First, although the ore on the Rand is apparently inexhaustible, it is commonly of very low quality. Second, South African mines have found it profitable to expand enormously their recovery of ore of such a low yield per ton that, had it been in California, Australia, or even India it would have been left in the ground.

Hence a riddle: Until the 1960s, when the price of gold climbed to dizzying and unprecedented heights, South African mineowners, like their competitors elsewhere, faced a fixed price on the world market. (Younger readers may need to be reminded that even as late as the early 1960s the United States Treasury was said to be subsidizing South Africa by guaranteeing to purchase gold at thirty-five dollars an ounce!) Meanwhile, costs of machinery and explosives were steadily rising. Yet the expenses of equipping any particular mine varied little. Roughly the same number of miners and supervisers and the same quantitites of drills and explosives were needed to work a good mine as a poor one. The only way to cut costs in an unprofitable mine, therefore, was to close it down. In only one way, then, could the Rand have managed to continue and expand its production: by keeping average wages as low as possible. South Africa's gold ore is profitable to mine not only because there happens to be a great deal of it but because average wages are low.[27]

The desire of the Transvaal's mining magnates to cut costs in relation to profits was not of course unique. What was different was not the motives of these capitalists but their success. In most Western economies average wages have risen steadily and substantially since the early stages of industrialization. (The question is not whether wages have increased but whether they have risen as much as they might have.) David Ricardo's famous iron law of wages, which so strongly influenced Marx's mistaken views about the inevitable immiseration of the working class, has been confounded. Most workers have moved into what Lenin despairingly and disparagingly called the labor aristocracy. For Africans in South Africa's gold mines, this pattern of increasing prosperity made possible by expanding productivity has not happened. The average real wages of African miners until the late 1960s were actually lower than they had been in the relatively open labor market of the 1890s.[28]

Low average wages were South Africa's great advantage. The Rand had available an industrial reserve army: politically powerless, overwhelmingly foreign, black, and ultra-exploitable. On this large group what Johnstone calls an exploitation color bar could be imposed.[29] This form of discrimination, he insists, was essentially different from the job color bar, which blocked the advancement of qualified individuals. In Johnstone's view the exploitation color bar was fundamentally a class instrument: Employers "mystified" low wages for a class of workers on the grounds of racial inferiority. A liberal might well reply that race was the determining factor: These workers were politically powerless and therefore ultra-exploitable because they were black; they were paid low wages because South African society had always discriminated against them. Once again, the distinction Johnstone draws between two kinds of color bar, which have usually been employed interchangeably, seems valid. The main fact, that South Africa's gold mines paid very low average wages to Africans, is not in serious dispute.

Whether the exploitation color bar was necessary for the gold industry's survival and expansion remains controversial. But it was obviously in the interest of management to attack the individual or job color bar whenever possible in the hope of replacing whites with blacks – at one-fifth or less the cost. In 1921, for instance, some £10.6 million out of a total wage cost of £16.6 million went to about 19,000 whites, the balance of £6 million being distributed among some 300,000 Africans. (Most of the whites were permanent; relatively few Africans worked the entire year.) On this issue white labor and white management faced each other. Although they supported as much as anyone the goal of a white man's country, claimed the employers, a rational hiring program was absolutely essential or the industry would topple. A civilized standard of living was a heavy burden for the white workers to bear, their spokesmen rejoined. How, unless they were protected, could they possibly compete with these highly advantaged members of an inferior race?

In 1922, the year of the Rand Revolution, the protracted dispute reached its violent climax. The white workers lost; the employers consolidated their victory. By 1924 the white labor force, now reduced to 16,500, still received £7.3 million out of a total bill of £13.7 million. Such figures go far toward demonstrating the contention that the exploitation color bar was not only advantageous but essential. White wages had been cut by £3 million. Africans received only an additional £400,000.[30]

With strong support from Smuts, the gold industry had carried out a severe assault on the positions of white workers. The extreme economic crisis, if not the political repercussions, of the early twenties passed. The industry survived and expanded. It is conceivable that in a different political climate, the mines might have contrived to maintain or slightly reduce production levels while raising the wages of Africans. Such an argument, however, cannot be sustained on the basis of the statistics that were provided by the Transvaal Chamber of Mines. (They are the only figures available and, although the Chamber's bias in favor of making a case for reform is apparent, the figures are ordinarily assumed to be accurate, perhaps because they are the only ones that exist.)

Although it received a bare fraction of the attention given to the Rand Revolution of white workers, an African strike of 1920 threatened the industry's viability even more severely. The Chamber of Mines calculated that even an increase all round of three shillings per shift, the lowest claim African miners were demanding at the time, would cost an annual addition of £8 million. Even at the premium price for gold that then prevailed on the world market, the Chamber concluded, twenty-three of the forty-seven mines that were then operating would at once be forced out of business.[31]

It is also very possible, though it would have been difficult to persuade white workers of this, that the mines might have been even more efficient in weeding out superfluous whites. Many of those who remained after 1923, however, were truly skilled workers who at the time could not conceivably have been replaced by Africans.

Thus the most persuasive conclusion is that, by abolishing the class or exploitation color bar against African workers, by paying not an average wage the industry could afford but one established by the free market, the Rand would have been exposed during the 1920s to the same intense squeeze that operated in Australia, Canada, or California. The end of the run, indeed, was widely predicted at the time. Rising wages, along with increasing costs of equipment, would have precipitated the decline of a once-thriving industry. Although gold ore would still have remained in the ground, extracting it from ever-deeper levels would have become unprofitable. Presumably South Africa's economy, like Australia's, would have developed anyway. But growth would have taken place more slowly and with very different social and political effects.

As both the Labour Party, which represented white workers, and African spokesmen complained at the time, an industry that paid such low wages that it was forced to draw most of its labor force from outside the country, that is, from areas still more depressed than South Africa's own reserves, could hardly be said to be operating in a free market.[32] The gold industry depended directly on a steady flow of migratory labor from afar, which the state helped to recruit and transport. In addition, the state helped to police the closed-compound system, through which the ultra-exploitable labor force could be controlled. During the strike by African miners in 1920, the system proved its value by permitting individual units to be isolated and defeated. It did so again during the Smuts government's suppression of the African strike of the Rand in 1946, a central event in postwar South African history.

The compound system was widely imitated. On the railways and docks, on farms in white areas, in fledgling industries, comparable labor patterns took root throughout the country. Such systematic class and race discrimination may or may not have been necessary for industrial capitalism to develop in South Africa. Very likely, however, it was the only way the country could both industrialize and maintain its traditional framework of racial stratification. Although ultimate causation may be disputed, the fundamental effects may not. The exploitation color bar became the basis of South Africa's political economy. As Percy Fitzpatrick, a sometime president of the Chamber of Mines and a close ally of Milner, explained to the Transvaal Labour Commission of 1903:

> Cheap labour (which for some time to come means coloured labour) has been the basis of South African calculations. It fixes the limits of development and determines the pace. We must either supplement the present supply or stagnate till conditions change so that white labour will become the cheap labour. I do not believe that anybody will ever be content or even be able to submit to the latter course. Shareholders can wait for dividends, but men cannot wait for bread.[33]

Inherent in the situation of the gold industry was a basic structure of relationships between management and labor, and between white and black workers. No matter how paternal individual mine owners might feel toward "their" white workers, it was obviously in their interest to attack the individual or job color bar. Even if they did not attack it – in fact, spokesmen for the Transvaal Chamber of Mines rarely troubled themselves with concealing their intent – white workers whose average wages were eight or nine times higher than those paid to Africans were naturally suspicious. As Frederick Johnstone explains, white workers were structurally insecure.[34] Many writers have severely criticized the white unions for their long, stubborn defense of the industrial color bar. But this modern form of racism was clearly inherent in the situation in which white workers found themselves. As long as the huge gap between average wages persisted, the interests of management and skilled labor, and therefore of white and black workers, would continue to be fundamentally antagonistic.

Of the white workers the most structurally insecure, and therefore presumably the most racist, were the marginal or semi-skilled, the last hired. Increasingly, as English-speaking whites left to fight in World War I, these most vulnerable positions were being filled by Afrikaners. By common consent the latter were less efficient than the more experienced Africans. Having come under intense pressure from the agrarian revolution of the late nineteenth century, these Afrikaner poor whites were the first wave of the last trek to the towns.[35] They were the country's first indigenous white proletariat. Their links with their country cousins remained strong. Like all such migrants, especially in the first generation – like the town laborers of industrializing England who often led rural uprisings, like the Irish in New York or Boston who provided money and leaders for the revolution at home – these Afrikaners looked back with nostalgia to the rural areas where so many of them hoped to return.

In 1913 English-speaking syndicalists had led a revolt on the Rand. In 1922 a new form of industrial action appeared: the commando system. A new class had formed. Further migrations from the countryside would add to its numbers and strength. The emergence of the urban Afrikaner proletariat was a central event in modern South African history.

The racism of working-class Afrikaners no doubt owed something to their cultural heritage: to their Calvinist religion, their experience during slavery, their long history of conflict with Africans, their lack of education, their isolation from European ideas, their frontier ethos. None of these cultural influences, at any rate, was in any way inconsistent with the economic insecurity that grew immediately out of the social relations of their situation in industry and town. There they found themselves in direct, persistent structural antagonism to the interests of the simultaneously emerging African proletariat.

The abortive revolution of 1922 was central to the consciousness of the Afrikaner working class. With great ferocity the strike was put down, appropriately enough, by the "big man's" representative, General Smuts. In 1920 the power of the state was used against Africans; in 1922 it was used against white workers. The alliance of gold and maize had won this battle. Although they were careful not to undermine the general pattern of the exploitation color bar against most African workers, on which (according to management) the survival of the industry ultimately depended, the mine owners carried through extensive reforms. White positions in the marginal, semiskilled areas were cut back or filled with Africans. The political repercussions of the big man's victory were immense. Within the year, General Hertzog's Nationalists had formed what Smuts called an unholy alliance with the English-speaking Labour Party.

THE AGRARIAN REVOLUTION

Both the large landowners, half of the alliance of gold and maize, and the Afrikaner urban proletariat, whose formation as a class by the 1920s radically altered the alignments and balance of South African politics, had their origins in profoundly significant and comparatively recent changes in agricultural methods and rural land tenure. Superficially South Africa's agrarian history appears to have followed the same broad contours as those of other societies. Agriculture became heavily capitalized. More machinery was employed. Improvements in transportation made internal and overseas markets increasingly accessible. Yields increased. Ownership consolidated. Like the Australian Outback or the American Midwest, South Africa's countryside became a big man's frontier. Small men became tenants or wage laborers. Or they were pushed off the land entirely.

In South Africa, however, white agriculture has been profoundly complicated by its increasingly close interaction with the agrarian history of Africans. Since the late nineteenth century, observers have recognized connections between these two themes. In the decades before the Boer War each of the colonies made extensive investigations and enacted numerous laws in the attempt to control the situation. During the era of state formation, no subject received closer scrutiny.

Most of the interest centered on one part of the problem, the fate of poor whites. The Transvaal Indigency Commission of 1906–8 concluded that their notorious shiftlessness and apathy, their strong aversion to manual work, were the result of the long history of "unfair competition" from Africans. "Uncivilized" labor was accustomed to a far lower standard of living. Africans accepted with alacrity wages on which white people could not survive. Presumably Africans were less efficient as workers, but they were cheap and plentiful. How could whites possibly compete with them?

The liberal historian W. M. Macmillan, whose first intensive research was on this poor-white problem, largely agreed with this broad interpretation.[36] Macmillan, however, went on to analyze closely the conditions in selected African reserves. He found shockingly severe poverty, the result of the Africans' having been squeezed onto insufficient and deteriorating land. The causes of unfair competition, Macmillan concluded, were quite beyond the Africans' control. Two studies carried out in the 1930s, one by the government-appointed Native Economic Commission, the other by the Carnegie Corporation, presented the same conclusion in much more detail.[37] As long as Africans possessed so little land, both the unfair competition and the poor-white problem could be expected to continue.

The problem in the reserves was not merely the severe shortage of land. From Macmillan's time on, investigators stressed that agricultural methods there were grossly inefficient. Presumably, traditional subsistence farming and pastoralism, as well as the attitudes and social institutions to which they were closely related, had been perpetuated. Communal land tenure, the use of the hoe instead of the plow, the dominant role of women in the work, overstocking of cattle – all these were apparently evidence of the Africans' stubborn attachment to their past. Although Africans often came out to work on farms in white areas, they carried little back with them. They remained impervious to European influences. Instead they persisted in the wasteful routine that they had followed, presumably since time out of mind. More land was certainly needed. Merely adding to the reserves would not, however, solve the problem. Basic African attitudes toward work, land, animals, and even women would also have to be altered.

In effect, students of the agrarian problem concluded, South Africa had two agricultural economies. One of them was progressive, modern, efficient, and white. The other was backward, stagnant, inefficient, and black. How little impact the one had had upon the other!

From 1926 through World War II and beyond, successive government and private investigations alike recommended that Africans should somehow be permitted more land. They also warned that African agricultural methods must be radically altered. Otherwise the added space would simply be filled up, and then the cycle of overstocking and erosion would repeat itself. Even the Tomlinson Commission of the late 1950s, which preceded the implementation of the Nationalists' Bantu homelands policy, concluded that unless the economy of the reserves was organized and developed on a fundamentally different basis, they could not conceivably be the permanent homes of the millions of Africans who were meant to live in them.

Before the 1920s the dominant perspective of white South Africans had been radically different. The very survival of the white man's country had seemed to be in mortal danger. Two powerful phenomena had apparently been closely connected: the intrusion of big capital and the ubiquitous spread of black labor. Large absentee land companies had bought up huge tracts of land in the northern Cape, Natal, and the Transvaal.[38] They proceeded to divide these tracts into small plots, which they leased to Africans, who paid rent in cash or farmed on shares. In the common phrase of the day, the land companies were Kaffir farming. Africans were content with lower living standards. Their whole families worked. How could a small independent white farmer possibly compete with the juggernaut of big capital and black labor?

Because they could extract larger profits per acre, the absentee companies and large farmers naturally preferred African labor. The sad truth was that African agriculture seemed to be more efficient.[39] And those who worked on the soil would presumably inherit it one day. The prospect – a few white cities literally surrounded by a sea of black – was frightening. Gradually but inexorably the powerful alliance of big capital and black labor was squeezing the Afrikaner little man out of the land of his fathers. As the key to the survival of the white man's country, he must therefore be protected.

In important ways, recent interpretations of South African agrarian history have more in common with these earlier perceptions than they do with those of the 1930s and 1940s. The facts about the wretched, deteriorating conditions of the reserves, which make a mockery of the Nationalist government's pretense that separate development can ever transform the homelands into viable economic entities, are not in serious dispute.[40] On questions of chronology and causation, however, recent students have agreed with the earlier version. The conditions that so shocked the liberals of the 1930s, they argue, were of comparatively recent origin. The fear of African competition that was so widespread in the early twentieth century was no mere illusion. For in terms of productivity compared with unit costs, African agriculture *was* more efficient. Contemporaries were right. The white man's country *was* in danger.

What saved it – what made white agriculture modern and progressive while that of Africans became stagnant – was not the stubborn persistence of the attitudes and methods of African tradition. It was the decisive intervention of the South African state. Recent students have seen more than a casual relationship between the two parts of what some authorities continue to call the dual economy. They have seen a direct, organic connection. In fact, the revisionists conclude, for at least the past century South Africa has had a single economy. Sometimes the connection between its parts is called internal colonialism, sometimes the development of underdevelopment.

This fundamental reinterpretation of South African agrarian history is by no means restricted to Marxists. It is implicit, for example, in two consecutive chapters of the *Oxford History of*

South Africa, written by Monica Wilson and her son Francis. The first, the title of which seems a little misleading, is "The Growth of Peasant Communities." It begins with growth, to be sure, but it winds up as a study of decline. The second chapter, "Farming, 1866–1966," is an analysis of the early stagnation of white agriculture followed by impressive success. This reinterpretation is still more explicit in Colin Bundy's seminal study of the Transkei region of the eastern Cape until 1913.[41]

Throughout the nineteenth century both the white military and the European market economy penetrated unevenly into the interior of southern Africa. African responses also varied. Some, particularly the Xhosa in the eastern Cape, were crushed in a long series of Kaffir wars. Others, for instance the Zulu and the Sotho, maintained a degree of political and economic autonomy, preserving more or less intact their traditional mixture of pastoralism and subsistence agriculture.

Still another group became peasants. It is they whom the revisionists have emphasized. And it was they who threatened the white man's country so severely after the 1880s. No longer were they mere subsistence farmers. To produce a marketable surplus became the focus of their economic lives. Their wants increased. Accordingly, they altered their family economy as well as the cluster of attitudes that had helped to maintain it.

Other dramatic changes followed. Moving out of the orbit of tribal authorities, they evolved a different political consciousness of their relationship to colony and Empire. They were frequently associated with Christian missions, who helped to inspire them with the work ethic and who often bought land on their behalf. More than most Africans, peasants experienced what Godfrey and Monica Wilson called an enlargement of scale.[42]

Africans were increasingly being proletarianized, or, as it turned out, semiproletarianized. Much of the pressure on African land tenure came from whites, who confiscated large chunks of territory. But some of the squeeze was internal. Among Africans as among whites, some could expand their holdings only by depriving others. Tall trees were crowding out short ones.

Considering all that has been written about the supposedly extreme conservatism of African agriculture, a surprisingly large proportion of Africans reacted "rationally" to the pressures and opportunities of the expanding market economy.[43] As important indexes of the transition from tribalism to peasantry, Bundy stresses rising purchases of plows and wagons. The emphasis is well placed. For these were not merely isolated implements; they were keys to a major economic and social reorientation, both cause and effect of a complex package of transitions in attitudes and behavior.

Using a plow instead of, or in addition to, a hoe meant that significant changes were occurring in the organization and the division of labor. Men, who had traditionally looked after animals, took on a larger share of the work. Cattle had been sources of protein and measures of wealth and status; now they became work units as well. Similarly, buying a wagon meant that the purchaser intended more than subsistence farming. Producing a cash crop for the market had become a principal concern. Bundy's figures and analysis are persuasive: Among large numbers of Africans, by as early as the 1870s, such fundamental reorientations were taking place.

Moreover, a substantial minority of African peasants were succeeding. During the late nineteenth century they accounted for a large share of the Cape Colony's growing agricultural exports. The amount of land that was being farmed by Africans in white areas increased substantially. From the white perspective Kaffir farming was spreading alarmingly. By underselling them, African peasants threatened white farmers with "unfair competition."

Worse, their success severely reduced the labor supply. Missionaries might argue that the economic interests of white employers and African peasants were complementary. They might claim that the best way to ensure a steady flow of efficient labor to white farms was to improve agriculture in the reserves, that the key to the advancement of both sectors was an increase in African "wants" and incentive. Large white farmers – like Jamaica planters in the early nineteenth century when told that free men would work harder and produce more sugar than slaves, like the white settlers of the Kenya highlands in the 1920s when J. H. Oldham and others tried to convince them of the benefits of the dual policy – were bleakly unimpressed with this line of reasoning. Their own analysis was very different. In their view, as long as Africans could maintain an independent economic existence, a condition that whites usually stereotyped as splendid idleness, they would not come out to work.[44]

The phenomenon that Monica Wilson calls the growth of peasant communities was comparatively short lived. As early as the 1880s some missionaries were already recording that the early prosperity of African agriculture was leveling off. In retrospect, it is clear that the long decline into a self-sustaining and, for most Africans, an unbreakable cycle of severe rural poverty had begun. Natural disasters such as droughts and rinderpest – a cattle disease that swept down from East and Central Africa about 1900, devastating herds in its wake – had some effect, though of course they affected whites as well.

Much more significant was political intervention. Squatters' laws were designed to inhibit Kaffir farming, their intent being to exclude from white areas all except "bona fide" laborers. Railways were carefully routed so that they linked white agricultural regions to the ports and to the growing urban–industrial complex on the Rand but bypassed centers of African population. You could always find reserves on a railway map, W. M. Macmillan used to say: They were the blank areas. The main object of Cecil Rhodes's famous Glen Grey Act of 1893, which was often cited as an enlightened piece of legislation, was to stimulate the flow of labor to white farms. Above all, the four white political units – two British colonies and two Afrikaner republics – maintained or even improved upon the military results of the nineteenth century. The African population was expanding. It was being hemmed into a small and fixed or even shrinking proportion of the land.

The rise of African peasant agriculture and the intervention of political power in an attempt to protect white farmers from unfair competition spread together across southern Africa: first in the eastern Cape, then in Natal, and only by the last decades of the nineteenth century in the Orange Free State and the Transvaal.[45] Even so, in the face of all the natural and artificial (that is, political) obstacles in their way, African peasants in the years just after the Boer War were probably still holding their own. The acute, widespread labor shortage of 1902–7 – what Donald Denoon called a strike – is a rough index of their continuing ability to exist independently from whites. In the revisionist view, those who held that African and white economic interests were not complementary, but fundamentally competitive, were probably right. As long as Africans could manage to support themselves in their own areas, the white man's country was in danger.

After the formation of the Union in 1910 the last effective imperial checks against local political initiative were removed. Now concentrated and unleashed as never before, white power intervened momentously in the Natives Land Act of 1913. Industrialists and large farmers alike – the alliance of gold and maize again – demanded labor. From the small farmers of the Orange Free State, in particular, came bitter, concerted attacks against Kaffir farming.[46] With sobs and tears, the reputed liberals in the Botha administration, notably J. W. Sauer of the Cape, acted precipitously and savagely. Under the Land Act more than a million peasants were abruptly proletarianized. Made pariahs in their own country, they were forced into the already overcrowded reserves.[47] Or, if they did remain in white areas, they became bona fide (that is, wage) laborers.

The Natives Land Act of 1913 was the foundation, the single most important piece, of the legislative program of segregation that white South Africans were steadily and very consciously constructing in the first quarter of the twentieth century. When the provisions of the act were finally fulfilled by General Hertzog in 1936, as a quid pro quo for the disfranchisement of African voters in the Cape, the permanent homes of some two-thirds of the country's population would supposedly be in thirteen percent of the territory. (By now, the African percentage is at least three-fourths of the population.) As early as the 1920s the utter impossibility of such a territorial segregation was obvious.

By prescribing reserved areas for whites and Africans, by imposing the one-man–one-lot formula of the Glen Grey Act whenever individual tenure replaced communal systems, the Natives Land Act of 1913 set extremely tight limits on the agricultural productivity of African peasants. These limits severely curbed the Africans' initiative and incentive. Advanced methods – crop rotation, machinery, increasing capital investment – were becoming characteristic of large-scale farming in white areas. Those methods had once been embraced enthusiastically by a substantial minority of Africans. In the reserves, however, they were impractical or even disastrous. At best the heavy plow was redundant; at worst it accelerated erosion. Gradually the hoe replaced it. Because cattle no longer pulled the plow, they ceased to be work units; they were, once more, countable but quite uninvestable capital. Increasingly men left the plots for the women to tend and came out to work for wages in white areas.

In one of his most vivid passages, De Kiewiet explains that the arid, rocky conditions of the South African interior had forced early Dutch settlers to reverse the familiar "progressive" sequence of European economic history. As they left the amply watered western Cape they retrogressed from the intensive, diversified market farming typical of Holland to large-scale grain cultivation and finally to pastoralism and even to slash-and-burn.[48]

During the late nineteenth and early twentieth centuries a similar retrogression was taking place in African peasant agriculture. What observers of the twenties and thirties interpreted as tradition, as a deep, persistent conservatism stubbornly unaffected by the progressive white sector of the so-called dual economy, was in fact the result of a primarily political process of internal colonialism or underdevelopment. In this process lay the roots of rural poverty.[49]

The reserves became increasingly overcrowded and eroded. After the end of the labor shortage about 1907, and certainly after the Natives Land Act of 1913, they were no longer places where Africans could live independently. They had become dormitories, reservoirs to which Africans could be returned from jobs in white areas when they became sick or "redundant." There they could be maintained at no cost to the government.[50] The reserves enabled the South African economy to justify average wages at or below the bare subsistence level, on the grounds that jobs in white areas were merely supplementing the Africans' basic economic life. The African working class could be prevented from evolving into a true, maturely developed proletariat, possessing nothing except their own labor and therefore requiring from their jobs a wage sufficient to support themselves and their families. African workers could be frozen at what, in comparison with European experience, was a very early stage of industrialization.

These homelands – where African interests were supposedly paramount – were used to justify depriving Africans of their political and civil rights in white areas. One day they would even become a means of declaring Africans foreigners in eighty-seven percent of their own country.

Segregation, argue the Marxist revisionists, may have had roots in the distant past, but it became a conscious, coherent system and ideology only in the decades after the Boer War. It is in that period we should seek its origins as well as the process by which it took form. The word "segregation" can be found, though comparatively infrequently, in nineteenth-century sources. It became a key word, a political slogan, a focus for an emerging ideology, only when the means to enforce it became available and when the checks against it were removed. The crystallization of segregation as an ideology was closely related to other vital, simultaneous processes: to the centralization of political power, to the rationalization of mining, to early industrial and urban development, and to the underdevelopment of African agriculture. Segregation was no unfortunate, anachronistic legacy from the frontier past. It was an organic part of South Africa's modern development as a capitalist (and racist) state and society.

In later chapters I shall return to examine more closely the revisionist interpretation of the evolution of segregation in the early twentieth century. However, because the American strategy came to a head about a decade earlier, and because the American example was an important though certainly not a determinative influence on South African thinking, it is appropriate at this point to turn to the American South.

4. The origins of segregation in the American South: the Woodward thesis and its critics

The recently formulated interpretation that I discussed in the previous chapter – that segregation crystallized in South Africa as a system and ideology only after 1900, that it was a distinctively modern response to the development of new and modern conditions, and that only afterward was it made to appear to be the logical, natural, and even inevitable conclusion of that country's traditional pattern of race relations – is one that may strike students of the American South as familiar. In the American case, however, the positions are reversed. The argument that segregation emerged dramatically in the 1890s and that it was closely related to the bourgeois New South movement is no iconoclasm of young radicals, Marxist or otherwise. It belongs instead to the widely acknowledged dean of Southern historians, C. Vann Woodward. First developed implicitly in his great work of synthesis, *Origins of the New South* (1951), and then explicitly (but with what, I shall argue, are important differences) in the immediate aftermath of the U.S. Supreme Court's historic *Brown* decision of 1954, the argument of *The Strange Career of Jim Crow* (1955) corresponds to what in South African historiography would be called the liberal orthodoxy.

The American revisionists, on the other hand, have been trying to establish the very proposition that has been under attack in South Africa. They have emphasized the bitter legacy of slavery, the strong and very old tradition of racism, the continuing institutions and attitudes of white supremacy. In their view the Woodward thesis vastly overstates discontinuity. There was, they insist, no break whatsoever with Southern traditions in the 1890s.

That decade saw not the birth of Jim Crow but merely the legal recognition of his manhood. Segregation, they admit, may indeed have been enacted into law comparatively late. But, they argue forcefully (and in my own view persuasively), what Woodward calls the forgotten alternatives of the era of Reconstruction were never really in the cards. In the 1890s the American South was not deflected from a course toward anything remotely resembling a democratic, tolerant, integrated society. *Strange Career,* its critics contend, is anachronistic, reflecting admirably the liberal aspirations of the second reconstruction of the 1950s and 1960s but having very little to do with the hard facts of the first one. By the 1890s, the revisionists conclude, segregation already had behind it several decades of experience as the settled, de facto practice of the South.[1]

To recapitulate (with apologies for the inevitable oversimplification) Woodward's classic but still exciting argument: Neither in law nor in custom had segregation been the tradition of the South before the Civil War. Whether on large plantations or on small farms, slavery was a system of direct, and *vertical,* domination. Its essential characteristic was not separation of the races, but close contact between them. The personal relations of slavery combined many forms of attitudes and behavior: exploitation, cruelty, mutual dependence, perhaps (Woodward admits skeptically) even warm paternal affection.[2] Only in the cities of the South, and even more clearly in those of the North, did patterns of residential separateness emerge as harbingers of a future order. Yet although they may have been disproportionately influential, Southern cities were numerically insignificant. The Old South was overwhelmingly rural. Typically, all through the predominantly agrarian society that would form the Confederate and border states, the rule was close, continuous contact between the races. Imposed by power, enforced by law, legitimized by religion and by social theory, the vertical patterns of dominance within a system of chattel slavery were normally quite sufficient to guarantee the security of the white ruling class. When white was so clearly set over black, what need was there for horizontal arrangements for the enforced separation of the races?

Immediately after the Civil War, Woodward continues, the defeated Confederate states enacted black codes. Frankly and explicitly discriminatory, these laws would have excluded the freed-men from the vote, from state-supported educational institutions, and from many social services. Indeed, they would have retained vertical domination by binding former slaves to remain as serfs on their old masters' farms and plantations. No doubt, Woodward agrees, the black codes represented the authentic expression of white opinion in a region that had always been racially exploitative and prejudiced. They demonstrated that the urge to keep the black man in his place, the virulent white racism that would eventually sire Jim Crow, did not need to be created. It was already there. Left to themselves, white Southerners would have imposed a system of race relations fully as harsh as segregation, and very likely more so.

White Southerners were not, however, left to themselves. Directly challenged by the black codes, which threatened to reverse the results of the war, Northern power intervened decisively. However most Southern whites may have felt about black people, discrimination was not permitted to be institutionalized in the region's law and politics – for a while, at least. By means of congressional enactment, constitutional amendment, and military occupation, the black codes were overturned. During Reconstruction, whether whites accepted them or not, black people participated. They sat where they wished on streetcars and were served in the hotels and restaurants that would later exclude them. In the face of considerable violence and intimidation, they voted in impressive numbers. They became postmasters, judges, state senators, and U.S. congressmen. To be sure, they never dominated. ("Negro rule" would be a myth formulated to serve the interests of a later generation of Democratic politicians.) But they did participate. All political parties openly competed for black votes. To some extent, as measured, for instance, by state support for public schools in largely black areas, blacks even benefited. During Reconstruction the Southern political process became for a time more open, more competitive, and more democratic than it would be again for at least a century.

Woodward's emphasis, however, is not on Reconstruction, when Northern armies were in control and when the white South was obviously unable to choose its own course, but on what happened afterward. Reconstruction was but an interval. Begin-

ning in the late sixties and culminating in the fateful compromise
of 1876–7, the white South regained control. The South's regional autonomy – in the quaint religious terminology that came
to characterize Southern history – was "redeemed." Tired and
cynical, the North withdrew its soldiers. Republicans were overwhelmingly replaced in office by patriotic whites, usually called
Conservatives, who virtually to a man were former rebels.

What is strange, Woodward argues, is that no abrupt change
took place in Southern life and politics. The violence and intimidation of the era of Reconstruction certainly continued. But so
did the pattern of comparative openness. Blacks still sat where
they wished on trains and on streetcars. They continued to vote
and to hold office. Conservative Redeemers, typified by the aristocratic Colonel Wade Hampton of South Carolina, did not exactly welcome the black man to politics. But they acknowledged
that he was probably there to stay. And they continued to seek
his vote.

For more than a decade after the North had abandoned Reconstruction, leaving the South as free from outside control as it
would ever be, Southern whites continued to acquiesce. How,
asked Woodward from the perspective of the 1950s, when at last
a second reconstruction was being launched against the hitherto
impregnable citadel of segregation, could the endurance of this
alternative be explained? Why had it been "forgotten" so soon,
and so totally? Apparently, Woodward stresses, the road to segregation was not the only direction Southern history might have
taken.

The Strange Career of Jim Crow thus revolves around a problem
in chronology. In the 1890s, Woodward argues, segregation
swept through the South with all the intensity, explosiveness,
and feverish energy of a revolution, which in fact it was. The
ultimate cause of this revolution is obvious and is not in dispute:
the old, persistent force of white racism. But Woodward makes
an important and often overlooked distinction. He is trying to
explain not the general ethos of white supremacy but the emergence of segregation as a new order of race relations at a particular time and in particular circumstances. His question is why
the events of the 1890s were so long delayed. Why had Jim Crow
not come of age soon after Reconstruction?

To this conundrum, say Woodward's critics, there is an obvious and perfectly satisfactory answer. Southern whites, who had only just succeeded in gathering the reins of power into their own hands, were understandably cautious. They must have remembered what the haste of the black codes had cost them. If they acted precipitously, they feared, the Northern coachman might well return. Momentum therefore gathered comparatively slowly. In 1890 came the Mississippi Plan to disfranchise black voters. To the white South's delight, it was declared constitutional. Two years later Senator Henry Cabot Lodge introduced a Force Bill, which would have authorized federal intervention in electoral districts where discrimination had obviously occurred. It was defeated. In 1896, in *Plessy* v. *Ferguson,* the Supreme Court rendered its famous separate-but-equal decision. Only then did Southern whites feel free to move. With the pent-up emotion that had not at all lessened in the three decades since the black codes, they did so with a vengeance.

The lack of restraints on Southern initiative and, more significantly, the white South's perception that the North was not going to intervene were important preconditions for the surge of segregationist legislation after 1890, according to Woodward. But these preconditions alone, he contends, do not satisfactorily explain the interval of more than a decade between the South's achievement of home rule and the onrush of Jim Crow. Nor do they account for the frenzied pace and irresistible momentum of the campaign once it had been launched. External influences, in Woodward's view, were necessary but not sufficient. The origins of the Southern revolution of the 1890s were primarily internal. Aided and made possible by the North's withdrawal and its refusal to intervene, segregation was made in the South by Southerners.

What were these internal, authentically Southern forces? Economic? Woodward certainly cannot be accused of neglecting economic history. Until very recently, indeed, the analysis of such subjects as urbanization, railroad finance, banking, and early industrialization that is contained in *Origins of the New South* was not only unrivaled but virtually unique.[3] In that book, moreover, Woodward provides extremely important clues (to which I shall return) about the kinds of people whose interests segregation may have served, as well as about the ways in which the new order of race relations may have been structurally related to the emergence of the New South in that same period.

Woodward abruptly (and rightly) dismisses economic determinism. Perhaps, he concedes (without in fact agreeing at all), in the long run, in "normal" societies and times, economic laws might be decisive. (Which "normal" societies and times he has in mind is not entirely clear.) "But circumstances," he concludes in a later restatement of his argument,

> were not "normal" in the postwar South, and race relations did not respond "normally" to economic imperatives, at least not for some time. Slavery collapsed, the old planter regime crumbled, industrialization got underway, and a bourgeois regime of the "New South" took charge. But except for an initial shock and hysteria [the black codes of 1865–7] race relations responded to political and sociological rather than to economic determinants.[4]

In Woodward's view the crucial political determinant was the swift resurgence and equally dramatic collapse of populism. Agrarian radicals attacked the causes as well as the symptoms of economic distress. The Populists' principal targets were the crop-lien system, the furnishing merchants who ran it, and ultimately the banking and corporate structure that controlled the middlemen. Building a widespread network of supplying and marketing cooperatives and an organization of lecturers, the Farmers' Alliance exploded in the late 1880s throughout the South. Gradually evolving into a political party, this mass movement swept on into the Midwest.[5]

Unquestionably, Woodward and many others conclude, populism was the most disturbing political force of the late nineteenth century in the South. Its leaders understood the realities of social and economic inequality a bit too clearly. What was worse, from the viewpoint of Southern Democrats, they upset the political process by competing as a third party and, in North Carolina in 1894, by fusing with Republicans. It was all more than a patriotic Southerner could bear. Flushed with success from its campaign for Redemption, the Democratic establishment now found itself in a fight for its very political survival. It had to defeat populism or, better yet, absorb it.

In state after state, the rise of populism created a bitter, no-holds-barred struggle for power. The fundamental issues raised in this intensely heated atmosphere were of a kind the white South has ordinarily thought it preferable to ignore. Their searching analysis of the inegalitarian structure of America's capitalist society enabled some Southern populist leaders, some of the time, to go far toward demystifying complex intersections between race and class. Black Farmers' Alliance groups were formed. On occasion white Populists rescued black Alliance men from mobs.

The race question was never the Populists' main concern. White Populists did not – could not – escape from their racist society and culture. Some Populists, such as Tom Watson of Georgia in his later years, were or became rabid race baiters.[6] In the era of their insurgency, however, Populists sometimes perceived the fundamental truth that the Negro Question could not be divorced from the general structure of Southern and American society that they were trying so desperately to change. In one respect however, Woodward argues, the Populists were like other Southern politicians. Like all parties until after disfranchisement, they sought the black man's vote.

Populism shook up Southern politics, giving it an unusual degree of fluidity. The situation was made to order for a new breed of racist demagogue. In state after state, Woodward argues, men of the stamp of "Pitchfork" Ben Tillman of South Carolina or James Vardaman of Mississippi seized the initiative. Successfully usurping the class rhetoric of populism, they aimed a stream of invective against Northern corporations, at their Southern stooges, and of course at blacks. Actually these demagogues were the most dedicated and most successful enemies of populism. South Carolina Populists, for example, might have supposed that they were bringing Tillman into their fold. In fact, he was co-opting them.

On a wave of violence, race baiting, lynchings, riots, intimidation – and even armed insurrection in Wilmington, North Carolina in 1898[7] – these new men rode to power within the Democratic Party. Sad, disillusioned, and defeated, the Conservatives who had held power since Redemption gave way. Disfranchisement was on every tongue. If this was what the black vote led to, if blacks in politics so corrupted the white man, then good Progressives must treat the Negro Question as they would liquor, prostitution, or the foulest of prison systems. Only political competition stood in the way of good race relations. As long as intense political rivalry persisted, as long as politicians could use the black vote in their struggle for power, the blacks' "best friends" would be unable to help them. Thus, by a strange twist of logic, disfranchisement would clearly be in the best interests of the blacks!

The black vote had to be eliminated. It was eliminated. Although they just stopped short of violating the letter of the Fourteenth and Fifteenth amendments – or so the courts somehow decided – state conventions repudiated their spirit completely. The black vote was effectively removed, as was much of the poor-white vote. Under the mystifying fiction of separate but equal, the U.S. Supreme Court took cover. After 1896 the brakes were taken off.

The process of taking the Negro out of politics swiftly accelerated. So did the avalanche of Jim Crow legislation. Separate-but-equal facilities were required in transportation, education, hospitals, courtrooms: in every imaginable area of Southern life. Blacks protested and often resisted heroically. The white man's law, the white man's police, the white man's bank, and the white man's mob were too strong for them. Some blacks naturally tried to collaborate in the hope of winning concessions. For most blacks, most of the time, there was little choice but to accommodate and make the best of the severely limited opportunities that remained in a segregated, discriminatory society. Perhaps it was as well that blacks were shown clearly that they must rely on their own leadership and resources, since it would ultimately come to that.[8]

That, however, is a retrospective view. At the turn of the century the lights were going out. In an astonishingly short time, argues Woodward, Jim Crow became the law and institutional practice of the South. It was not long before even the most liberal whites would believe instinctively that segregation was an integral, traditional part of the region's most basic folkways. Even they soon forgot the dramatic revolution of the recent past in which the new order of race relations had taken shape.

Blacks, Woodward concluded, faced a cruelly ironic paradox. Segregation, a comparatively new system of race relations that had been characteristic neither of slavery, nor of Reconstruction, nor even of the era of Redemption after the 1870s, had been imposed rather suddenly by law. In the powerful mythology of Southern history, however, it had become tradition. And tradition, it was so often said, could not effectively be altered by law. Change would therefore have to be slow and piecemeal. The minds of white Southerners would have to be educated and, after that, their hearts softened before Jim Crow could possibly be eliminated. And that, liberals resignedly agreed, might take a long time.

Not surprisingly, Woodward's interpretation – so provocative and so sweeping, penetrating so directly to the heart of central themes of Southern and American history – has been controversial. Most of the discussion has centered on the earlier part of the argument, that is, on how much de facto segregation existed during Reconstruction and after. Some of the research has confirmed Woodward's hypothesis.[9] But the bulk of it, most notably Joel Williamson's important book on South Carolina, has argued persuasively that Woodward overstated his case, painting far too optimistic a picture of race relations after the Civil War.[10]

Almost immediately after 1865, Williamson contends, blacks and whites both drifted and were pushed violently apart. Voluntarily they formed separate churches. By law the public schools were mixed, but white parents refused to send their children to them. Dividing the lives and minds of South Carolinians was a great gulf of mistrust and hatred, the inevitable legacy of two centuries of slavery. Some blacks did participate in politics, even getting elected to office, but there is not much evidence that whites accepted them. Granted, the wave of segregationist legislation came after 1890. But surely Woodward makes far too much of that? The basic cause of Jim Crow – white racism – was there all the time. It would have put its mark upon the statute books much earlier if only the white South had been convinced that the North would not intervene once more. Until the Force

Bill of 1892 had been defeated, however, how could Southern whites be sure?

Law ordinarily ratifies the facts of existing social conditions, or confirms the direction of historical trends already in motion, insist Williamson and other revisionists. Practice is therefore far more significant. No sweeping change took place in the behavior or outlook of South Carolinians in the last decade of the nineteenth century. The reality – before, during, and after the 1890s – was a good deal closer to permanent race war than to the forgotten alternative of the open society posited by Woodward.

What is true of South Carolina can presumably be projected, with only minor modifications, throughout the region. Long before 1890, the revisionists conclude, segregation was a fact of life among the vast majority of Southern people. That the law lagged somewhat behind the facts is to them a matter of comparatively minor significance.

To this criticism Woodward has replied, not very convincingly, that perhaps South Carolina was a little different.[11] With only slight adjustments he has restated his position, and the revisionists have restated theirs. The outside observer finds it hard to choose. Typically the detailed research continues to be conducted on a state-by-state basis. Do the differences properly belong to the individual states or to their individual historians?

The debate has centered overwhelmingly on the earlier part of the Woodward thesis: an important part, certainly, but only one. The revisionists may well have made their point about the realities of Reconstruction. But they have largely ignored Woodward's very important distinction between the general ethos of white supremacy, which he agrees existed long before the late nineteenth century, and the specific system of segregation as a distinct stage of race relations. Moreover they have argued, again mostly by omission, that the problem of chronology on which Woodward centered *Strange Career* is either insignificant or nonexistent. As so often happens, the debaters have talked past one another. The revisionists have failed or refused to meet Woodward on his own ground.

The reason for this failure in communication is perhaps understandable. The problem posed by Woodward in *Strange Career* spans two great watersheds of American history. Until very recently, American historians ordinarily attached themselves to one of these two periods. Specialists on the Civil War and Reconstruction would focus on one set of questions. Specialists on the Progressive Era would stress another: whether Southern politicians could simultaneously have been racist and Progressive and, if so, how they managed to combine two apparently contradictory postures. To an outsider it is amazing how many American history books, regardless of theme and subject, either end with 1890 or begin with 1900.

Yet there seem to be good reasons for regarding the 1890s – an age of rapid economic concentration and industrial expansion, of the populist revolt and labor conflict, of imperialism – as a central, formative decade in American history. And Woodward's interpretation centers on the 1890s. At both ends his critics have largely avoided him. The process by which the class and race relations of the white supremacist era of Reconstruction and Redemption evolved into those of the white supremacist New South has therefore not been sufficiently investigated.

I shall return to these very significant points in Woodward's thesis about the origins of segregation in the South. Meanwhile, it should probably be concluded that his suggestion that the South before the 1890s was in practice a comparatively open society, in which white and black competed on surprisingly equal terms, contradicts most, though certainly not all, of the available evidence about the lives of most Southerners in the generation after the Civil War. Already they were substantially separated. Indeed, even before 1860 the black population had by no means been evenly distributed. Many counties in the black belt possessed only handfuls of whites. After 1865 the pronounced demographic shift of blacks from the upper into the lower South persisted, continuing the prewar trend of "selling South." In the earlier period masters had been responding to higher prices for slaves. Now freedmen were migrating toward the larger number of available jobs, primarily in cotton and sugar, at slightly higher average wages. Both white and black schools of segregationist (or black separatist) thought could therefore claim that territorial segregation was being accomplished through natural causes. (Whites often stressed not rational economic decision making but the gravitation of blacks toward the hotter, more tropical climate most congenial to their racial temperament: a stereotype that even their great migration northward after 1915 would not destroy completely.)

Contact between the races tended to diminish considerably in many areas where it had once been substantial. The religion of the Old South, for instance, had once been characterized by a surprising incidence of interracial worship. Often that meant slave galleries; more rarely it meant black ministers preaching to mixed congregations. Before 1860 black separatist churches, notably the African Methodist Episcopal Church, had been founded in the North. After 1865, when many denominations engaged in an intense rivalry for the souls of the freedmen, the trend toward self-segregated white and black churches sharply accelerated.[12]

Residential separation increased more rapidly in the new towns of the Piedmont than in the older coastal and river port cities.[13] As in South Africa, urbanization placed substantial strains on the system of white supremacy. By law all tax-supported schools and social services were supposed to be equally available to all races. Insofar as the South can be said to have possessed social services, however, these in practice were largely reserved for whites. A common means of evasion, and one that would be repeated a century later, was to substitute private for public institutions. The state University of North Carolina, for example, remained closed until Redemption, and it continued to be starved for funds until after the turn of the century. The slack was taken up by denominational institutions – the Baptist college of Wake Forest, Trinity (now Duke) of the Methodists – which were not affected by federal law.

To blacks and their Republican allies segregated facilities usually represented an advance, for the choice was between those and none. The revisionists' argument thus seems overwhelmingly persuasive. The eras of Reconstruction and Redemption were not characterized by close interracial contact or open participation. However much it may have been voluntary or de facto, the amount of segregation in practice seems impressive. Integration was not a practical alternative. The events after 1890 were politically dramatic. But there was no reversal of prevailing circumstances, attitudes, or behavior.

Woodward's scorn for well-meaning folk who pour oil on

troubled waters, who seek to reconcile interpretations that are in fact contradictory, who exclaim disarmingly "they're both right," makes one wary. Yet Woodward and his critics do seem to be discussing different problems. The revisionists are talking mostly about practice and attitudes, Woodward about political rhetoric and law; they about social and economic structure, he about political and ideological superstructure. All parties to the argument would presumably agree that these things are ultimately related. None but the crudest of economic determinists would maintain that – even in what Woodward calls normal societies and times – they must be *causally* connected. Nor can there be much doubt that the swift acceleration of the political pace after 1890 proceeded primarily from causes that were immediately and even fundamentally political. The reason, after all, is perhaps distressingly simple. If economic and social forces are to survive, if they are to compete for the leadership of a sophisticated and conscious society, let alone win power, then they must be organized and articulated. Once organized, however, whatever their origin, they become recognizably political in kind.

If the point is conceded to the revisionists that a great deal of segregation already existed in practice throughout the South before the 1890s, then Woodward's argument about the chronology of the period becomes all the more significant. Both sides in the historiographical debate agree that the frenzied rhetoric, legislation, and violence all came to a head after 1890. Why then? What function did they serve? What, or whose, interests? The South already possessed de facto segregation. Why, in such a hurry and with such feverish intensity, must it create segregation as legal system and ideology? That question is as central today as when Woodward originally formulated it.

Perhaps the strangest thing about *The Strange Career of Jim Crow* is how much of his earlier interpretation Woodward chose to ignore when he delivered his famous lectures on the origins and acceleration of segregation in 1954. Whereas in his great work of synthesis, *Origins of the New South,* he had seen the evolving system of race relations against the context of the whole of Southern society, in *Strange Career* he narrowed his focus considerably. In so doing, he altered his explanation in ways that seem very significant.

One of the dominant, and most controversial, themes of *Origins* concerns the impact of what Woodward regards as a massive infusion of Northern and foreign capital into the region after the mid-1870s. For that, indeed, was really what the historic compromise of *Reunion and Reaction* was all about.[14] In his view this investment removed much of the economic decision-making power to corporate boardrooms in New York. The South did begin to industrialize. But, suffering from discriminatory railroad rates and from investors' unwillingness to back sophisticated manufacturing, as well as from the destruction of the Civil War, it did so very slowly. The region's rate of economic growth lagged well behind that of the nation. In Woodward's view the effect of outside capital was to perpetuate and even to rigidify further the South's traditional colonial relationship with the North.

A second theme of *Origins* is the emergence in the Piedmont region of a new entrepreneurial elite of businessmen and industrialists: bankers, railroad men, and owners of cotton, tobacco, and iron factories. Mostly homegrown, but often possessing strong ties to Northern capitalists, this was a middle class on the make. It was closely associated with the ideological movement called the New South. In the late nineteenth century, in Woodward's view, the rising bourgeoisie was gradually seizing the initiative in a protracted struggle with the old planter aristocracy.

Throughout *Origins,* but never more eloquently than when he is describing the influence – to use no stronger term – of railroad or land-company interests on state legislatures, Woodward emphasizes the unity of economic and political power. In *Strange Career,* however, as well as in more recent restatements, he places a barrier between political and economic elites. "The new order of race relations," he concludes, "was shaped and defined by political means and measures, and they came not to meet the needs of commerce and industry but the needs of politicians."[15] Are not businessmen political animals? In *Origins* they certainly are. Do politicians lack economic interests? Apparently race relations is not the only subject to have been segregated in *The Strange Career of Jim Crow!*

Even an admiring critic must be puzzled. Why should the central theme of one of the finest works of synthesis in American history have been so studiously ignored in its author's next book? Why has the unity of power given way to such distinct demarcations among the elites who controlled Southern society?

This point is not, I think, merely technical. As I shall explain in more detail in Chapter 6, *Origins* contains very important clues to the ways in which segregation may have been structurally related to larger systemic changes that were going on in Southern society: urbanization, industrialization, political party formation. It also points to the sorts of powerful economic (and therefore political) interests that the new racial order may have served. Just who or what stood to gain from segregation, anyway? This basic question, the kind of question the author of *Origins* had asked boldly and repeatedly, the author of *Strange Career* had somehow ceased to raise.

Woodward of course is well able to answer for himself. (Not that he needs defending.) One may, however, speculate that his reluctance to address the relationship of the origins of segregation to class interests may have grown out of problems he was beginning to have with his earlier interpretation of the social dynamics of Southern history.

By the 1890s a new entrepreneurial elite had begun to emerge. But had it sufficiently consolidated its power by that time? Could it call the tune? More important, did it? Can it be demonstrated that the campaigns throughout the South for disfranchisement and Jim Crow were led by this new middle class and its political henchmen? If not, since the attack on black and many poor-white votes was obviously central to the basic political struggle of the era, can the Southern bourgeoisie be said to have been winning?

The answers to all these questions are undoubtedly negative. There are too many Tillmans and Vardamans around, politicians who ran against the candidates favored by the business interests and who were the most fanatical of race baiters. Second, another of Woodward's arguments in both *Origins* and *Strange Career* – one that we must assume he himself has by now abandoned[16] – is that the driving force behind the exclusion of blacks from the franchise was the rabid racism of lower-class whites and their political representatives. The new men who, according to Woodward, seized control of the Democratic Party from the Conservatives and who most strongly favored disfranchisement were, in his view, the bitter enemies of the industrial elite of the New South.

The Southern bourgeoisie, one may agree, had begun to rise. As late as 1900, however, the proposition that they had attained a dominant position in the region's life and politics is doubtful. Indeed, if one follows closely Woodward's evidence and analysis, it is not at all clear why he thinks they had. On the one hand he believes that a massive transformation "of a profound and subtle character" took place in the South's power structure, "even comparable with those changes in the two generations between the establishment of the factories and the Reform Act of 1832" in England. Yet he produces evidence that suggests nothing of the sort. By 1900, taking into account cities of 50,000 or larger (a misleading standard that severely underestimates the degree of urbanization in this period), the south-central region of the United States was still only eleven percent urban. Cities were proportionately insignificant; agriculture remained the dominant occupation.

Over the area as a whole, therefore, nothing like a decisive alteration of the mode of production occurred. Thus "the 'victory of the middle classes,' and the 'passing of power from the hands of landowners to manufacturers and merchants,' which required two generations in England, were substantially achieved in a much shorter period in the South, yet with nothing approaching the same amount of industrialization." On the basis of what concentrated economic power, one must ask, did these manufacturers and merchants build their political muscle? Woodward avoids this question, and the answer remains obscure. In seeking to understand the South in the late nineteenth century, he concludes, "one must explore beyond the limits of economic history."[17]

Readers who may be familiar with recent interpretations of English history will detect in the previous two paragraphs several useful object lessons in the pitfalls of the comparative method. Great Britain was certainly more industrialized by 1832 than the South was by 1900. But the social and especially the political implications of that fact are easily overstated. First, industrialization was by no means universal. As late as 1850 the majority of British workers, about half of whom were in agriculture and domestic service, remained in occupations that had not been transformed by machines.[18] Second, the suggestion that power had been transferred to the middle class would have astonished the Whig government of the second Earl Gray – the most aristocratic government for a century – which enacted the Reform Bill of 1832. The British ruling class broadened very gradually indeed, with the strong influence of the landed aristocracy continuing through the nineteenth century and even beyond.

Third, although the British population was certainly much more urban than the South's, the early phases of industrialization often took place outside the already established urban centers. This was true in particular of the central, pacesetting cotton-manufacturing industry. Mill towns such as Oldham or Preston in Lancashire gradually merged – albeit much more rapidly, because the available space was so much more limited – into an urban sprawl greatly resembling that of New England in the mid-nineteenth century or that of the southern Piedmont after 1900. Fourth, no credible English historian, emphatically including Marxists, would presume that one need not go well "beyond the limits of economic history" – into Methodism, the influence of the American and French revolutions, and utilitarianism to give a few examples – in trying to explain what happened or did not happen in British society between 1790 and 1832.[19]

Finally, Woodward implies that British industrialization took place more or less spontaneously, with economic forces acting in normal ways, unimpeded but also unaided by other factors, whereas the economies of later imitators such as the South had to be mobilized and guided from above. This is both true and misleading. Great Britain in the late eighteenth century was obviously not consciously pursuing something called industrialization, a process for which no word yet existed.[20] This first industrial revolution was not planned.

Nevertheless, the role of the British government in creating and guaranteeing overseas and colonial markets was crucial. Since the late seventeenth century the British political climate had been extremely responsive to the needs of capitalism in its several successive phases: landed, mercantile, and industrial. Although the persona of capitalism – gentry, merchants, and what Marx called the millocracy – were to some extent distinct and competitive, it is their combination (as in 1832) that is more impressive. Moreover, the ideology of the emerging class of industrialists in the early nineteenth century – protesting that they were not the hard, heartless men so cruelly caricatured by Cobbett, Carlyle, or Dickens; calling for the godly discipline of factory labor; promising a prosperous future in reward for their own generation's necessary sacrifices – was comparable in its nature and its impact to the creed of the New South movement. Such ideologies – favorable to capital accumulation, low labor costs, high profit margins and rates of investment – seem to be essential weapons in the armories of societies on the make.[21] Even in Great Britain one must explore beyond the limits of economic history to understand how change was induced from above.

Woodward's assumption that the relationship of segregation to the economic imperatives of commerce and industry can therefore be abruptly discounted because the South's urban and industrial growth by 1900 was proportionately small can be attacked from yet another angle. Whereas in one sense he has surely overstated the degree of change that was taking place, in another sense he has understated it.

In any modernizing society the early phases of industrialization and urbanization are much more important in forming persistent political and social patterns than would be readily apparent from purely quantitative measurements. Banks, lawyers, newspapers, fashionable seasons, and legislatures are all centered in cities. Even in a society so aggressively Jeffersonian in its rural orientation as the South before 1860 – or, say, the modern Republic of Ireland – cities set the pace and tone. Indeed, according to Woodward's own argument, the political influence of the bourgeoisie, and therefore presumably of the cities where the bourgeoisie tend to live, was considerably stronger than urban population figures would indicate.

It is to cities that historians normally look for those bursts of energy and sharp clashes of ideas that both produce and signify change – an oversimplified perspective, to be sure. The insurgency of Southern populism in the late nineteenth century, not to mention the peasant movements that have made much of Asia communist in the twentieth, demonstrates that European Marxists have vastly underestimated the huge revolutionary potential that lay beneath what the *Communist Manifesto* superficially calls the idiocy of rural life. Still, in stressing the disproportionate role that factories and comparatively small numbers of industrial workers can play in transitional societies, Marx had a point. The industrial proletarians of Russia were less than ten percent of the population when they overthrew the tsar in street demonstrations in Petrograd and Moscow in February 1917. Insufficient though they were to sustain and defend the revolution, they led its crucial first phase. Thomas Hodgkin perceptively began his classic analysis of African nationalism by ignoring the traditional framework of rural tribalism, in which the large majority of the people still lived, and instead proceeding abruptly to the lumpen-proletariat of the mushrooming cities.[22] Why should the South be presumed an exception to the disproportionate influence of early industrialization and of still small but expanding urban areas?

In fact it was not. As Woodward himself persuasively argues, the energy and psychological investment that were concentrated in the early industrialization of the underdeveloped, agrarian, and war-damaged South were necessarily enormous.[23] Rates of capital investment and reinvestment, and therefore profit margins, had to be high. (Whether they had to be as high, and plant expansion as rapid, as was often the case in Southern cotton mills is more doubtful.) Huge sums were essential, or – if we take seriously the econometric argument of Robert Fogel that rivers and canals would have been a sufficient and much cheaper alternative – they were perceived to be essential, for trunk railway systems that were often uneconomic.[24] A rural labor force accustomed to seasonal rhythms and to personal, paternalist relations with planters had to adjust rapidly to the factory whistle and the assembly line.

In arguing that a massive transformation "of a profound and subtle character" was going on in Southern society, even comparable to that of the English industrial revolution, Woodward is therefore correct. The main lines of this process of social and political change are in no sense unique to Southern or American history. They have been analyzed in great detail and with sympathetic passion, for example, by Edward P. Thompson in *The Making of the English Working Class*. All of the trauma and "unrest" recorded in that book happened in the South, with the added complications that industrialization came after slavery and that it had to be imposed on a society that was already racially divided and discriminatory.

The early phases of Southern industrialization could not have happened automatically as the normal effects of economic laws. They had, indeed, to be guided from above. A strenuous, highly conscious, intensely ideological, and even religious campaign – the New South movement – was launched to attract outside capital and to encourage local entrepreneurial initiative.[25] The political implications of such a bootstrap operation must have been immense. They certainly had been in Great Britain, where industrialization had begun from a much sounder base of previous domestic growth and overseas investment and where no ties of dependency on a stronger economy had to be broken. One might presume, indeed, that the political impact of industrialization on an underdeveloped society such as the South would be even more significant. Indeed, *Origins of the New South* contains abundant evidence that the political clout of business interests often far exceeded their purely economic significance.

Woodward's suggestion that because the Southern economy was still comparatively backward in 1900, urbanization and industrialization could therefore have played no important role in the simultaneous creation of a new order of race relations called segregation is at least theoretically unconvincing. By statistical standards – how many people lived in cities with populations over 50,000; how many manufactured articles had to be imported; what proportion of the working population was engaged in agriculture – the New South was indeed a myth. The new day had barely begun to dawn. Paradoxically, however, the political implications of the early stages of the South's industrialization were probably more profound than in later phases. The stakes were higher. The New South was not as industrialized as Great Britain had been in 1832. It was far more so than South Africa would be until at least the 1940s.

What, then, were the main economic and social trends of this emerging New South? In what ways may these developments have been related to the simultaneous campaigns for Jim Crow and black disfranchisement? As I have argued, if socioeconomic forces are to play any important role, they must be organized politically. There is therefore no question but that the origins of segregation in the American South were directly and even primarily political. It would indeed be surprising to find that so complex a social and ideological system of race and class relations was created, in any simple or normal way, to meet "the needs of commerce or industry." But the suggestion that segregation may have emerged as an integral, appropriate part of the systemic change of a whole society is one that, simply because it is not immediately apparent from statistics, should not be dismissed out of hand.

5. The South makes segregation: the economic interpretation

The previous chapter analyzed the long and still apparently unfinished debate between C. Vann Woodward and his critics concerning the origins of segregation in the American South. There I made two important points. First, the two sides seem to be discussing essentially different problems. Woodward argues that the pace of segregationist rhetoric and legislation accelerated only after 1890. The revisionists contend that in practice the races had drifted and had been pushed violently apart long before that. These interpretations, however, are not necessarily incompatible. This may be one of those relatively few cases when both sides are right. Indeed, if de facto segregation had already thoroughly pervaded the life of the region, then Woodward's thesis centering on the chronology of Jim Crow and black disfranchisement seems all the more significant. What, after all, was all the fuss about? If the South already had segregation in practice, why did it have to create segregation as a system and an ideology? Apparently some new set of circumstances, some hitherto unacknowledged challenges, must have come into existence.

Second, whereas in *Origins of the New South* Woodward had argued persuasively in favor of the unity of economic and political power, in his later *The Strange Career of Jim Crow* those two factors drifted mysteriously apart. Politicians and businessmen, as well as their needs, became more or less separate and distinct. In Woodward's view the origins of segregation were overwhelmingly political. Indeed, he argued forcefully in favor of a politicians' conspiracy. The conspirators were the "new men," a group of racist demagogues, representing primarily lower-class whites, who seized control of the Democratic Party from the Conservatives during the 1890s. But the force that lay behind the acceleration of segregation, the new circumstances that gave these conspirators their opportunity, was the profoundly disturbing, radical challenge of agrarian populism.

At this point I entered a basic and, I fear, a fairly obvious caveat. Unless economic forces or interests are organized and articulated they will not long survive, much less succeed in dominating a literate, sophisticated, conscious society. Once organized, however, these interests at once cease to be merely economic and become political forces. Contenders in the political arena are more like complex emulsions than simple mixtures, so that to separate them into their original components becomes impossible. Ordinarily economic-political interests are represented by specialists called lawyers or politicians, power brokers who speak to and for more than one constituency and who may even have reasonably autonomous objects of their own. Moreover, the success of economic interests in the pursuit of political power will very likely depend on the ability of their spokesmen to make their special class concerns appear identical with the desires of the politically represented sections of society. Making such an identification is the very nature of the politician's profession.

The proposition that politicians had perfectly straightforward political motives for carrying segregation to its logical conclusion does not, then, necessarily mean that certain classes or interests had nothing to gain. Nor is it incompatible with the hypothesis that the new order of race relations was an organic part of a larger systemic change that was simultaneously transforming Southern society, or at least some sections of it. In the next two chapters I shall argue that in the American South, as in South Africa, segregation was primarily an urban phenomenon and that it was linked in significant ways to the early, formative industrial growth of the region. Any analysis of the New South's political economy and of its relationship with the frantic rush toward segregation must begin, however, with what remained by far its most dominant component, agriculture.

Long before 1890 the South's agrarian mode of production had begun a gradual and multifaceted transformation in land tenure, in the credit system, in the organization and control of labor. In the Old South three broad types of agricultural production had prevailed: capitalist plantations worked by large (twenty or more) gangs of slaves; farms owned by whites who themselves worked alongside a small number of slaves or hired laborers; and mainly subsistence farms owned or rented (sometimes on shares) by poorer whites and a few free blacks. Of these three forms, in terms of sheer numbers, the smaller units had been more typical. The majority of Southern whites had owned no slaves at all. But the large plantation – the characteristic form that capitalism had taken in the periphery of the world economy since the seventeenth century – had been without question the dominant mode of production.[1] Marketing and transportation systems alike had been geared to the needs of the large plantation, and it had determined the base price of labor. Despite sectional variations, with the upper South generally comparing unfavorably with the lower South, the profitability and dominance of the plantation were both increasing in the period just before 1860. By no means was the South's plantation economy on the verge of internal collapse.[2]

Compared with, say, the grain-producing regions of the Midwest, Southern agriculture, though profitable, long remained labor intensive and backward. It did not follow the "normal" capitalist cycle: substituting technology for manpower, increasing the productivity of labor, raising the wages of workers while sharply reducing their numbers, and releasing people to be redeployed in other sectors of an expanding economy. Until the 1940s the ratio of labor to the amount of acreage under production remained high and productivity stayed low. Cotton or tobacco farmers were notoriously slow to adopt tractors, mechanical pickers, and other available technology. The primary reason for this lag was neither ignorance nor laziness but because both the short- and medium-term costs of manual labor remained significantly cheaper. In the New South as well as in the Old, the plantation system was the basis of the agricultural system. It depended upon a plentiful supply of unskilled and semiskilled workers who were relatively inefficient but also unusually cheap. Maintaining the large supply and low cost of labor had been and remained the primary function of the South's political economy.[3]

The Old South's political system had reflected the balance of economic power. The planter aristocracy had dominated it, providing a disproportionate share of governors and legislators. Links between planters, merchants, and professional elites – lawyers, newspaper editors, bankers – had been close. So successfully had the planter class asserted its hegemony, its control over the region's political consciousness, that it had managed to transform a conflict on behalf of its own special interest – the defense of slavery – into a general, glorious cause: the so-called war for Southern independence.

After 1865, at least in those parts of the South that have been closely investigated, no precipitous or dramatic fall of the planter class seems to have taken place. "The national power of the planter class was broken," concludes Jonathan M. Wiener:

> That was what the war had been about. But within the
> South, the new class that emerged from war and Reconstruc-
> tion owning the land and controlling the labor force included
> a surprisingly large proportion of the antebellum cotton fami-
> lies, while the structural basis of their wealth and power had
> been altered.[4]

By their own reckoning, of course, the planters' loss in property, that is, the prewar value of their slaves, was both abrupt and catastrophic. But this analysis, which historians until recently have tended to accept at face value, is much too simple.

Emancipation liquidated a form of capital. But it required from the planters themselves no direct outlay of cash. Perhaps over several generations a planter family had invested substantially in order to provide a guaranteed labor force. Although those particular workers and their descendants were no longer bound to the plantation by law, they or others like them were still available. Much more crucial therefore were the means of production: mules, tools, and, above all, the land itself. A substantial redistribution of the means of production – the forty acres and a mule that were proposed by some radical Reconstructionists – would indeed have crippled the planters. To the surprise of the planters themselves, merely freeing the slaves did not necessarily do so. If planters could retain their land and, under some form of labor management other than chattel slavery, if they could continue to obtain enough workers at a sufficiently low price, they could survive or even prosper almost indefinitely with little basic change in their operations.

Both before and after the Civil War the Southern planter class seems to have been much like the celebrated English gentry of the seventeenth century.[5] Some of them were rising. Others were, or declared themselves to be, declining. A social class, argues Lawrence Stone, one of the foremost historians of the origins of the English Revolution, is rather like a bus: Exchanges of riders go on constantly and are easily mistaken for the end of a journey. On the whole, the planters after 1865 appear to have maintained or, in many cases, to have increased their economic preponderance over the black-belt regions they had always dominated.

The credit and marketing system did change. But the transformation began well before 1860. In the Old South the business of buying, selling, and lending was concentrated mainly in the hands of the factor. Typically this gentleman was located in seaports or river ports: Charleston, Savannah, New Orleans, or Memphis. The factor arranged for the purchase and delivery of supplies to the planter. Based on his specialized knowledge of overseas markets, he advised where and when the crop should be sold. Often he loaned to the planter a sum sufficient to tide him over through the coming year, using the forthcoming crop as collateral and speculating in his own behalf on the future price. This credit arrangement is usually identified with the sharecropping system of the postwar period, when it was applied with very different consequences to a different class of farmers. But it was already a well-established institution under plantation slavery. It was the crop lien.[6]

By the late nineteenth century, as the result of a process that was already under way by the 1850s, the role of this middleman had been substantially undermined. The main cause of the factor's undoing was a revolution in communications. The improving canal system and, more important, the coming of the railroad enabled the large producer to negotiate directly the terms of purchase, sale, and shipment of his crops. Through the local newspaper the telegraph gave the planter direct, immediate access to the sort of detailed, current market information on which the factor had once based his business. The factor, then, was steadily being replaced by the infamous furnishing merchant.

The furnishing merchant was likely to be a local man. His area of operations was far more restricted than the factor's, but it was also much more intensive. Often the furnishing merchant was himself a planter. He financed the smaller producers of the area and often bought up their crops in the hope of making a profit on the turnover. Ordinarily he would furnish his tenants or sharecroppers with seeds, fertilizer, tools, a mule, and food, usually taking half the crop as well as a substantial and sometimes usurious rate of interest. In the case of cotton he typically owned the only available gin. The furnishing merchant bought in bulk, often pledging the forthcoming crop from his entire plantation as security. The small independent producers of the neighborhood, as well as his own tenants and sharecroppers, who were usually required to do so, bought on credit from his store, using their forthcoming crops as collateral.

Before the Civil War, then, the planter was typically in debt to the factor, who was in debt to an English merchant house, which in turn was financed by a London bank. Now the farmer was in hock to the furnishing merchant, who was under obligation to local or New York bankers. The institutions of credit and marketing, including the notorious crop-lien system, were mainly continuations of earlier arrangements. But the lines of the credit network ran differently, enhancing the pivotal role of the furnishing merchant, who was often a local planter. This gradual transition in financial structure helps to explain why, contrary to what was once supposed, the period after 1865 probably saw an increase in the concentration of economic wealth and power in Southern agriculture.

Still more significant was the gradual but extremely uneven alteration of the labor system. Both the former slaves and a large and steadily increasing proportion of the smaller independent farmers were moving into one of the variants of what became the dominant form of labor organization: sharecropping. Apart from the long controversy over the profitability of slavery, the debate on this "kind of freedom" is one of the very few widely researched issues in Southern economic history. The often-heated argument it has generated has centered on how much racial discrimination the sharecropping system embodied.[7]

As in the long discussion of the standard-of-living question in the historiography of the English Industrial Revolution, the debaters in the sharecropping controversy have argued on the basis of a largely common body of evidence that they interpret very differently. As in the English case, they divide themselves into pessimists and optimists. The pessimists contend that the South's agrarian institutions were fairly riddled with opportunities for racially discriminatory practices by white planters and furnishing merchants. These men had the power, and they kept the books. Their principal weapon was the crop lien, which was enforced by a court system that these same planters and furnishing merchants dominated. With it they kept politically powerless tenants chronically in debt and therefore dependent. Debt peonage, indeed, was hard to distinguish from slavery.

It may be conceded, reply the optimists, that the South was a racially discriminatory society. But the economic effects of discrimination must not merely be deduced; they must be carefully counted and weighed. There was much less direct economic injustice than one might expect. What there was centered primarily in the court and police system and was not inherent in the economic institutions themselves. Some of the account books have survived. They appear to show that, for the most part, country stores probably dealt honestly with black and white clients. They also reveal that high rates of interest were being charged to the stores themselves.

The inability of many tenants to pay out at the end of the year is not in dispute. Many of them labored hopelessly under a heavy burden of debt. Yet the most important characteristic of the sharecropping system was the mobility of labor. Far from being frozen, it circulated constantly. The typical sharecropping or tenancy agreement was renegotiated each year. The bargaining may well have been unequal, but it was surprisingly hard.[8] Moreover, although furnishing merchants naturally received higher rates of return from credit than from cash transactions, it was not at all in their interest to multiply indefinitely the extent of debts that obviously could never be repaid. For their part tenants usually had available alternative stores and employers. The evidence appears to show, argue the optimists, that they put competition to work and benefited from it.

The pessimists, their opponents charge, forget the sad but

inescapable fact that farming requires capital. The small farmer had little and the tenant virtually none. Apart from wholesale redistribution of land, which would have decapitalized Southern agriculture drastically, what alternative to the crop-lien system could there conceivably have been? Sharecropping was not an inherently discriminatory system. It was a perfectly understandable response to the basic economic conditions of the postwar South. In the free-enterprise economy, contend the optimists, even in the share-tenancy system that was admittedly one of its more constricted forms, there was usually room and opportunity for maneuver. Politically blacks were powerless and oppressed. But economically they were far less helpless than might be supposed. Besides, the optimists conclude, the crop lien was not a racially exclusive institution. It affected whites as well as blacks.[9]

Perhaps it did, return the pessimists, but not quite in the same way. Blacks, on average, farmed fewer acres and concentrated still more exclusively on cotton or tobacco.[10] Frequently, at the planter's insistence, they planted cotton right up to the cabin door. The planters' profits increased in proportion to the number of tenants on their property, no matter how the tenants themselves might fare. Is it any wonder that politically powerless black tenants were so often preferred? Plowing in a much narrower furrow, more heavily bound under the control of furnishing merchants and planters, they had no choice but to stay with the cash crops. For black tenants, even more than for whites, there was little incentive and less reward. True they circulated, in the pathetic and usually frustrated hope of getting a better deal. As long as they remained within the orbit of the plantation economy, however, the mobility of labor remained a harsh illusion. The new furnishing merchant or landlord possessed the same power as the old. He was often in the same county. His terms, which were often arranged in agreement with his peers, differed from theirs marginally if at all. Above all, he still kept the books.

But why, ask the optimists, should these complex effects be ascribed so readily to the single cause of racial discrimination? Would not one expect that a people only one generation removed from slavery, who had started in 1865 with no capital and very little training, would be more poorly prepared to farm independently? Surely the surprise is not that most blacks remained poor.

It is how well some exceptions, and even blacks in the aggregate, managed to do. Indeed! comes the scornful and unanswerable reply of the pessimists. In a land of hope, progress, and expanding economic opportunity, while the gap in real wages and living standards between the South and most of the rest of the nation continued to widen, Southern blacks eked out a pitiable and precarious existence.

I shall return in the next chapter to the complex question of the economics of discrimination. Here the South African perspective prompts some additional reflections. First, there are apparently worse things than sharecropping. In America the tenancy system is ordinarily associated with poverty, oppression, and hopelessness. In Africa, as we have seen, it is identified with prosperity, uplift, and hope. The sharecropping system was not the planters' first choice. And it was not to be their last. They much preferred, as American agricultural employers still do, hired hands – what South Africans called bona fide laborers – who could be employed during season and then be dismissed when they became redundant. Although there is no reason to dispute the dominance of sharecropping in the Southern agrarian mode of production, hired hands outnumbered tenants and croppers combined, according to Georgia censuses.[11]

Second, everywhere in the world except England and America, sharecroppers and small independent farmers are called peasants. From long before the Civil War until well into the twentieth century, however, "peasant" seems a very appropriate term for most white and free black farmers in the American South. They were "marginal" people who had an arms' length relationship to powerful economic and political forces that controlled the vast regional, national, and international markets in which they were situated. The large comparative literature on the subject – which American historians, because they study "farmers," do not ordinarily seem to have considered – stresses that small landowners, renters, and sharecroppers may well be poor, oppressed, and insecure.[12] Peasants do, however, possess a measure of economic independence. They are not proletarians or even lumpenproletarians. Their field of maneuver may be narrow and hemmed in. Nevertheless, they have something to defend.[13]

The economic independence of peasants is ordinarily extremely precarious. Partly for that reason their political lives are often violent. Their risings cannot be explained as merely spontaneous reaction to economic factors alone. Like other men and women, peasants are swayed by historical experience, by the folk memory of their (no doubt partially imaginary) past, by religion, and even by what more sophisticated people call ideas. Despite appearances – it has been ironically observed that bread riots do tend to occur on market days – the link between intolerable conditions and sustained action is never automatic. The substantial gap must be bridged by education, organization, and collective class identity. Nevertheless, pressure on their marginal and insecure means of subsistence is a common feature of peasant rebellions from Lutheran Germany to the Great Fear of 1789 in France, to populism in the American South, to modern China. The placid stability that city dwellers perceive in rural life is a mistaken and, for them, a dangerous illusion. Instead the lives and minds of peasants are volatile and explosive. In the American South the livelihoods of black and white peasants were under relentless, fluctuating, but steadily increasing pressure.

Loosely employed, as the term ordinarily is, sharecropping covers a wide variety of arrangements between capital and labor concerning the means and distribution of production. On the ladder of Southern agriculture, itself a subject that has been hotly disputed, sharecropping embraces those who are just above hired hands at one extreme and those just below renters at the other.[14] From the tenants' point of view, however, renting was not always the preferable alternative. When prices fell, or when the boll weevil attacked, planters sometimes tried to change over to the rental system – in which they received a fixed sum instead of a share of the crop – as a means of shifting the risk to the tenant.

Nor was the sharecropping system adopted uniformly. Where workers were comparatively abundant, as in parts of the black-belt areas of the Deep South, or where the efficient operation of an industry demanded it, as on the sugar plantations of Louisiana, planters sometimes continued to employ gangs of workers to whom they paid wages in cash, credit, or goods. These workers were what sharecroppers were not – true rural proletarians.

As both white and black peasants well understood, there was a difference.

The object of sharecropping, like that of slavery, was to maintain the conditions essential for the plantation economy: plentiful, cheap, docile, and therefore not particularly efficient, labor. Planters, who had not expected the new system to succeed and who complained constantly of the so-called labor shortage, turned to sharecropping only after gang labor had failed. As it turned out, however, sharecropping had unexpected advantages. The croppers' incentive to produce was undoubtedly higher. Moreover, because they negotiated their contracts, did their work, and purchased their supplies individually, the organization of collective bargaining or strikes, which took place on a large scale on Louisiana sugar plantations in the eighties and early nineties, was far more difficult.[15]

Nonetheless, the sharecropper's chance of accumulating a little capital, of owning a mule and perhaps even land, was somewhat better. Croppers were certainly oppressed people. But the share-tenancy system would not have begun in the first place except for their ability to exercise some bargaining leverage. Moreover, to look ahead to the 1930s and after World War II, sharecropping remained the dominant labor system only as long as the respective negotiating positions of capital and labor within Southern agriculture remained at comparable levels.

Gradually circumstances altered. First, the closing of the Atlantic migration during World War I enabled Southern black (and white) peasants to begin to escape from the orbit of the plantation economy by moving to the industrial North. This large migration put pressure on the plantation system at its most vulnerable point: its low-wage structure. Planters responded at first by trying to block the recruitment by Northern industries of "their" black workers and then by adopting technology that had long been available. At last, because the scale of costs had shifted, machines were replacing manual labor. Eventually, indeed, technology would force the pace. Peasants would be pushed as well as pulled from the land.[16] The balance would be tipped, even more strongly than before, in favor of big men like William Faulkner's furnishing merchant Will Varner. Planters would turn off their tenants, replacing them, as well as most of their permanent wage laborers, by machinery and migrant workers. Within a remarkably short time, sharecroppers would become obsolete and rare. The position of small independent farmers would be only a little less precarious. Banks would foreclose on their mortgages. Huge expanses of territory would be opened up to the further urban and industrial development of successive versions of the New South. (The latest is called the Sunbelt.)

Sharecropping was thus a transitional phase in a long, profoundly significant process by which the land, class, and power structure of the South's agrarian economy evolved, consolidated, and evolved again. In its most general outline, that process is sketched succinctly and reasonably accurately in Marx's classic analysis of the transformation of preindustrial England in *Das Kapital*. The coin has two sides. One is named the agricultural revolution and the rise of modern industry. The other side – everywhere in the world except England and America, where of course it has been most complete – is called proletarianization. An agricultural people escaped, or were driven, from the land and became dependent on their labor.

The ladder of Southern agrarian society had slippery rungs. Black slaves became hired hands or sharecroppers; croppers might accumulate capital (a mule, a few tools) and become renters; successful renters became landowners, who borrowed from banks as well as from furnishing merchants or stores; a few prospered; over the course of a century "progress" squeezed most of them off the land. (As I write I learn from the radio that only eight thousand independent black farmers remain in North Carolina.) In the long run all this may have been necessary, perhaps even ultimately for their benefit: But squeezed they were. Except for the beginning point of slavery, the cycle for most white farmers was not very different. More of them prospered; a smaller proportion were hired hands; their stay on the land might have been longer; when they were squeezed off, or pulled away by improved opportunities or by "bright lights," they moved to comparatively better jobs in town.

The gradations of extreme poverty are difficult to comprehend. The Okies in John Steinbeck's novel *The Grapes of Wrath*, for example – the picture of a young woman nursing a grown man who otherwise would have starved to death comes to mind

– were as destitute as blacks were in Mississippi. The crucial point is not whether poor blacks on average were more oppressed than poor whites, although they were. Grinding economic pressure was overpowering them all. The discrimination that permeated the agrarian society of the South was not a simple color line. It was a complex interpenetration of race and class.

The transitional sharecropping system had replaced slavery as the dominant form of labor organization long before 1890. Its principal social characteristic was deep structural antagonism between the two oppressed groups of the same economic class: poor white and poor black. There was nothing new about that either. In the Old South, as the former slave Frederick Douglass had once patiently explained to the poor-white president Andrew Johnson:

> The hostility between the whites and blacks . . . has its roots and sap in the relations of slavery and was incited by the cunning slave masters. Those masters secured their ascendancy over the poor whites and the blacks by putting enmity between them.
> They divided both to conquer each. There was no earthly reason why the blacks should not hate and dread the poor whites when in a condition of slavery; it was from this class that their masters received their slave catchers and overseers.[17]

In the rural South after 1865 – whether reconstructed, redeemed, or new – the roots and sap of acute structural antagonism persisted. Planters in the black belt made no secret of their preference for "the nigger every time. The nigger will never 'strike' so long as you give him plenty to eat and half clothe him: He will live on less and do more hard work, when properly managed, than any other class, or race of people."[18] Using black tenants planters could produce on average more cotton or tobacco. Less of their land would be wasted on vegetables, grass for grazing, or corn to be turned into meat. Still more would be bought on credit from his store. Not surprisingly, white tenants were often replaced by black, a trend that seems to have increased during the depression of the 1890s.[19]

The structural antagonism of agrarian race and class relations in the New South thus differed remarkably little from the situation Frederick Douglass analyzed so perceptively in the Old. Clearly there was substantial continuity between the two periods. The culture of a traditionally racist society, in which plantation slavery had been the basic mode of production for more than two centuries, could not conceivably have been superseded at once – particularly when the whites were in the majority. (Where whites were a small minority, I suggested in the first chapter, as in the Caribbean or in East Africa, institutionalized racism evaporated surprisingly rapidly.)

The virulent and perhaps accelerating racism of the postwar era is often explained mainly on the basis of that cultural inheritance. Prejudicial attitudes, it is argued, formed and frozen in a slave society, lagged behind the progressive pace of economic and social change. In time, however, they would improve. Such has always been the view of optimists, from Booker T. Washington to the 1950s and beyond.

Although this reasoning certainly has some truth in it, it seems profoundly misleading. Not only culture, but the forces that had shaped that culture, persisted and even intensified. The new men, the demagogues who came to dominate Southern politics, who typified its style in the late nineteenth and twentieth centuries, could tap among their poor-white followers a deep, persistent, explosive racism. Its roots and sap were far more immediate and intensely personal than the legacy of slavery.

Although the demographic proportions of white and black in the two countries might suggest otherwise, the structural antagonism between the two races in the agrarian New South was a good deal more severe than it was in rural South Africa, where it was nipped in the bud. In South Africa the Natives Land Act of 1913, which prohibited white landowners from Kaffir farming their land by leasing it to African tenants, successfully removed the threat to white agriculture. Peasants were miraculously transformed into bona fide laborers. Everywhere except in the thirteen percent of the country that was protected as Bantu homelands, Africans were proletarianized by a stroke of the pen. In the American South this same process happened much more gradually. The competition between white and black that contemporaries so deplored therefore persisted and accelerated. The New South's agrarian labor system was based upon it.

Populists sometimes argued that white and black farmers, who had everything in common except the color of their skins, should combine against their common enemies the bankers and furnishing merchants. This analysis of the South's class relations could hardly have been improved upon. Like Frederick Douglass, the Georgia populist leader Tom Watson perceived that what at bottom were class issues were being skillfully mystified and manipulated by means of race. "The accident of color can make no difference in the interest of farmers, croppers and laborers," he pleaded, in a well-known and perhaps overquoted statement. "You are kept apart that you may be separately fleeced of your earnings."[20]

But it did make a difference. To repeat a central, if not entirely original, argument of this book: Unlike class relations, which have their ultimate origins in contradictions that emerge within and between a society's basic modes of production and exchange, race relations are essentially extrinsic. Their origins are not in production, but in power. They are not inevitable or natural. They must therefore be imposed. In the evolution of history, however, race can and has become so embedded in fundamental institutions that it is virtually inseparable except by means of a decisive overthrow or wholesale reordering of the political and social system.[21] Racism is indeed what Lenin called false consciousness. It is nonetheless real and powerful.

This painful lesson some white and especially black Populists learned often and to their cost. In eastern Texas, for instance, "armed horsemen rode through the ranks" of blacks lined up to vote in 1896 "and destroyed with force the years of organizing work of the black political evangelist" John B. Rayner.[22] That event and its effects would be repeated countless times. It would be hard to overestimate the bitter conflict of this period of Southern history. The numerous and well-documented "Negroes in Politics" volumes, in which the race relations of the late nineteenth century have been recorded state by state, are one long, depressing, frightening tale of fraud, intimidation, violence, and murder. The effort to unify the people of the South by elevating class consciousness at the expense of racism would be attempted, repeatedly and courageously, by the Knights of Labor, by some Populists, and by their successors.[23] Time and again, until that distant day in the 1960s when at last the massive if often ambivalent power of the federal government would begin to modify rather than reinforce white supremacy, those attempts would fail. They would fail not because the analysis of the interrelationship of race and class on which they were based was mistaken. It was all too accurate. When physicians are unable to order a cure, however, a correct diagnosis, no matter how often repeated, must remain ineffectual. However many times they were exposed, the forces that controlled and directed Southern society were too strong to be dislodged.

Not the least of the weapons in the arsenal of the Southern power structure was this exceptional ability to blur the lines of class and race. By the late nineteenth century this weapon had been used so frequently that it had become habitual and virtually instinctive. Racism had a powerful, functional role to play. So successfully were race and class intertwined that Southern historians still explain racism in the twentieth century mainly on the basis of the cultural values inherited from slavery. Racist attitudes had of course been pervasive then, and they continued. No new ideology of white supremacy had to be invented. But the racism that permeated the New South was not merely the survival of an anachronism, working against the grain of a modernizing economy and society. The racist culture was constantly being replenished and reinvigorated by the evolving structure of contemporary social and power relations. Otherwise, although it would certainly not have vanished into thin air after 1865, Southern racism would not have been so pervasive or so explosive.

The intense interpenetration and structural antagonism of race and class relations explain much about the violent, schizophrenic, pathological personality of Jim Crow. As the contemporary South African observer Maurice Evans argued, the lower level of competition in his own country may partially account for the otherwise puzzling fact that lynching never became a South African disease.[24] (The fact that the law in South Africa has been much less ambiguous and even more effective as an instrument of social control is probably still more significant.) It may also explain the paradoxical difference in political rhetoric and tone. In South Africa, as in the American South, all save a tiny handful of whites were racists. Yet despite South Africa's large black majority, even most Afrikaner politicians from the High Veldt of the Transvaal or the Orange Free State ordinarily spoke in softer, more paternal voices. (Not until the more competitive era after World War II did that tone become comparably strident.) Like their American counterparts, South African politicians found it advantageous to defend the sacred purity of their women against a "fate worse than death" at the hands of "big black brutes." But no South African novelist approached the shrill racist imagery of Thomas Dixon of North Carolina.[25] Those U.S. Senators from the state of Mississippi, James Vardaman and Theodore Bilbo, might have felt slightly out of place in the political dialogue not only of the pro-Commonwealth leaders Louis Botha and Jan Smuts but even of such nationalist politicians as J. B. M. Hertzog and Tielman Roos.

The racism that permeated the agrarian institutions of the Old and New South was probably intensifying in the late nineteenth century. The causes of this acceleration are complex: the escalating rhetoric of politicians; what Woodward aptly called the invention of the Old South mythology in the New; the "pushiness" of blacks to become landowners, to exercise their rights and leave their "place." The driving force was the severe, long-term squeeze on Southern farmers.

Yet the direct political connection that Woodward drew between the rising tide of poor-white racism and the acceleration of black disfranchisement after 1890 – his classic paradox of the Herrenvolk that "political democracy for the white man and racial discrimination for the black were often products of the same dynamics" – must apparently be cast upon the growing heap of excellent ideas that happen to be contradicted by the facts.[26] J. Morgan Kousser, who is himself a student of Woodward, has recently demonstrated that no groundswell of popular opinion favoring disfranchisement took place in areas that were populated either by "hillbillies" or by "redneck" farmers.

Nor did a new type of radical politician, a man of the people from humble origins, seize control of the Democratic Party from planter Conservatives. Men like Furnifold Simmons of North

Carolina, whose family's plantation had been worked by a hundred slaves, or even "Pitchfork" Ben Tillman of South Carolina came from backgrounds that were not exactly impoverished. Within the state Democratic parties – until after Reconstruction they were usually called Conservative – there had always been factions. And a new generation of leaders was coming to power. But it was time for that to happen. By the 1890s Redeemers like Wade Hampton of South Carolina were growing old. The language and style of politics somewhat altered. But the background, economic interests, and programs of the Democratic establishment when they were in office remained much the same.

In their desperate struggle for survival against Populists and fusionists (i.e., populist–Republican coalitions), Kousser argues persuasively, the Democratic elite deliberately raised the level of their racist rhetoric. With all their considerable powers they incited and inflamed. But racism was not sufficient, Kousser finds from a close analysis of election returns. Most white populist voters were racists, and some of them undoubtedly were persuaded to move over or back to the Democrats. Some – but not enough. By the late 1890s the Democratic elite had been surprisingly unsuccessful in cutting away the base of populist support. Hence they decided in favor of a much larger program of disfranchisement than they had originally intended.

The leaders of the disfranchisement campaigns were usually well educated, they were often wealthy, and they were frequently from the black belt. The main centers of opposition were not black-belt areas dominated by paternalist patricians, as Woodward had supposed, but counties that possessed large white majorities. (Kousser's analysis is borne out by the state of Texas, whose black-belt area in the east is proportionately small. Disfranchisement came late and was never complete.) Moreover, there was strong opposition. By means of fraud, violence, reregistration, multiple ballot boxes, and so on, the imaginative disfranchisers were therefore careful to limit the size of the vote *before* the election of delegates to a constitutional convention or *before* a referendum on a restrictive amendment. In a fair popular vote, fairly counted, or so they suspected, disfranchisement stood a good chance of being defeated. And the disfranchisers, Kousser concludes, were right.

The Democratic Party feared the common man, and with reason. For, Kousser argues, the black vote was not the only target of the disfranchisement campaigns. Reducing the poor-white vote, the main support of populist parties, was also an extremely important objective. Grandfather clauses, under which illiterate descendants of Confederate soldiers or of those who had voted before 1860 might qualify, have tended to obscure this strategy. But the disfranchisers, Kousser concludes, predicted quite correctly that most disqualified whites would be ashamed to confess their illiteracy before a registrar.

The common man could not, apparently, be trusted. As Furnifold Simmons, who had been campaign manager in the crucial elections of 1898 and 1900, explained with unusual candor in his opening address at the Democratic Party convention of 1900 in North Carolina, "if the white people of the State would always stand and vote together as they did in 1898, we would always have White Supremacy," that is, a Democratic majority, "without the necessity of a Constitutional Amendment." The sad fact was, however, that "the white people will not always stand together and vote together." Many whites, particularly in the mountains, would probably continue to vote Republican: As indeed they have. Others from time to time might follow third-party fads. The disfranchisement amendment, which reduced the turnout of voters after 1900 by about one-third, was therefore essential. The amendment, Simmons explained, "embodies our plan for establishing White Supremacy [i.e., Democratic power] upon a permanent basis . . ."[27] And so, for more than half a century, it would.

Kousser's valuable research fixes responsibility, answering a question that has long preoccupied Southern historians: "Who done it?" Not poor whites, who lacked the means, but men with power, whose motive was their own political retrenchment. "The new political structure," writes Kousser,

> was not the product of accident or other impersonal forces, nor of decisions demanded by the masses, nor even the white

masses. The system which insured the absolute control of predominantly black counties by upper-class whites, the elimination in most areas of parties as a means of organized competition between politicians, and, in general, the non-representation of lower-class interests in political decision-making was shaped by those who stood to benefit from it most – Democrats, usually from the black belt and always socioeconomically privileged.[28]

Thus Kousser strengthens and refines Woodward's emphasis on the political factor – the partisan motives and objectives of the disfranchisers. Even more clearly from Kousser's detailed evidence than from Woodward's does the conclusion emerge that, directly and immediately, disfranchisement served the needs of politicians.

We can now appreciate the complexity of the problem that may have led Woodward to conclude that the search for the origins of segregation in the late nineteenth century must go "beyond the limits of economic history." Agriculture was the occupation of some three-fourths of the South's people. Most of those who were engaged in manufacturing depended on local agricultural products. The evolving structures and institutions of agrarian society reinforced and drove forward the antagonism and interpenetration of class and race.

Yet nothing in the long transition within the plantation economy from slavery to sharecropping required a new, horizontally organized order of race relations. During slavery the lines of power and authority had been overwhelmingly vertical. Despite the efforts of some Populists and others to build class lines across the color bar, the power relations of the rural New South continued to be mainly vertical. The pressure on tenants and small independent farmers may well have increased during the 1890s, with the deep international depression, the fall in farm prices, the replacement of some white tenants with blacks, and (beginning in Texas) the gradual, devastating invasion of the boll weevil. It would be tempting to draw a connection.

The political and economic time frames do not mesh, however. The rise of the People's Party, the cyclone of disfranchisement, and the legislative consolidation of Jim Crow were all short-term events. The transition in the agricultural mode of production took place over many decades. Moreover, like the influence of World War I in European history, agrarian distress is too easily made the cause of too many complex and contradictory phenomena. It may partially account for the surge of racial violence in the late nineteenth century. But it also helped to create populism, which was the most significant internal challenge to the hegemony of white supremacy until the 1960s. Economic pressure, again, might be a key to the strong religious revival of the period. An economic factor that accounts for everything winds up explaining nothing.

No necessary and sufficient explanation of the origins of segregation emerges, then, from an analysis of some of the principal institutions and tendencies of Southern agriculture. Furthermore, no economic interpretation that does not satisfactorily account for the most significant facts of agrarian history could conceivably be adequate. Economic determinism will not work. On that, as with so many of his conclusions, Woodward is absolutely right. But before this chapter, like Woodward, necessarily begins to venture "beyond the limits of economic history," I shall examine briefly some of the dimensions of the principal labor systems that were taking shape in the early, formative phases of Southern industrialization.

Southern industry seems to have contained four broad types of class–race relations. In the first, which was typified by tobacco manufacturing in North Carolina, Virginia, and Kentucky, a traditional work process that at least on relatively large plantations had been carried on by black slaves was moved into large warehouses in town called factories.[29] In the early years, as had once been the pattern in the first phases of the transition from cottage industry to the factory system in the spinning and weaving of cotton in England after 1790, the traditional work process remained essentially unaltered.[30] By placing the workers under one roof, however, where they could be more closely supervised, employers gained important advantages. Both the productivity of the work force and the consistency of the product could be improved. And once a technological innovation became available, it could be adopted speedily throughout the entire industry.

In these early factories the cycle of production, as well as the types and skills of the people who were engaged in it, changed little. The work process continued to be undifferentiated, not broken up into discrete stages as on an assembly line. The worker was engaged in the whole process from start to finish. What Marx called the alienation of the laborer from the product and from the complete process of his work had not yet begun. The early manufacturing of tobacco continued to be overwhelmingly unskilled. It was "nigger work."

In the 1880s technology transformed this situation dramatically. By 1883 a cigarette machine, which had been patented by a Virginian named James A. Bonsack, was introduced into the factories of Richmond, Danville, Durham, and Winston. Simultaneously a well-organized advertising campaign was increasing the demand for the product. With the machines came skilled, and therefore white, laborers. The first were Jewish immigrants who were experienced in manufacturing cigars. When they proved to have advanced ideas about such things as labor unions and working conditions, however, the employers turned to local whites.

In tobacco as in many other industries, such as lumber manufacturing or flour milling, a modern, differentiated work process characterized by the combination of machines and skilled white labor was superimposed upon a traditional, undifferentiated, unskilled cycle of production that continued to be manned by blacks. The separation of the work process into distinct, discrete phases did not of course cause the social differentiation of the labor force according to race. It did, however, make institutionalized color discrimination both possible and convenient. Enough unskilled manual work remained, however, for tobacco manufacturing to continue to be a strong center of black employment.

A second important labor pattern was the gang system. The dominant form of organization of slave workers on large plantations before 1860, it continued to be employed where sharecropping was not adopted: on some cotton plantations in the Mississippi Delta and particularly on the sugar plantations of Louisiana. It was also the prevailing system of the railroad companies. Railway gangs were herded about, living in temporary camps, moving with the job. As members of a national industry, railway workers were easily infected by "outside agitators," and they were notoriously strike-prone. The frequent intervention of state power and the threat of being replaced by strikebreakers – who, since they were more vulnerable to unemployment, were often black – helped to keep them in line.[31]

The gang system was not, of course, uniquely Southern. But factors peculiar to the South no doubt made it harsher than it was, say, for the Irish immigrants who built the Erie Canal. One reason was the continuity with slavery, when the whip had kept the field hands up to the pace. Even more significant was the gang system's most notorious form, the institution that for a time undergirded much of the organization and discipline of labor in the South in the late nineteenth century: the convict lease.

Under both Reconstruction and Redemption, convicts were leased in all the Southern states to railroad companies, coal mines, and large plantations – not to mention Scarlett O'Hara's lumber-yard in *Gone with the Wind*. Because it raised revenue, reduced prison costs, and removed "vagrants" from street corners, the leasing system was an effective though insufficient answer to the chronic complaints of employers about the labor shortage. (As in South Africa, "labor shortage" ordinarily meant that sufficient workers were not forthcoming at the wages employers had agreed to pay.) Southern labor strenuously resisted the employment of convicts in competition with free workers. And, of course, since their employers literally had the power of life and death over them, they were the most effective strikebreakers imaginable.[32]

Early in the twentieth century, citing grim and plentiful statistics of brutality and astonishingly high death rates, and arguing with irrefutable logic that as long as there was a financial incentive, judicial systems would be in business to produce rather than to rehabilitate criminals or prevent crime, Southern Progressives gradually abolished the leasing system. The states themselves continued to employ convicts on the roads. Until after World War II a child such as myself, growing up on the outskirts of the capital of the South's reputedly most liberal state, North Carolina, became accustomed to chain gangs, supervised by guards with shotguns, working only a few feet from the front door. The guards were always white. The convicts were segregated. Sometimes they were white; more often they were black. The association in the child's mind between black males, crime, and forced labor at gunpoint was inescapable.

A third important labor pattern was typified by the iron mines and foundries of northern Alabama and the bituminous coal mines of Tennessee and Kentucky. A South African observer would have found the situation extremely familiar. Both sections of the iron–coal complex employed large numbers of unskilled workers underground and in the heavy jobs on the surface. They were supervised by a small number of skilled technicians, clerks, and managers. All of the latter categories were white. Many, though by no means all, of the unskilled workers were black.

Birmingham was the American South's Johannesburg. The rise of the Alabama–Tennessee coal and iron industry was not quite the tale of unbroken boom that its boosters and historians have usually told.[33] Somewhat successful attempts to set limits on Birmingham's growth were made – first by the alliance of cotton planters and the ocean port of Mobile, which wanted to move coal by rail directly to the sea, and then by the discriminatory policies of U.S. Steel in favor of the established steel-manufacturing centers of Pennsylvania and Ohio. Even so, from literally nothing as late as 1870 – when the site of the future city was like the Afrikaner farm that became the diamond fields of Kimberley in the eastern Cape Colony of South Africa – Birmingham by 1900 had risen to become the leader of American pig iron production.

Birmingham's historians have stressed the city's good fortune in having the essential resources of coal, iron, limestone, railways, and the bold initiative of local entrepreneurs in such close juxtaposition. But the fundamental fact about the industry's spectacular growth, the unique advantage that made the "Pittsburgh-plus" base-pricing system seem so essential to U.S. Steel, was the low-class wage that was paid to unskilled labor. Here, unlike the situation in so many Southern industries, where black workers were typically being forced down and out by the potent combination of machine technology and skilled white labor, the proportion of blacks in Birmingham's labor force was steadily increasing. By 1910 they were seventy-five percent of all workers in iron and steel.[34] That is indeed a South African statistic. All that was missing was the closed compound.

A South African observer would also have found Birmingham's pyramidal population structure familiar. It might not have been surprising to hear the industry's propagandists proclaiming the immense social virtues of such a situation, for "the Negro in Birmingham fills the industrial position which elsewhere in great manufacturing towns is filled by a low class of whites." Whereas the immigrant proletarians of Northern cities were dissatisfied and turbulent, Birmingham's blacks were satisfied and contented. But even this was not the end of the black people's not inconsiderable contribution to the white people's tranquillity. It was to blacks alone that the city's whites owed their own internal solidarity. Other cities were unhappily divided by sentiments of class. In Birmingham that unfortunate and divisive preoccupation had been replaced by the altogether loftier consciousness of race:

> The white laboring classes here are separated from the Negroes, working all day side by side with them, by an innate consciousness of race superiority. This sentiment dignifies the character of white labor. It excites a sentiment of sympathy and equality on their part with the classes above them, and in this way becomes a wholesome leaven.[35]

Our South African observer would have listened, with some respect, to this skillful mystification of race and class, a piece of propaganda worthy of a president of the Transvaal Chamber of Mines. But, particularly if he had been a member of the Labour Party, he would have demurred: Where blacks became the basis of the labor force, white workers would be driven out. And then the white man's country would be in mortal danger.

Finally, in a pattern that was typified by the cotton mill and the accompanying mill village, both of which became ubiquitous from the 1880s across the whole Southern Piedmont, from southern Virginia to northern Alabama, there was the absolute color bar.[36] Unlike tobacco factories, which were located in town and which drew their black and white labor from an existing urban community that they strongly influenced but did not completely control, cotton mills were ordinarily built on the outskirts of town and even in rural areas.

The advantages of avoiding towns were considerable, explained the Charlotte, North Carolina, industrialist, propagandist, and historian Daniel Tompkins, in what he called a textbook for prospective mill owners – a work that might have been written as a caricature by Karl Marx. City taxes could be avoided. Proximity to union organizers, to lawyers, and therefore to lawsuits in the case of accidents could be reduced. And "a mill in the country can operate its own store, and thereby get back in mercantile profit much of the money paid for wages." Companies should build and rent their workers' houses themselves, the rough rule being one room per operative. Half an acre should be provided per house: enough to provide a supplementary garden but not so much that any member of the family except very small children might remain independent of employment at the mill.

The clear implication, which according to all accounts was certainly realized in practice, was that cotton mills would pay a family wage. The ideal mill village would be self-contained and "self-governing," with its own police force, fire department, churches, gymnasium, school, and lyceum – all, of course, under the control of the company. Employees would never have to leave the neighborhood. And since the mill owned their houses, their bargaining positions were naturally somewhat weakened. In the mill village, motives of philanthropy were nicely balanced by keen business acumen. "Moral influences and education," Tompkins explained disarmingly, "make better work people."[37]

Of all the labor patterns in Southern industry, envious white South Africans perceived in the cotton mill and village a beautifully fashioned model of how a white working class might be made industrious, competitive with black labor, and self-sufficient.[38] In the mill town the poor whites, whom slavery had made as shiftless and as apathetic as any of their own Afrikaner bywoners, might be taught the dignity of labor. Instead these workers might become fit, productive representatives of a thriving Anglo-Saxon society. Here was the key, which white South Africans sought so desperately, to the guaranteed survival of the economically threatened white man's country. American ingenuity had skillfully invented the secret formula. It was low wages.

In the cotton mills a way had been found to make white labor truly competitive, only a little more expensive than black.

With a religious fervor that often made the subscription campaign for a new company hard to distinguish from a camp meeting, the cotton mill was sold to the South as the right road to salvation for poor whites.[39] The high profits of owners and the low wages of employees notwithstanding, there was a grain of truth in that claim. Across the South the white (and black) population was growing rapidly, while both tenants and small independent farmers were severely pressed. Without the mills, presumably, poor whites would have starved or migrated. In the mill village they became subordinate and deferential members of the mill owner's white family. He took care of them. The color bar was thus a large part of the mill owner's claim for social acceptance and political support.

The usual justification for the color bar was the classic Southern taboo: Because white women were part of the labor force, they could not work under the same roof with black males, and that was that. Even though, like most other large enterprises, prewar cotton mills had been worked by slave labor, some authorities contended that blacks were not intelligent or nimble enough to use machinery. After all, two famous experiments had been tried and both had failed. In Charleston, South Carolina, the employers learned to their great regret that black workers would not live up to their high reputation of being willing to work longer and at lower wages. Exceedingly ungrateful, heedless of the great opportunity for the advancement of their race that they bore upon their careless shoulders, when strawberry or oyster season came round, those black folks just took off. For them, it seemed, life was one long picnic.[40] In Concord, North Carolina, the Duke family and other white benefactors contributed to a test case: a cotton mill that was to be managed as well as worked by blacks. But somehow the capital was never quite sufficient, and the mill failed.[41] The mixture of black people and white cotton was apparently destined to last only as far as the gin.

Other industrialists disagreed: If you paid the same wages and provided the same conditions for black workers, if you built mill villages for them, then you would get the same amount and quality of work. Daniel Tompkins made clear that the color bar was essentially a political decision. Blacks, he advised fellow mill owners, would never "be available as cotton mill operatives except in the more menial occupations. Possibly, after a long time, when the white operatives should have left the coarse work behind, negroes may become successful in this work."[42] Meanwhile, employing blacks would seriously "disorganize the force of white labor." Tompkins could hardly have been more explicit. Blacks were to be kept as what Marx called an industrial reserve army.

Throughout the Southern cotton mills, a gentleman's agreement persisted to maintain the color bar. It may have cost the employers a little – but not much. In return they gained the important advantage of moral influence over members of their "family." Often during strikes they threatened to overturn the barrier, but they seldom did it. In the long run the color bar paid. The paternalistic labor system, on which the cotton mills depended even more than other Southern industries did, made it virtually essential.[43]

Together the cotton mill and its company town made up a marvelous and very consciously constructed laboratory for the creation of an ideal order of race and class relations. It was a model so perfect that blacks were excluded from it altogether. The mill became the symbol of the Anglo-Saxon race's salvation. Its rigidly segregationist labor and residential systems were the closest possible approximations to the new order of race relations that simultaneously was being created in law and political action across the South.

6. The South makes segregation: the social interpretation

The long transition of the economic institutions of the rural South, and of the social relations that were rooted in them, provided a strong basis for structural ambiguity, strain, conflict, and violence. Southern farmers and peasants were subject to fluctuating but intense and unrelenting pressure, to the long-term squeeze of agrarian capitalism and modernization that eventually drove most of them off the land. This severe pressure accounts for much, though certainly not all, of the volatile explosiveness of Southern politics in the late nineteenth and twentieth centuries.

Yet the dynamics of the South's agrarian history apparently provided the power structure with no imperative need for a new, horizontally organized order of race relations. In rural areas, with the very important exception of self-segregated all-black towns, the personal power of planters and furnishing merchants continued to be institutionalized in crop-lien laws that were enforced by sheriffs, biased courts, and lynch mobs. In rural areas, for the most part, the traditional mechanisms of intimidation remained in good working order as effective instruments of social control. Overwhelmingly race relations continued to be vertical. White was over black.

THE ROLE OF CITIES

The situation was very different in urban areas, with their concentrations of black lawyers, newspapers, colleges, and large churches. City blacks were somewhat more autonomous than their country cousins. The small but growing middle and artisan classes, in particular – bankers, undertakers, insurance salesmen, teachers, barbers, carpenters, masons – were often their own bosses. Since they did much of their business within the black community itself, they were less directly vulnerable to threats and economic sanctions from whites.[1] They had to deal with white landlords, judges, and policemen – but not with the crop lien.

Urban schools for blacks were overcrowded and shockingly underfinanced, with public expenditure per black pupil often one-eighth or less of that per white; but at least they were better than those in the country. City blacks were better educated, better organized politically, and more "uppity." They therefore posed a much more substantial threat to white supremacy. The need for urban whites to devise new, horizontal mechanisms of coercion and control was therefore far more urgent.

In the South, cities had always been exceptional. They had always contained slave populations, and urban slavery was far from collapsing before 1860. But it had never worked completely satisfactorily.[2] No matter how hard the owners might try, they could not duplicate the comparatively isolated conditions of the plantation. Slaves had mixed with free blacks and, in the saloons, dives, and brothels of such quarters as New Orleans's famous Bourbon Street, with whites of the "baser sort." Although to educate them was usually illegal, urban slaves had been more likely to be literate. Advanced ideas had circulated more freely among them. They were more conscious of a wider world and of their relation to it. Slave revolts among them were more frequent and better organized.

The value of slaves with industrial and other urban skills remained high, and the demand for them continued undiminished. Nevertheless, slavery in the cities had been a contradiction within the South's old order. Along with the early black ghettos in the North, the cities of the antebellum South took their place in C. Vann Woodward's synthesis as important harbingers of the system of segregation that became entrenched in the late nineteenth century.[3]

After 1865 the problem posed by the presence of large numbers of masterless blacks in town grew more intense. Within a year after Lee's surrender serious race riots flared in Memphis,

New Orleans, and elsewhere. Urban whites were alarmed. Like their counterparts in South Africa, they tried to halt the flow to the city. (Many black leaders, including Frederick Douglass and Booker T. Washington, also tried to discourage urban migration.) Blacks, whites kept insisting, did not belong in town at all. They were by nature rural animals, and their proper habitat was on the land. The temptations of the sinful city life were said to be too strong for them. In town no one was in a position to look after them. Urban poverty was wretched; it was said to be worse than rural deprivation. Disease, mortality, crime, and vagrancy rates all soared, foretelling the inevitable decline of a race that was still in need of protection, still unable to stand alone. In the city those who had once been "good niggers" became "uppity" and "spoiled." But these constant exhortations to remain on the land were conspicuously unsuccessful. Although more whites than blacks moved to town, the percentages of blacks held steady or declined only slightly.[4]

In an impressively documented and well-argued recent study, Howard Rabinowitz demonstrates the central, pioneering role of Southern cities in creating the new, horizontal order of race relations.[5] Urban centers were certainly no laggards. Well before 1890 they had invented and tested most of the various devices – including separate housing and social services, poll taxes, educational qualifications for the ballot, white party primaries – that were to be fused into the legal system of segregation across the South.

Theaters, hotels, streetcars, lunch counters, railway stations, factories – all these are urban phenomena. For the very reason that contacts between the races in town were inevitably more casual, because people jostled together much more haphazardly, the rules governing those contacts were defined all the more thoroughly. Precisely because urban blacks were more autonomous and less vulnerable, their place was circumscribed in more detail.

All this may sound suspiciously like common sense. It is therefore important to point out just how profoundly Rabinowitz's argument contradicts much of the available literature of urban sociology. According to the Chicago school, which dominated the field in the United States during the 1930s and beyond, urbanization was conceived of as a unilinear process of social leavening, melting, and unification. It might be traumatic. But it made obsolete inherited, irrational symbols and institutions. On the contrary, recent anthropologists contend, the continuity between country and city is impressive. Ethnic competition and therefore ethnicity – for example, tribal ties in Africa – do not vanish in the city. Indeed, they tend to grow stronger.[6]

Although Rabinowitz ends his study in 1890, at the very point when the streams of segregation were only beginning to swell into an all-engulfing torrent, his case for the urban origins of the system is persuasive. Jim Crow, it seems, was not born and bred among "rednecks" in the country. First and foremost he was a city slicker.

Moreover, continues Rabinowitz, in an argument that Woodward himself had already emphasized, segregation developed most aggressively and most thoroughly not in the Old South cities – New Orleans, Charleston, Savannah – but in new towns of the industrializing Piedmont, such as Birmingham, Atlanta, Spartanburg, Charlotte, Durham. As late as 1900 many of these new towns had 10,000 people or less and were too small to be classified as urban in the census reports. They were, however, growing centers of iron, cotton, or tobacco industries. Connected by the lines of rail that were opening up the region's interior, they were the New South's heartland.

The black belt's paternalism has no doubt been overemphasized. But the older towns possessed preexisting racial patterns that altered more slowly. When Louisiana moved its capital in the 1880s from New Orleans in-state to Baton Rouge, it is said, black legislators who were accustomed to being served in good restaurants found themselves excluded. Woodward cites the example of a writer for a Charleston newspaper in the early nineties who asked sarcastically whether maybe Jim Crow Bibles in all the courthouses might not be next.[7] And so, within a short time, they were.

Anecdotes like these could no doubt be multiplied indefinitely, on either side of the debate about the pervasiveness of racial segregation in practice. More persuasive is the statistically documented argument that residential separation of the races in the older cities lagged considerably behind that in newer centers. By

1910 Charleston's block-by-block "index of dissimilarity," compiled from city directories, was still only 16.8; Birmingham's, the year before, was 84.[8] The Old South cities had long histories of interracial economic and social relations, of master–servant ties between white and black families that sometimes went back several generations. Many of these bonds, of course, had already dissolved. But the housing patterns that had been based on them remained. By contrast, the new towns of the Piedmont, where the people of both races were recent arrivals, could be model cities from the first. In practice, segregation took shape most rapidly in cities, especially in the new towns of the Piedmont, where the New South was truly new.

The early phases of urbanization and – as I argued in the previous chapter – of industrialization in the Piedmont provide something that the gradual evolution of the much more prevalent agrarian institutions of the South does not: a reasonably clear chronological correlation between developing socioeconomic relations and the rapid crystallization of segregation as a legal system and an ideology after about 1890. The early economic development of the Southern Piedmont and the acceleration of segregation occurred simultaneously. Social differentiation was matched by political and legal differentiation. Here, at least, the time frames meshed.

Was there between these two vast processes, the one mainly social and the other primarily political, more than a merely casual relationship? If so, what was its nature? Did segregation, as Woodward put it, somehow serve "the needs of commerce or industry?" Was the new system in some way necessary for capitalism? Did segregation pay?

THE ECONOMICS OF DISCRIMINATION

Economic discrimination may work in two ways. There is wage discrimination: Unequal sums may be paid to persons from different groups for the same work. Or there is job discrimination: Certain categories of work, usually called skilled labor, are formally or informally reserved for particular groups. Either form of discrimination involves financial costs.[9] Wages paid to favored workers are artificially high. That is, they have not been determined by supply and demand in the free market. Efficiency suffers because some workers are prevented from occupying positions they are qualified to fill. The costs of discrimination, however, may be matched – or more than matched – if the wages of a sufficiently large number of workers can be held artificially low relative to profits. That, as I have argued – though economists still debate the point – has been the case in South Africa. In certain circumstances individual employers might find discrimination detrimental. But the gold industry in particular, and white South Africa in general, found both job and wage discrimination profitable.

In the American South, for the obvious reason that whites were not a minority but a large majority of the labor force, the question of the relative economic costs and benefits of discrimination is far more complex. The South's economy simply could not have afforded to pay the grossly discriminatory wage ratios that supported the civilized standard of living for South Africa's white workers. (In the gold mines wages were typically on the order of a pound a day for whites against a pound a week for Africans.) As white South Africans perceived, the American South was in a far healthier condition. Prospects for the survival of the white man's country were therefore much more secure. The South's white workers were much more competitive with black.

As optimistic economic historians appear to have demonstrated, grossly discriminatory wages in the same jobs were comparatively rare in the American South.[10] Black masons usually made less than white masons, black carpenters less than white ones. But the gaps were narrower than one might suppose. Far more frequent, as well as much more difficult to analyze quantitatively, were job reservations: blacks being called carpenters' helpers instead of carpenters. Indeed, there were whole ranges of occupations, especially supervisory, white collar, or skilled positions, in which blacks were simply not to be found, except in their own segregated institutions.

Throughout the South, as well as much of the North, the job-reservation system employed both formal and informal arrangements. Despite the mythology that what was called industrial education was suitable for a race destined for work with the hands, most blacks were inadequately trained even for better-paying artisanal jobs, let alone for white-collar positions. Even when they were qualified, however, they were systematically excluded. A huge number of institutions and businesses – white-run universities and hospitals, white banks and insurance companies, state and local governments, even the federal government under Woodrow Wilson – simply never considered blacks for work "above a certain level." Disproportionately blacks remained in unskilled, dirty, low-paying jobs in agriculture, woodcutting, mining, or domestic service. They also provided, when they were not being jailed as vagrants, a large proportion of the South's casual laborers and chronically unemployed.

The question, insist the optimists, is not whether the South was racially discriminatory but the extent to which discrimination was translated into cold cash terms. For that would depend not only on the intensity of white racism but on the varying relationship between the size of the labor force and the needs of the economy. When they were given direct choices, it seems, individual whites tended to behave like whites in South Africa. They were reluctant to pay for discrimination, or at least to pay very much. "Other things being equal," they tended to act more or less as rational economic persons, who might well "hire a nigger" if he would do the same work at a cheaper rate. The point of the job-reservation system was to reduce the incidence of such "rational" economic choices.

Segregation – indeed any system of race or caste discrimination, even including slavery – regulates the behavior not only of the oppressed but of the oppressors. In South Africa, as the third chapter of this book explained, the Natives Land Act of 1913 forbade white landowners from leasing their property, in what would have been the most efficient and most profitable manner, to African peasants. Enacted two years earlier, the Mines and Works Act prevented white industrial and mining employers from hiring Africans in jobs reserved for whites.

In the American South the coercive mechanisms were somewhat less rigid. There, too, a mixture of formal arrangements and informal understandings was pervasive. There, too, the job-reservation system acted to curb the unwholesome economic appetites of white people, reducing as far as possible the number of occasions when they would be free to make decisions purely on the basis of personal advantage. But, primarily because of the very different racial compositions of the labor forces of the two countries, there was a difference. South Africa used both job and wage discrimination. The South had a great deal of the first but comparatively little of the latter. Southern employers, and therefore black workers, were somewhat less constrained.

The economics of discrimination, then, depended not only on the racism that permeated Southern society but on the ability of the job-reservation system to prevent individual whites from behaving as rational economic persons. But that, in turn, depended on the condition of the economy. If growth were rapid, relative to the size of the labor force, then the job-reservation system would be put under pressure. Although they would still bear the brunt of discrimination, blacks would benefit.

Was the South's economy expanding or stagnant? That is a very complex question. As usual, statistics mingle uneasily with qualitative judgments. In absolute terms, despite long periods of acute business and especially agricultural depression, it was certainly expanding. Proportionately, argues the optimist Robert Higgs in the most systematic analysis of the subject available, the Southern economy was growing at a faster rate than that of the nation as a whole. From what was it expanding? If we take 1860 as the base point, we have harbingers of growth, especially in cotton manufacturing, but hardly a process of sustained industrialization. If we take 1870, the first census after the Civil War, then the complicated problem of war damage clouds the issue. In either case, it is clear, the South in the late nineteenth century was building from a much lower level than the nation as a whole. Even a rate of growth more rapid than the national average might therefore legitimately be regarded as stagnant.

Higgs's admittedly inexact calculation is that by 1900 the average per capita income of Southern blacks may have been some two-thirds that of Southern whites.[11] At this point E. P. Thompson's brilliant and provocative discussion of averages in the long controversy over the standard of living during the English Industrial Revolution comes to mind. Real people must cope with individual, not with aggregate, statistics. Many of them, in fact roughly half, fall below the average. They did not live in "the South" but in the Appalachian mountains, the Piedmont, the black belt, or the piney woods. Even within those regions, and often within particular counties, the quality of soils, availability of water, history of land tenure, and therefore comparative standards of living, differed widely.[12] Moreover, it is perfectly possible, as Thompson puts it, for statistics and experience to run in opposite directions.[13] That is surely as true of Southern farmers, the large majority of whom have left the land during the last century, as of English cotton weavers.

Nevertheless, if Higgs's estimate is even close to the truth, then one of his central arguments is very persuasive indeed. The vast majority of blacks, the exceptions being the few who were already free, had begun in 1865 with no capital whatever. Plantation slavery, which some historians have called a school of civilization, had systematically withheld education. Some urban slaves possessed industrial skills. On plantations slaves had been required to work in agriculture, but they had not been prepared for the comparatively sophisticated occupation of the independent farmer, which required decisions about types and quantities of fertilizer, whether particular tools or machines would be cost-effective, marketing, and so on. Even in the best of all possible worlds, theirs would have been a struggle against severe economic odds. As it was, they had to survive in an oppressive, violently discriminatory society whose foremost object was to prolong and intensify their condition and status of inferiority. Given all these facts, the economic achievement of Southern blacks during their first generation of freedom is indeed impressive.

Equally significant, however, is Higgs's further estimate that the average per capita income of Southerners of both races in 1900 was about half the national figure. Compared with Northerners and Westerners, Southerners were very poor. How much of this substantial disparity is to be explained by the low level of manufacturing before 1860? How much by the destruction of the Civil War? How much by the lack of decent public education for most children of both races until well into the twentieth century? How much by what some scholars have argued was a continuing condition of structural dependency, even a colonial relationship, with the advanced industry and powerful financial centers of the North? How much by the costs of job discrimination? The wide and continuing gap between Southern and national average incomes, which began to narrow perceptibly only after World War II, thus returns us to the questions posed earlier in this chapter. Did segregation pay? If so, whom? By what means? Who, or what, found discrimination advantageous or functional?

The distinction between "functional" and "essential" is narrow but significant. The low average wage of Birmingham's predominantly black labor force gave its fledgling iron industry an important advantage over competitors in Pittsburgh, Cleveland, and Europe. But Birmingham could presumably have grown without it, although not perhaps so rapidly. Blacks could have, and in fact did, run cigarette machines. No compelling economic reason, certainly, required the color bar in cotton manufacturing.

As many students of Southern labor relations have argued, the primary role of discrimination was not to enable employers to hire low-paid black workers instead of better-paid white ones. This they did comparatively rarely. The main social and economic effects of discrimination were more indirect. But for the job-reservation system, blacks could easily have occupied a wide range of positions that were normally held by whites. That system of discrimination, however, was rarely recorded in written documents, such as union contracts, let alone guaranteed by law. The gentleman's agreement between employers and white employees was implicit and could therefore be broken at will.

The black reserve army was thus a potent weapon with which white workers could be threatened, intimidated, and isolated. That weapon was used often and effectively. It helped the South's agricultural and industrial employers to block or severely weaken organizing efforts by labor unions, to break strikes, and to perpetuate the ethos of paternalism and deference. The long-range results of the division of the Southern working class on racial lines were very substantial. As late as the 1980s, for example, the South's most industrialized state, North Carolina, still possesses both the lowest rate of unionization and the lowest average wages in manufacturing.[14] The correlation between racism, weak unions, and low average wages has been difficult for students of various perspectives to resist.

For industrial and agrarian capitalists in the South, racism was therefore advantageous. In Marxist terms, it helped them to maintain and justify a low-class wage for all workers, the majority of whom were white. But was the low-class wage itself economically beneficial? Were its benefits important enough to the South's economic development to repay the undoubted financial costs (to go no further) of the racial discrimination that helped to legitimize and perpetuate it?

On this question the opinions of economists are divided. Development theorists tend to agree that temporarily low wages may constitute a form of enforced social saving, enabling capital to be accumulated and invested in plant expansion or infrastructure (roads, harbors, technical education, etc.). Especially when the newcomer to the industrial race attempts to grow by manufacturing lines of products that are already established in more advanced economies, as the South was trying to do with cotton or iron, then low wages provide an important competitive edge. Low wages seem to be a characteristic feature of the early stages of industrialization – in England in the early nineteenth century, when David Ricardo was formulating his famous iron law of wages, in Soviet Russia during the five-year plans, when grain confiscated from peasants was used to finance purchases of machinery abroad, or in contemporary Brazil.

Moreover, in a society's strenuous effort to maintain temporarily low wages, a powerful ideology, which both stimulates the masses to exert themselves and inures them to hardship, discipline, and sacrifice, is a common component or even a necessary precondition of modernization.[15] In eighteenth-century England that ideological role was played by Methodism, in twentieth-century Russia by the Stakhanovite movement. In the American South the ideological brake upon the rising expectations of workers – and upon those instruments such as labor unions that would have helped them to achieve those expectations – was provided by various forces: so-called primitive and revivalistic religions, the unity of Southern whites in defense of their "glorious cause." But the centerpiece was racism. Discrimination directly held down the wage levels and the mobility of black workers. The indirect effects of racism were even more economically significant. Far more effectively than English and Irish immigrant workers had been kept at odds during England's industrialization, for example, the South's working class was kept divided and politically weak. The average wages of whites were somewhat higher than those of blacks, by perhaps one-third according to Higgs. The incomes of both groups remained low.

That is a short-term view. From a longer perspective Keynesian economists argue that the low purchasing power of the South's working people severely retarded the growth of the region's internal markets and, hence, its secondary industrialization. The South industrialized, but only up to a point. Overwhelmingly its industries continued to manufacture primary goods that were finished elsewhere. They made textile fabrics instead of clothes, pig iron instead of machine tools, tractors, or automobiles. In the short run low average wages may well have stimulated the South's industrialization. In the long run, however, they were a severe depressant, which helped to keep the region backward, stunted, and underdeveloped – though not, of course, necessarily unprofitable to those who controlled its economy.

On the whole, we may conclude that the coming of segregation was probably no more economically essential, no more economically determined, than its eventual weakening. The South's pattern of industrialization adapted so naturally to Jim Crow that the two phenomena soon became apparently inseparable. So readily and smoothly, indeed, that it is still difficult to imagine how the South's society and economy could possibly have evolved in any other way. It is precisely this kind of historical imagination, however, that Woodward undertook in *The Strange Career of Jim Crow*. It was very likely, he agreed, that segregation should have developed in a society where slavery and racial oppression had been the rule for centuries. Likely, but not quite inevitable – so that even the highly probable must be explained by analysis of the specific circumstances in which the event took place. I agree. Segregation was not, in any automatic or mechanical way, economically determined. Given a different balance of political power, economic development certainly could have taken place – perhaps not so rapidly in the short run but without doubt more healthily in the long term. The result could have been a very different kind of class and race structure.

In summary, segregation as a system and ideology of domi-

nance and control was appropriate to the needs of an already racially discriminatory society that was becoming more advanced
economically and more complicated socially. The old system,
which largely continued in rural areas, had been primarily vertical in organization. The new system was in the main organized
horizontally. In industry after industry machines enabled the work
process to be broken up into discrete phases. Skilled and unskilled labor, and therefore laborers, could be differentiated as
never before. Simultaneously the new towns of the industrializing Piedmont, unencumbered as they were by the traditional
bonds of personal interdependence, deference, and paternalism
that were decaying more gradually in the older cities, could develop residential separation and discrimination in services, rapidly and to an unprecedented degree.

Yet the forces that shaped the specific social arrangements of
the new order of race relations were not economically determined. The division of labor into the skilled, who were almost
entirely white, and the unskilled, who were disproportionately
black (and female), was based not on earned individual merit but
on ascription. It was an artificial classification. At bottom it was
based not on economic but on political grounds.

Nothing inherent in the nature either of the city or of the factory demands discrimination among those who live or work
there. Nor is there anything fundamental to either institution that
prevents discrimination from being maintained as a pervasive
pattern, more or less indefinitely. Both, as Herbert Blumer has
argued persuasively in a seminal essay, tend to conform to the
prevailing political and ideological forces of the particular society
in which they take root.[16] In a society that was already dedicated
to white supremacy, and determined to remain so, town and plant
adapted readily enough to the demands of the politically powerful. Industrialization and urbanization enabled those demands to
be achieved even more rapidly and more thoroughly. But the
demands themselves were political. They were organized and
mobilized in an attempt to gain or perpetuate political power.
Both the crystallization of segregation after 1890 and its eventual
dismantling in the 1960s and after were political events, the results of decisive changes in the balance of political power.

THE SOUTHERN POWER ELITE

In a recent essay on "The Cost of Segregation" George Tindall points to a theme that implicitly underlies many interpretations of the South: that of "a power elite which has remained little studied and little understood." That subject, he continues, "is one of the next tasks in southern history – the study of race, class, and power. Who exercised power over whom, to what ends, and how?"[17]

Such a disarming admission might cause some surprise. It might have been supposed that the study of Southern history had been concerned with little else and that its students, including Tindall himself, had been engaged in the "next task" for some time. Yet the point is well taken. The power elite of the New South, usually going under such code names as Bourbon or Democratic establishment, has often been strenuously defended and, on occasion, strenuously attacked. It has rarely been analyzed systematically. The one-party political system of the twentieth-century South may reasonably be compared to the Whig supremacy of eighteenth-century England. The historiographies of the two regimes are also comparable. Like the school of Sir Lewis Namier, if rarely with such tenacity, Southern historians have tended to take the Democratic establishment for granted. In great detail they have traced the internal personal and factional quarrels within this power elite, on which elections, in the absence of genuine issues, ordinarily hung. Like the Namierites, they have tended to assume that the one-party system was normal, that its economic and social basis did not have to be accounted for.

Although comparatively rare, however, there has been much more thoughtful investigation into the nature of the Southern power elite – into who constituted it, how it formed and under what specific circumstances, how it achieved and retained power, how it exercised hegemony over a society whose most fundamental characteristic was class and racial inequality. The questions just listed, indeed, might well serve as a reasonably succinct summary of the principal themes of Woodward's *Origins of the New South*. As so many prefaces have testified, the boldness of that pioneering work would be hard to overestimate.

The trouble is, as Tindall's critique of Southern historiography implies, that Woodward stood on amazingly few shoulders. In English history his achievement would be like that of Geoffrey Elton on the Tudor monarchy without Sir John Neale or Conyers Read; like that of Christopher Hill or Lawrence Stone on the origins of the English Revolution without Sir Samuel Gardiner or R. H. Tawney; like that of E. P. Thompson on the working class during the Industrial Revolution without the Hammonds or Sir John Clapham. Woodward did not so much revise an existing interpretation as pump air into a historiographical vacuum.

Virtually at once Woodward's brilliant, sweeping synthesis of the relationship of race, class, and power became a new consensus. Unlike the melee of controversy that surrounded *Strange Career* only a few years later, when he argued that race relations were comparatively open during Reconstruction and Redemption, his assessment of the nature and sources of power relations in the New South after 1890 went virtually unchallenged and largely unscrutinized. This, as Woodward himself candidly recognized, was by no means a healthy situation. For his synthesis had gone far beyond the existing foundation of detailed archival research.

Briefly, and again with apologies for the inevitable shortcomings of so bald a summary, the main elements of the Woodward interpretation are the following. First, both directly through the movement and pillaging of armies and then indirectly through Emancipation, the Civil War destroyed or at least severely weakened the economic roots of the Old South's dominant class, the planter aristocracy. For a time the fall of the mighty from their places of eminence was not apparent. The Conservatives who held power during Redemption, and who subsequently lost it in the "revolt of the rednecks" during the 1890s, were mainly black-belt patricians or their direct political descendants.

Appearances, however, were deceiving. The historian who would understand the politics of the New South had to look beneath the surface. Beneath the placid transition from Conservatives to Bourbons, even beneath the apparently cataclysmic overthrow of both groups by racist demagogues, Woodward argues, was an essential continuity. Basic, highly significant shifts were taking place in the class determinants of political power. Though they were constantly punctuated by bitter quarrels among personalities and factions, the slowly evolving shape of these far more fundamental class configurations was what Southern history was properly about.

In Woodward's view the source of these evolving power relations was essentially external. It was the supposedly massive invasion of capital from the industrialized and financially powerful North. The impact of this outside force on the South could hardly be overestimated. A region whose rulers until 1860 had been able to play off two contenders – England and the North – against each other was fast evolving into a Northern colony, tied by bonds of structural dependency so tight that the eighteenth-century British Board of Trade would have admired the relationship as a finely tuned example of mercantilism.[18] For Woodward this shift in the lines of dependency was the fundamental fact of Southern economic history in the late nineteenth century. The political implications of this realignment were enormous. The class, and of course the politicians, that could successfully ally with the irresistible force of Northern capitalism while simultaneously pretending to defend the South's autonomy against external domination would control both the economy and the politics of the New South.

Converting the South into an abject and cooperative Northern colony required internal, authentically Southern collaborators. That, at least, was the lesson of the era of Reconstruction, when Northern capitalists had tried to achieve their objective by working through Republicans or by importing their own compradors, the carpetbaggers. At bottom, argues Woodward, this attempt at direct domination of the Southern economy was what Reconstruction was really about.

By the mid-1870s, however, it was clear that the strategy of direct rule had failed. But as other imperialists – notably the British in the Indian princely states, Malaya, Nigeria, and elsewhere – have also discovered, the goal of economic hegemony could be achieved as well, and with much less trouble and expense, through subtler forms of indirect political domination. The substitution of an indirect for a direct strategy was the reality behind the facade of Redemption. The end of Reconstruction – that is, the refusal of the Republican administration of President Rutherford

B. Hayes to intervene after a series of Conservative election victories over state Republican parties – was basically another effort to achieve Northern economic ascendancy, this time by working through "patriotic" Southern collaborators.[19]

Woodward identifies these collaborators. They were in fact the Redeemers. Their passionate defense of white supremacy and the glorious cause notwithstanding, they were fundamentally favorable to Northern capital. Sometimes, indeed, in their roles as railway lawyers, for example, they were its well-paid agents. After 1877 the results of this tacit alliance became apparent. What had hitherto been only a trickle of Northern investment became a growing river. The Redeemers were the answer for which Northern capitalism had been desperately searching: authentic Southern collaborators who could be relied upon. In the last two decades of the nineteenth century the conversion of the South into a colonial dependency of the North proceeded apace.

In the 1870s, Woodward continues, a new class of businessmen and industrialists had begun to form. This was something the South had never known: a homegrown bourgeoisie with a separate economic base, able to compete with the planter ascendancy and eventually to overcome it. In the Old South the interests of the mercantile elite, that is, the factors whom we met briefly in the previous chapter, had been fully complementary to those of the planters. Both, for instance, had favored low tariffs so that prices of agricultural products would remain high relative to manufactures. The merchants of the Old South had been comparatively few, and they had been politically weak and subservient.

The cotton, tobacco, and iron magnates who rose to prominence by the 1880s were mainly new men, in Woodward's view. They owed much of their growing economic power to their close connections with Northern business interests, who helped to finance their ventures. They sought to promote an era of national reconciliation, a climate favorable for business and industrial expansion. Their principal spokesmen were newspaper editors and publishers: Henry Grady of the Atlanta *Constitution,* Henry Edmunds of the *Manufacturers' Record* of Baltimore, and Daniel Tompkins, who in addition to being the owner of several cotton mills was publisher of the Charlotte *Observer.* Their program of

Southern industrialization directly challenged both the economic strategy and the political dominance of the planters. It was called the New South movement."[20]

The professed objective of the New South campaign was regional autonomy. It was a catch-up strategy. The South's debilitating weakness, maintained the New South's advocates, was its almost total dependence on Northern manufacturing. Not a plow, not a bolt, not a collar button could be bought in the South that had not been produced elsewhere. Huge transportation, handling, and what economists now call value-added costs were constantly being passed along to Southern consumers. The weakness of the South's industrial base ought to have become evident during the Civil War, when it had been pounded into submission on the anvils in Northern factories. Nevertheless, the South had continued to rely on the prewar economic strategy of concentrating on agricultural exports. Since the heyday of King Cotton, in the last years of the slave regime before 1860, the volume of cotton production had indeed expanded. But the promise of prosperity had not been fulfilled. As long as it continued to exchange agricultural products for outside manufactured goods, the South would remain poor, backward, and dependent.

There was nothing inevitable, the New South publicists maintained, about the South's pathetic condition. Before the 1830s, they argued, overstating their case considerably, there had been plenty of industrial ventures; William Gregg's celebrated South Carolina cotton mills are an example. During the eighteenth century, indeed, Southern manufacturing might even have been at a level more or less equal to that in the North. But then, in a crucial and fateful decision that had been dictated by the planter interest, the South had deliberately turned its back on balanced agricultural and industrial growth. The North had built factories, foundries, canals, railways, and ships. The South had followed a very different strategy. Greedily and singlemindedly, its ruling class had pursued the quick and apparently inexhaustible rewards of a cotton-export economy. Not only had manufacturing not been supported. It had been powerfully discouraged.

Plantation slavery had become entrenched along with its highly compatible partner, King Cotton. That in particular, the New South men admitted, proved to be a curse. Though not so much for the blacks: Innately suited as they were for servitude, they were fortunate to have been schooled in what was very probably the most benevolent labor system in the history of the world! No, the real victims were ordinary whites. For them the cotton and slave regime was disastrous. It effectively shut them out of their rightful role in the central economic life of their society. Although in recent years they seemed to have forgotten the lessons, slavery had once taught blacks the habits and the dignity of labor. It had done no such thing for whites. It had made them slovenly and apathetic. The legacy of slavery largely accounted for the unfortunate (and no doubt temporary) inferiority of Southern white laborers, who after all came from the finest Anglo-Saxon and Scotch-Irish stock, to the more industrious and better-disciplined workers of New England. Slavery had been no crime. There was nothing whatever in its proud record of which the South need feel ashamed. Worse than a crime, as Talleyrand once said, slavery had been a mistake.

The New South movement's chosen route to the goal of regional autonomy was outside capital investment. Its publicists diligently courted Northern financiers, who supported their mills, mines, and foundries. Once again, Woodward argues, appearances were deceiving. External investment was supposed to be a shortcut to regional autonomy. Instead it turned out to be another long detour. The South did begin to industrialize, but only in a few areas. It competed only with the less efficient sectors of Northern manufacturing, building industries that were particularly attractive to outside investors. Because manufacturing usually continued to stop short of the finished product, the South continued to pay for the last, most expensive stages of the value-added process. The profits of the South's economy therefore continued to be drained away. The overall effect of the New South economic strategy, Woodward concludes, was to intensify the region's severe structural dependency, to maintain the South all the more firmly in its role as a colony.

The New South movement professed to be the champion of the common man, whom the Old South had so scorned and so neglected. In fact, Woodward maintains, it represented once again the interests of big men – bankers, industrialists, railroad magnates – who were backed by big capital from the North. For, stripped of its rhetoric, the basis of the New South's economic strategy amounted to a very old prescription, now intended to be the foundation of industry as well as of agriculture. It was the low-class wage.

In one respect the New South might be dismissed rather easily as a mirage that never became reality. Nevertheless, Woodward continues, the movement was no merely peripheral phenomenon, outside the Southern mainstream. It was a strong bid for power, for control of the South's economic and political destiny, by the rising bourgeoisie. It became an important component – triumphant in some states, successfully resisted in others that did not industrialize – of the Conservative-Bourbon-Democratic regimes that took control throughout the redeemed South during the mid-1870s. With the gradually declining but still extremely potent survivals of the old planter aristocracy, the newly formed bourgeoisie fashioned uneasy but reasonably effective political alliances. Armed with the power of the statehouse, masking their interests and their intentions by means of a variety of ideological screens – the appeal to racial solidarity, the promise of a New South, the defense of the "cause" of the old one – members of the Democratic establishment were busily entrenching themselves in power. Beneath the facade that was called Redemption, the basis of a new economic and political hegemony was being consolidated.

Then came populism. For Woodward that movement was by far the most powerfully formative force of the entire era. Unlike the radical Reconstructionists, who depended on the dubious stamina of Northern intervention, Populists built their challenge on the angry revolt of a large portion of Southern farmers, not all of whom were powerless. The threat posed by populism to the hegemony of planters and big industrialists was therefore even more dangerous than the earlier one. Centering on the stranglehold of furnishing merchants, bankers, large manufacturers, and railroad magnates, the populists' issues were overwhelmingly economic. But from the beginning in the 1880s, when the Farmers' Alliance was both a program and a network of cooperatives but not yet a party, the immense political implications of the people's movement were apparent. Only by taking power could such an insurgent group hope to defend itself against such well-entrenched adversaries. In North Carolina alone did Populists take their challenge to its logical conclusion by fusing with Republicans to drive the Democrats from office in 1896. But the threat of the union of the have-nots of both races was the most potent force in the violent, explosive politics of this period of Southern history.

That threat led to disfranchisement. As had been the case during the triumph of the Redeemers, so now in the struggle of the 1890s that culminated in the disfranchisement campaigns: the race issue was essentially a masquerade. The quarrel was among white men. As so often happened in America, however, blacks were the big losers. "It is one of the paradoxes of Southern history," writes Woodward in one of his most brilliantly sweeping passages, "that political democracy for the white man and racial discrimination for the black man were often products of the same dynamics." Those dynamics were fundamentally economic and social:

> As the Negroes invaded the new mining and industrial towns
> of the uplands in greater numbers, and the hill-country
> whites were driven into more frequent and closer association,
> and as the two races were brought into rivalry for subsistence
> wages in the cotton fields, mines and wharves, the lower-
> class white man's demand for Jim Crow laws became more
> insistent . . . The barriers of racial discrimination mounted in
> direct ratio with the tide of political democracy for whites.[21]

Was populism, then, somehow responsible for disfranchisement? Not directly, in Woodward's view. Instead, the popular force behind the rise of racial discrimination was the "revolt of the rednecks," a movement led (or rather captured) by such demagogues as "Pitchfork" Ben Tillman of South Carolina. Under the banner of a heroic fight to throw off "Negro rule," these radical reactionaries overthrew the Conservative leadership within the Democratic Party. Adopting the language of populism, stealing its issues whenever possible, resorting frequently to violence and intimidation, the demagogues co-opted and beat back the Populists. Once in power they disfranchised black voters. At the feet of their poor-white followers they tossed the crumbs of Jim Crow.

Yet again, argues Woodward, beneath these political rumblings that seemed to shake the earth, the degree of continuity was impressive. A significant change took place in the tone and style of politics in the 1890s. But no fundamental shift occurred in the class determinants of power. Once they were in office, their anticapitalist rhetoric notwithstanding, the policy toward business interests of "men of the people" like Tillman was fully as cooperative, fully as subservient, as that of their Conservative predecessors.[22] In the shrunken, sheltered pool that remained after disfranchisement, big fish swam and splashed with abandon. The consolidation of the alliance of big men, of the hegemony of the Southern power elite, resumed. Gradually, in many states, the influence of the rising business and industrial bourgeoisie came to outweigh that of the planters. The crucial fact, however, is that the South had once more been made solid. The power elite would not again be seriously challenged for more than half a century.

Thus, although it must have seemed a convenient way to introduce a review of recent interpretations of Southern history, George Tindall's remark that one of the next tasks must be the study of the relationship of race, class, and power is a bit misleading. The power elite has been on the agenda for some time. What is true is that Woodward's magnificent synthesis has "stood the test of time" for nearly three decades.

As early as 1971, in his Preface to the second edition of *Origins of the New South,* Woodward himself took note of the substantial volume of new research that had become available and called for a new synthesis. It was high time, he teased, for the young historian "to be about his work."[23] Only very recently, however, has Woodward's analysis been significantly questioned. The main outlines of an explicitly revisionist interpretation are at long last becoming available. But far more research will have to be done before a new synthesis, comparable in scale and comprehensiveness to Woodward's, will be possible.

The kind of reinterpretation Woodward presumably had in mind is illustrated in the important book by his student J. Morgan Kousser. He substantially revised his mentor's version of the politics of disfranchisement at what appears to have been its weakest point. Disfranchisement, Kousser demonstrates by means of regression analysis of electoral returns from selected districts, was not the result of a popular outcry among poor whites. Nor were the campaigns to disqualify black voters led by representatives of counties with white majorities. The principal disfranchisers were overwhelmingly members of the elite, usually from black-belt areas. They tended to be planters.

The populist revolt may well have threatened the Democratic establishment, goading them into taking steps that would ensure their own political dominance. But *they* did it. Like their social betters, most poor whites were no doubt racists. They lacked the power, however, which the elite alone possessed, to strip black men of their votes. Districts with substantial white majorities were more likely to oppose disfranchisement, whereas black-belt areas dominated by planters were more likely to be in favor. (Thus black men supposedly voted in large numbers for their own disqualification.) Disfranchisement did not, then, mount "in direct ratio with the tide of political democracy for whites." Indeed, by eliminating many poor-white as well as black voters, the disfranchisers were determined to make anything resembling genuine democracy virtually impossible.[24]

As I have already observed, the overall effect of Kousser's revision is to strengthen Woodward's argument by removing from it a logical contradiction. The rhetoric of the racist demagogues, Woodward himself had contended, had always been sham. Once in office they behaved like members of the big man's club. Kousser backdates their membership. Never, despite appearances, had they been anything else. For the most part Woodward's interpretation of political history from Reconstruction into the twentieth century emphasizes the continuity of the Southern power structure. His explanation of disfranchisement stands out as exceptional for its stress on discontinuity. Kousser's revision makes the story even more continuous than Woodward had supposed.

Yet Kousser's work has wider implications that do not square so easily with important parts of the Woodward synthesis. Black-belt patricians, Kousser argues persuasively, usually led the fight for disfranchisement. If that is true, then the planter aristocracy must have remained at least an extremely powerful component within state Democratic parties. But the economic strength of the planter class, or so Woodward had told us, was destroyed irrevocably by the Civil War. A new alliance, in which bourgeois industrial and business interests were becoming increasingly dominant, had already gone far toward displacing it. Even before Kousser's book this generalization was questionable. According to Woodward's own evidence, the Conservatives who were supposedly driven from power in the 1890s were mainly planters. Kousser's analysis of the class origins of most of the disfranchisers and demagogues alike (of men like Furnifold Simmons of North Carolina, Hoke Smith of Georgia, Tillman, Vardaman) shows that the planter class was still far from dead politically after 1900 as well as before.

How did a class that had supposedly lost its base of economic power a full generation earlier continue to exhibit such political potency? By appeal to sentiment? By a continuation of inherited habits of deference among other segments of society? The argument is more persuasive that, like the reports of Mark Twain's death, the fall of the planter class has been greatly exaggerated.

The relative political preponderance of businessmen and industrialists, who after all – according to Woodward's own estimate – controlled a sector of the economy employing less than twenty-five percent of the South's working people by 1900, is unlikely to have been so great as Woodward indicates. In time, of course, as the South (or rather specific parts of it) industrialized, the economic and political influence of the rising bourgeoisie would certainly grow. During the late nineteenth and early twentieth centuries, however, they remained lesser partners in the Southern power elite. One should expect the planters' role in any significant political decision to have remained substantial. The New South, in short, was less bourgeois than Woodward supposed.

THE NEW REVISIONISM

Such important problems as these do point out the need for a fundamental reinterpretation of race, class, and power in the New South. The main dimensions of such a revision are only now beginning to become available: notably in the books of Jonathan Wiener on Alabama and Dwight Billings on North Carolina. Written under the strong influence of Eugene Genovese, Bar-

Origins of Seg: 2nd part of thesis. pt - need to address this further to be new origins. not just continuity. Cell accepts the need for part II

The Social Interpretation 155

rington Moore, and Immanuel Wallerstein – and owing a substantial debt to Woodward himself – the arguments are strikingly similar to the neo-Marxist version of South African history that I summarized in the third chapter.[25] The revisionist approach, I shall argue, does offer what in some respects is a more satisfactory explanation than exists at present of the structure of power relations in the New South and therefore of the origins of segregation. Like Woodward's critics who specialize in the period of Reconstruction, however, these revisionists work at the level of individual states. So far there are few of them, and on several important matters they do not agree with each other. Generalizations about the South are therefore more than ordinarily hazardous. The obvious fact must be emphasized that, at this very early stage, hypotheses must be extremely tentative.

The revisionists begin by challenging a fundamental assumption of Southern and American history. The familiar characteristics of Southern society – widespread poverty, low rates of unionization and industrialization, high rates of illiteracy, poor transportation and social services – are, as Marxists like to say, no accident. Those conditions are not the legacy of the slave regime, nor of the economic damage of the Civil War, nor even (as Woodward put it) of a colonial dependency on the more industrially advanced North. Instead, they are the result primarily of political decisions that were made in the South by Southerners and that were carried out by the Southern power structure. Indeed, the revisionists argue, although a comparison between the parts of the same country is virtually unavoidable, it is essentially false and misleading. The South was not just lagging behind the North but was following a different evolutionary path altogether.

The North followed the classic pattern of industrial capitalism under the conditions of "free enterprise." Gradually but surely, agriculture became highly capitalized and mechanized, increasing the productivity of labor and enabling it to be redeployed. Even before the American Revolution, New England merchants had won a respectable share of the rich commerce of both the North and South Atlantic trading networks. By the early nineteenth century their ships were to be found in large numbers in Asia and throughout the world. Beginning with cotton factories in New

England, the North developed all phases of manufacturing and processing. Centering on the huge coal and iron deposits of western Pennsylvania and Ohio, the heavy industry of the Midwest competed with and surpassed that of the English Midlands and the German Ruhr. Cities grew rapidly and internal transportation developed impressively. Even before the Civil War the American North had become a core area of the capitalist world economy.

Although it was punctuated periodically by depressions (during the seventies and again in the nineties), the expansion of the Northern economy during the late nineteenth century was explosive and sustained. The apparently insatiable demand for labor pulled millions of immigrants from overseas. The North overtook Great Britain as the world's foremost workshop. "Yankee ingenuity" became a watchword. Profits were high and fortunes huge. Labor was characteristically "free." In comparison with Western Europe, trade unions developed slowly and remained weak. Yet Northern workers benefited from the rapid expansion of the economic base. The conditions and hours of their labor, and above all their average real wages, continued to improve. Although Western Europe's world ascendancy was not yet finished by the early twentieth century, half of Alexis de Tocqueville's famous prediction of the 1830s that the United States and Russia were destined to become the strongest economic and ultimately political powers on earth had been fulfilled.

The South's pattern of growth, the revisionists contend, was not simply a retarded version of this Northern success story. Its economy was not stagnant. (Revisionists agree with the classical economic historian Robert Higgs that the South's rate of growth was surprisingly respectable.) Nor was it unprofitable to those who controlled it. The South was following a different path, one that was far less spontaneous, far less natural to those who regard industrial capitalism and free enterprise as the norms. Its economic system was much more closely controlled and much more carefully orchestrated. The political factor was far more decisive. In some ways, the revisionists argue, the South's political economy had less in common with the North's than it did with the economies of Germany or Japan. Its pattern was modernization from above, what Barrington Moore has called the Prussian route.

To the revisionists the most important class determinant of this evolving political economy, especially in the cotton belt, where the plantation system remained strongest, continued to be the upper ten percent or so of agricultural landowners: the planters. As I have already indicated, Jonathan Wiener's detailed investigation of manuscript census returns from selected counties in Alabama's cotton-growing region reveals a high degree of stability in this class of top families. There was fluctuation after 1865, of course. Some families rose into the select group; others fell out of it. But the rates of upward and downward mobility seem to have been about the same as those before 1860.

During the late nineteenth century significant changes were occurring in the upper levels of Alabama's agrarian society. The labor system shifted from slavery to sharecropping. Many landowners assumed new roles, becoming furnishing merchants, owners of warehouses, or directors of utility and railroad companies. There is no question that planters had suffered a loss in national political power. These changes, however, were symptoms of metamorphosis, not necessarily of a precipitous economic, social, and therefore political decline within the region. Planters, Wiener concludes, continued to dominate the economy and the politics of Alabama's black belt.[26]

How far can Wiener's conclusions be extrapolated to other areas and other sectors of Southern agrarian society? That remains to be seen, at least in detail. The materials for such an inquiry (manuscript census returns, tax lists, registers of wills, etc.) are available in embarrassing and even intimidating profusion. It is therefore not surprising that the exceedingly tedious county-by-county, region-by-region investigation that the crucial importance of this subject certainly demands remains to be undertaken.

Hypotheses that run too far ahead of systematic research are necessarily suspect. It seems reasonable, however, to suppose that Wiener's argument for the continuance of planter hegemony would probably hold throughout the cotton belt: that is, in substantial areas of South Carolina, Georgia, northern Florida, Alabama, Mississippi, Louisiana, southern Tennessee, Arkansas, and eastern Texas. His argument would also hold for the sugar plantations of Louisiana, which had always been conducted on a large scale and which successfully maintained the gang system.[27] What about the tobacco producers of the coastal-plain and Piedmont regions of Virginia, North and South Carolina, and Georgia? Traditionally tobacco farming had been conducted on a smaller scale than cotton, often by small independent farmers or by comparatively modest slaveholders. Did North Carolina ever really possess a planter class with the wealth, power, and arrogant pomposity characteristic of the Virginia and South Carolina tidewater regions or of the Deep South? It is unlikely. One would expect a higher degree of mobility and fluctuation, both before 1860 and after 1865. Like Wiener, Dwight Billings argues in favor of a high degree of persistence among the agrarian elite of North Carolina.[28] But his conclusions are based on a small sample of the most influential families from across the state, not on a detailed analysis of manuscript census returns and other materials from either representative or contiguous counties.

How far Wiener's conclusions about the stability of planters in the Alabama black belt can be extended to other areas and sectors thus remains in doubt. Yet too much caution would also be unjustified. Cotton held such a significant place in the South's agrarian society that, even if Wiener's findings should be restricted to that crop alone, the evidence seems sufficient in itself to discredit previous hypotheses about the supposedly rapid fall of the planter class. On the contrary, his evidence makes clear that the plantation system and those who controlled it would remain an important element in the South's political economy for decades to come.

In the 1870s, continues the revisionist argument – that is, at the same pivotal point on which Woodward and his predecessors, the numerous apologists for white supremacy and Bourbon democracy, had focused their interpretations – the Southern power elite regained political control. Certainly no single, unified ruling class really existed. In some states large planters continued to hold the reins of power virtually unchallenged. In others businessmen and industrialists, Woodward's rising bourgeoisie, or perhaps a somewhat lower level of farmers, both joined and competed with them. In all cases, however, the ruling class in state after state proclaimed home rule, which they called Redemption. For their own economic and political ends, Northern Republicans acquiesced. Southern whites remained apprehensive that the North's mood might shift once more. By the 1890s, however, it had become apparent that home rule was secure. Reconstruction was over.

Even before that, however, in the view of the revisionists, the Southern power elite had made what amounted to a fateful collective decision. Because no unified ruling class existed across the South, much less a centralized decision-making process, that collective decision was not made all at once. When it was made, it was only partly conscious. To a large extent it was (or seemed to be) a series of reflex actions, of natural responses to existing forces and circumstances: to the long history of plantation slavery, to the location of mineral and water resources in certain areas, to the determination among whites to throw off Northern domination, to their will to preserve the Southern way of life.

The economic and political strategy that took shape by the early 1880s, the revisionists emphasize, was by no means the only conceivable way in which the South might have evolved. One alternative favored by such radical Reconstructionists as Thaddeus Stevens or Charles Sumner advocated wholesale land redistribution, heavy investment in primary education, and a political process fully open to the equal participation of all classes and races (with the important exception of former Confederate leaders). In fact, under the very moderate regimes that had governed the Southern states during Reconstruction, the radical program had never really come close to being achieved in practice. Nevertheless, the Southern strategy that emerged after 1877 would be a conscious rejection of that program in all its aspects.

The South would not be like the North. It would not become a helpless prey to hordes of inferior immigrants from southern and eastern Europe. Only in the South would the purity of the Anglo-Saxon stock be maintained. The South would avoid the anarchy and rampant corruption that characterized Northern cities. It would uphold law and order, gentility and refinement. Above all, the South would remain a white man's country, where the black man knew his place and stayed in it.

If all these obviously wholesome social objectives were to be achieved, then it followed that those demonic forces of unregulated capitalism that were altering the North so rapidly must be very firmly controlled. If there must be change at all, then it must be directed. If there must be modernization, then it must be from above. In many ways the evolution of the South would more closely resemble the authoritarian examples of Germany or Japan than the liberal–democratic models of Great Britain or the American North. Sometime during the late 1870s and early 1880s, the revisionists suggest, the Southern power elite opted for Moore's Prussian route to capitalism.

The revisionists offer an interesting, though strained, comparison of the inegalitarian and authoritarian American South to Germany and Japan. As sovereign states, Germany and Japan had centralized decision-making processes and clearly defined boundaries. This was not true of the South. All around its edges, from Texas to Kentucky and southern Indiana, to West Virginia and Maryland, it is hard to tell where the South ended and the North or the West began. The revisionists seriously understate the importance of the intensifying structural linkages – financial, transportation, corporate, market – between the regional economies of what after all was a single country. The model of internal colonialism, which Woodward developed long before it became fashionable among social scientists, remains a valuable insight into the dynamics and the course of Southern history.

Above all, neither Japan nor Germany built an authoritarian strategy of development around what, for the American South, was an absolutely crucial determinant: race. Japan's population was as homogeneous as any in the world. With the important exception of Jews, whose principal fault seems to have been precisely that they had been so largely assimilated into the economy, imperial Germany was divided by class, region, and religion but not by race.

Surely the closest parallel is therefore the one examined in this book: South Africa. Here too, as I have repeatedly warned, there are important differences. After 1910 South Africa was a sovereign state. Its economy long remained structurally linked to Great Britain's, but not to the extent that the South's was linked to the North's. Its black and brown populations were the majority. And its white people were ethnically divided between Afrikaners and English speakers. What the two cases do have in common is that they were both white man's countries that had inherited largely vertical patterns of white supremacy, but that developed the primarily horizontal system of segregation as a means of controlling the impact of urbanization and industrialization.

In South Africa there were important variations among the elites who controlled the four colonies that in 1910 became the provinces of the Union: the liberal Cape, whose large farmers and merchants had gradually joined forces in the west before the discovery and consolidation of the diamond industry in the east; Natal, largely controlled by sugar planters; the Orange Free Stare, where mining interests did not intrude upon a singleminded concentration on the needs of white agriculture; and the Transvaal, where large Afrikaner landowners desperately competed with gold magnates during the 1890s, and subsequently combined with them. The rivalries among these elites continued, so that South African history in the twentieth century has often been interpreted as a struggle between south and north. After 1910, however, a centralized state structure took charge. It attacked and, by the late 1940s, overcame these centripetal tendencies. South Africa developed a coherent, conscious strategy that enabled it to modernize without dismantling the apparatus of racial discrimination.

Although the actions of the power elites of the American South were frequently so similar and so nearly simultaneous as to suggest conspiracy – for example, in the process by which state after state was redeemed, or again in the wholesale borrowing of laws and evasive devices that took place during the era of disfranchisement and Jim Crow – the region lacked the unifying engine of a single polity. The decision-making process remained diffused within the several states, subject only to the loose checks that were exercised by a federal structure located outside the region. Local elites remained largely in control.

In the American South the Prussian route had therefore several forks. Which of these a particular region or state might take depended mainly on the relative preponderance in that area of the power elite's three principal components: planters, industrialists, and businessmen (meaning merchants, railroad men, and bankers). These categories were not exclusive. Planters could, and very often did, move into industry or business or both. Industrialists and successful merchants bought land or came from landed families.

complt white

In the Old South the factors had overwhelmingly supported the interests of the planters, who were by far their major suppliers and customers. Since the New South was industrializing, economic and political alliances were more complicated. Merchants tended to be swingmen, who would support those who dominated the means of production in a particular area. They might be planters; they might be manufacturers. The relative balance and relationship between the planter and industrial (or protoindustrial) groups in individual states or regions were therefore crucial.

There appear to have been three main variations of this relationship. First, in those sections where the plantation economy had developed most completely – in the tidewater areas of the southeastern coastal states from Maryland to northern Florida; in the black (and cotton) belts of the Deep South; in the sugar areas of the Mississippi Delta – the natural strategy was to maintain the monopoly of the prevailing system. Significant industrialization would mean increasing and unacceptable competition for the mainly black labor supply. In the view of the planters, after all, a chronic labor shortage already existed. In the Old South these areas had been by far the most prosperous – that is, for the planters. They feared that industry would attack the plantation economy at its most vulnerable point: the low class wage of its predominantly black workers. The fewer alternative opportunities for employment, the better. Capital for the development of industry was therefore not forthcoming. It was not (and for the most part still has not been) built.

In some states – Mississippi, Louisiana, Arkansas – the planter class was sufficiently well entrenched to shut out potential competition altogether. There the Prussian route meant virtually no industrialization at all. Transportation continued to be skeletal, with branch railway lines devoted almost entirely to bringing agricultural products to the seaports. The monopoly of the plantation system continued. Those who controlled it tried very successfully to ensure that, for the plentiful supply of labor at low wages on which that system depended, there would be as little competition as possible.[29]

A second case was that of Alabama and Tennessee. There the strong planter aristocracy and the rising bourgeoisie of the coal–

iron complex that came to center on Birmingham were locked in
a fierce, protracted struggle. The fact that many of the industrial
entrepreneurs were new men, who had not come from the ranks
of the planter class, may have intensified the rivalry. But the intense competition for labor was much more serious. By 1900, as
we have seen, Birmingham's labor force was seventy-five percent black. The average wages in the coal mines and iron foundries of the Alabama–Tennessee complex were lower than those
of Pittsburgh or Cleveland. But they were higher than those of
Alabama agricultural workers, whom they drew like a magnet.

As Jonathan Wiener has shown in an exceptionally well-
documented analysis, the struggle between planters and industrialists centered on the railway question. Black-belt planters concerted with large merchants in the port of Mobile to back a line,
the South and North Railway Company, that would bring coal
directly from southern Tennessee to the sea, where it would be
used for fuel in ocean-going steamships carrying cotton. Birmingham, which Mobile newspapers continually mocked as a
pipedream, would be bypassed. The opposition was organized
in the Louisville and Nashville Company, which favored a branch
line from the Tennessee coalfields to a new city in northern Alabama (i.e., Birmingham). Another branch line would connect
the growing industrial complex with Mobile.

The presence of planters on boards of directors of railway
companies, Wiener emphasizes, does not indicate that they had
been converted to a strategy of industrialization. On the contrary, the location of the railway was absolutely central to their
strategy of blocking or at least severely weakening the development of industrial competition for agricultural labor.

Either strategy necessarily involved state subsidies in the form
of railway bonds. The political history of Alabama in the late
nineteenth century is therefore one long contest between railway
lobbyists and between the competing interests they represented.
The continuing opposition of planters to the New South movement in general, and to Birmingham in particular, Wiener argues, has been largely overlooked. Furthermore, the consolidation of the well-known Big Mule–Black Belt coalition at the head
of the state's Democratic Party has been placed prematurely in
the 1880s. On the contrary, the struggle between Birmingham

industrialists and southern Alabama planters, between the New South and the Old South, was then at its apex. And it continued. Only the populist challenge, which threatened the hegemony of both groups, eventually brought them together. The deep division between the elites may help to explain why in Alabama disfranchisement was proposed and carried through comparatively late.

The second fork of the Prussian route, in Wiener's view, was marked by bitter and sustained conflict between what he calls capitalist and anticapitalist factions.[30] On the intensity of the struggle his evidence is abundant and persuasive. What seems very doubtful is his classification of the planters and their merchant allies in the South and North Railway Company as anticapitalists. They were certainly opposed to industrialization. But surely they were capitalists.

For large agricultural interests and the rising bourgeoisie in industry and commerce were not necessarily in conflict, argues Dwight Billings, outlining a third variation of the Prussian route. In North Carolina's cotton-manufacturing industry they were very often the same people. Two myths, he contends, must be discounted. The first is that the new industrialists were generally transplanted Northerners. In fact, as J. Carlyle Sitterson demonstrated some three decades ago, all the important entrepreneurs who pioneered the state's industrialization were Southerners.[31] The second, which underlies Woodward's identification of the South as a Northern colony, is that Southern industrialization was largely financed by a massive influx of Northern capital. On the contrary, Billings argues (in agreement with Wiener), the extent and influence of Northern capital have been vastly overestimated. Northerners appear to have been reluctant to invest in Southern industries that would seriously compete with their own.

Billings bases his argument upon a comparatively slender body of evidence drawn from an analysis of a dozen or so of North Carolina's wealthiest families. A much more exhaustive study, combining group biography of the cotton-mill owners and promoters with close investigation of the sources of capital that the companies tapped, would be necessary to demonstrate his hypothesis in detail. Yet there is a strong prima facie case in favor of it. Cotton manufacturing constituted the first important wave of Southern industrialization. It did not spring from nothing. Indeed, a minor historiographical controversy surrounds the extent of its growth before 1860. A systematic analysis of capital formation remains to be undertaken, but (as Broadus Mitchell argued long ago) there is not much doubt that most of the capital came from local sources. After about 1890 local capital came from a variety of sources: for example, from tobacco men like Julian Carr. Before that, during the pivotal period of the 1870s and 1880s, when the cotton boom began to gather speed, and when the collective decision in favor of the Prussian route was supposedly being made, there was no alternative. The only men with capital to invest were from large agricultural families: for instance Daniel Tompkins, whose South Carolina family had owned more than a hundred slaves. The leaders of the cotton-manufacturing industry were, or had been, planters.

The pattern in tobacco was different, Billings points out, much more like the one Wiener identifies in Alabama. Its leading entrepreneurs were usually new men from genuinely humble origins. Despite their immense wealth, the Dukes and the Reynolds remained social and political outsiders. Of this there are several indications: Unlike cotton mills, tobacco factories freely employed black labor; Washington Duke secretly subsidized a populist newspaper; his son Benjamin (Buck) Duke became a Republican. From the many companies it might have considered, especially the railroad conglomerates, the state's planter-dominated Democratic legislature after 1900 singled out the Dukes's American Tobacco Company for investigation as a trust. In tobacco manufacturing there was indeed a bitter, protracted conflict between planters and the rising bourgeoisie.

In cotton, however, the relationship was a close, cozy partnership between large producers and manufacturers. Although the subject remains to be systematically investigated, there is reason to think that Billings's argument would probably hold true for other states. From the tidewater and eastern regions of Virginia, North and South Carolina, and Georgia, capital and capitalists moved in-state, bringing with them the profits, methods, and attitudes of the planter class. Billings's hypothesis would account for the well-known plantation system, which so many observers have described in the mill village, characterized by deference toward employers, who in turn treated "their" workers as subordinate members of the family, that is, as children. The owners, Billings concludes, acted like planters because on the whole that is precisely what they were.

Billings is more controversial in trying to account for two other extremely significant features of the cotton-manufacturing industry: its location and the composition of its labor force. Why, after all, were cotton mills concentrated in the Piedmont? The favorite contention of contemporary propagandists – that they were providing a form of self-help as a substitute for poor-relief for destitute whites – may have some truth in it, but not much. The environmental argument – that because early mills relied on power supplied by fast-flowing water, they had to be built west of the fall line – is of course much more substantial. Yet the center of the textile industry was a good many miles west of the line. Did the streams not run quickly enough near Fayetteville or Rocky Mount? White-water enthusiasts will testify to the contrary. Moreover, the mills soon outgrew water power, switching to steam and later to electricity. As any traveler in the Southern Piedmont can see, many mills – those in Durham or Carrboro, North Carolina, for instance – were not built near any water whatever. Cotton manufacturing, however, continued to be a monopoly of the Piedmont.

Inertia might account for this pattern of location: Later phases of urbanization and industrialization tend to follow earlier trends, even though the initial reasons in their favor no longer apply. Before 1860, however, most urban settlements as well as most industries, such as there were, were in the east. In fact previous industrialization was not an important factor in locating cotton mills. As Daniel Tompkins made clear in his textbook for mill owners, the ideal factory built and maintained its own village, away from cities. On the whole Billings's hypothesis, under-documented as it is at present, seems the more persuasive. The large agricultural interests who led the growth of cotton manufacturing were mainly from the east. They were careful not to locate mills in the heart of plantation country, so that they could avoid competing directly for labor.

Moreover, even though they could have done so at somewhat lower wage levels, the employers refused to hire those very (pre-

dominantly black) workers who might be seeking alternatives to
the plantation. The usual explanation, racism, is not imaginary.
But the speed and unanimity with which the industry adopted
and enforced the absolute color bar, reversing the prewar situation when cotton mills, like most other enterprises, were often
worked by slaves, indicates not reflex action but a highly conscious policy. Occasionally a maverick like George W. Williams
of Charleston, a former factor, might try to breach the wall.[32]
After all, in New England as well as in Lancashire, England,
cotton was manufactured with apparent success near the sea.
Charleston was still an important cotton port: Presumably costs
could be cut if the product were not transported inland. And
plenty of half-employed blacks were available. But Williams's
experiment failed, and he had few followers.

Once a poor region, the Piedmont industrialized and became
comparatively wealthy. The green and pleasant mountains, where
roads were expensive and voters remained stubbornly Republican, became centers of mineral extraction, where coal was strip-
mined and miners were ruthlessly exploited. The once-prosperous
east, where the plantation had been most fully developed, stagnated and declined. A perceptive driver on an east–west highway
can see and feel the change in passing from region to region.
Although the differences have much to do with the facts of geography and the force of inertia, they have more to do, Billings
concludes, with a largely artificial division of labor, the result of
collective calculations by the Southern power elite about a century ago. This is an arresting interpretation. Just as race was being
segregated from race, so region was being segregated from region. The South provides a classic example of internal colonialism, of the development of underdevelopment.[33]

Whereas Wiener finds conflict between planters and the rising
bourgeoisie in Alabama, Billings sees cooperation in North Carolina. The obvious conclusion that the Prussian route to modernization had more than one variation prompts an additional reflec-
tion on the nature and role of class struggle in Southern history.
Throughout the still extremely limited Marxist and neo-Marxist
literature on the South, as well as non-Marxist works such as
Woodward's, the theme of class conflict looms large. What appeared to be, and indeed were, racial problems, argues Eugene

Genovese, were at bottom class questions. The political economy of the New South, conclude Wiener and Billings, had mainly class determinants. I agree.

But the attempt to cast the planters in the role of an anticapitalist aristocracy, however much it may explain their attitudes, their pretensions, and their aspirations, seems to me fundamentally misleading. They were not, and never had been, a titled nobility. In the states on the Deep South frontier (in Mississippi and Alabama), where their hegemony was strongest, they had been entrenched for two or three generations or less. The planters may fulfill the economic criteria of Marx but they only partially fulfill the status model of Max Weber. Although they superficially resembled the Prussian Junkers, they never quite made it as aristocrats. Whatever else they were, they were not anticapitalist. They were and remained capitalist agriculturalists. As slaveowners they presided over the characteristic labor system that capitalism had always adopted in peripheral regions of the world economy.[34] As landlords over the sharecropping alternative they attempted to perpetuate their version of capitalism.

Indeed, the most appropriate model within Marxist theory would seem to be not the well-known progression from feudalism to capitalism (which on the whole is not very enlightening when applied to colonial or peripheral areas) but Marx's relatively unnoticed analysis of the class parameters of the British in India.[35] There, he remarked, the Asiatic mode of production had been largely uprooted, and India had been set on the road toward its destiny as part of the mainstream of world history, by successive phases of the bourgeoisie. First were the merchants, who came in the seventeenth century to trade with one of the world's strongest and wealthiest civilizations. A century later followed the "squirearchy," drawn largely from the gentry (capitalist landlord) class of England, Scotland, and Anglo-Ireland, who took control of the East India Company, conquered a decaying empire, and became its governors. Then there were planters, especially in indigo and sugar, who employed coolies under forced labor.

Last of all came the "millocracy," both the most systematically destructive and, as measured by their impact, the most revolutionary. By means of free trade they undersold and destroyed

India's domestic cotton industry, leaving the bones of spinners and weavers to bleach under the Bengal sun. Then they moved in to build factories. In India they paid even lower wages and therefore created still more surplus capital than they could at home.

On the surface these various factions – the mercantile, governing, planter, and industrial elites – appeared to be locked in mortal combat. With what contempt did the grandees of the Honorable Company greet the upstart millocracy! Yet appearances were deceiving. Beneath the surface, even despite themselves, they cooperated. For they were all sections of the bourgeoisie, the persona of British capitalism in its several phases transplanted to a stagnant Asiatic society that they were systematically uprooting and transforming.

To sum up the argument of this long and rather complicated chapter: The accelerating pace of segregation as a social system and an ideology after about 1890 was not economically determined in any simple, mechanical way. Instead, it grew directly out of political responses to circumstances that were mainly political. The most that can be claimed for the social interpretation, it seems to me, is that segregation was an organic part of a massive, systemic change by which the Old South was giving way to the New. That claim, however, is by no means insignificant. Segregation was not a feature of the South before 1860. It was born and grew to maturity in the vigorous environment of a society that was attempting to modernize. It was in the New South that the highest stage of white supremacy evolved.

As Marxist historians have argued in relation to South Africa, segregation was appropriate to the New South in important ways. First, a closer correlation can be drawn between segregation and industrialization or urbanization than between segregation and the more gradual evolution of agriculture. Rural areas were hardly deficient in racism and violence. It was there, however, that the old, vertical order of race and class relations mainly continued. In urban areas the traditional ways no longer worked. A new, primarily horizontal system of control was needed if white supremacy were to be maintained. And the new towns of the Piedmont hurried the pace of change.

There was nothing inevitable about that either. City and fac-

tory are essentially neutral institutions, which bend with the social and especially the political wind. Even in the early phases of
industrialization, for example in the cotton industry, the job-
reservation system may have cost Southern employers something. The benefits in the form of improved morale among white
workers may well have made up the difference. If not, the employers passed the costs on to the consumers.

Second, segregation was related to the formation of the Southern capitalist power elite. As usual blacks were convenient instruments that enabled whites to resolve or at least to sublimate
their differences. The awesome and largely unchecked power of
the state enforced crop-lien laws, ran the convict-lease system,
and enacted penalties against outside labor recruiters. In black-
belt areas, Wiener argues, the Ku Klux Klan, often with active
planter leadership, tried to keep blacks at work in the fields; in
white areas it attempted to force blacks out altogether. With
amazing rapidity and uniformity cotton mills – but not tobacco
factories, coal mines, or iron foundries – imposed a color bar.
The South was being regionally segregated into industrial and
plantation zones. Racial segregation was thus closely related to
the New South's strategy of capitalist development.

Third, although segregation was not of course related to state
formation, as in the case of the autonomous nation of South Africa, it was related to the political consolidation of the power elite
in the Democratic Party. The timing of that consolidation varied
somewhat from state to state, depending on the relative strength
and relationship of the planter and industrial factions, as well as
on the intensity of the populist insurgency. From the Mississippi
Plan in 1890 until the last formal exclusion after 1900, disfranchisement was usually a political response to the internal political
challenge of populism. There is no doubt that it succeeded. The
artificial reduction in the size of the electorate confirmed the economic and political hegemony of the Southern power elite for
more than half a century.

7. A note on Southern moderates and segregation

Since the 1940s – when the contradictions posed by the Negro Problem became acutely embarrassing for the makers of American foreign policy, when massive migration was building black political muscle in Northern and Western cities, when Gunnar Myrdal's *American Dilemma* was systematically destroying the intellectual credibility of segregation – many white historians of the South have approached the region's racial problems with a heavy burden of guilt. Their defensiveness is both understandable and laudable. To paraphrase Sir Winston Churchill's famous comment on Clement Attlee's modesty, we have a lot to feel guilty about.

Viewing the past from the perspective of the civil rights era after 1954, historians have commonly identified segregation with extreme racism.[1] In time this identification proved true. They have regarded segregation as an oppressive, blatantly discriminatory, and satanic system of white supremacy. It was, I have argued, the highest stage of white supremacy. But such a view is retrospective and partial. Segregation needs to be understood not only in the light of the somewhat more liberal and more tolerant standards of a later era in American history but in the context that existed then. That is one of the principal values of a comparison with South Africa. For there, instead of loosening under the combined pressure from African nationalism and an increasingly critical world opinion, institutionalized racism has hardened further into apartheid. The comparison helps us to read the history of segregation in the American South forward as well as backward.

171

Viewed from the perspective of the era in which it took shape, it seems evident that segregation was by no means the harshest, most draconian solution to the Negro Question of which white Americans were capable. In that very period after 1890, when blacks were being lynched and disfranchised, when they were being subjected to the cascade of Jim Crow laws, national attitudes, behavior, and policies were hardening on many fronts. The huge and economically necessary immigration of Jews, Italians, Poles, and other strangers into the North, and of Orientals into the West, provoked a strong reaction of intolerant nativism.[2] The long economic depression, during which the fortunes of the very rich continued to multiply, sharpened the contradictions within unregulated capitalism, as Henry George described in *Progress and Poverty*. Strikes were bitter, violent, and prolonged. Farmers were in revolt. The climate of opinion with respect to social issues veered toward the hysterical and the cataclysmic. It was a time for "solutions."

This tendency toward simplistic, frighteningly logical responses to complex and enduring problems was not restricted to the United States. It was characteristic of Western civilization in general. This was the age of the new imperialism. Even while emphasizing its continuity with British expansion earlier in the century, the authors of a classic account of the scramble for Africa describe "a hardening of arteries and a hardening of hearts."[3] Racism captured the cultural high ground. Marked by frequent pogroms in Russia, the Dreyfus Affair in France, and the forged Protocols of the Elders of Zion, anti-Semitism surged forward; so did the eugenics movement, which sought to counter the degeneration of the race. Both movements would come to their logical, terrible conclusion in Adolf Hitler's concentration camps.

The late nineteenth century was the age of Social Darwinism, when professors of history in Germany and elsewhere described the grand struggle of nations in the past and looked forward to its speedy and glorious renewal. War was clean, manly, and vigorous, a purifying fire. Jacques Barzun sums up the militaristic literature of the period as "one long call for blood."[4] The author of a leading textbook organizes his analysis around the parallel between the diplomatic and domestic histories of Europe. Just as the continent was being divided into the two armed camps of

Triple Alliance and Triple Entente, so the internal political histories of country after country were marked by "the erosion of the moderate position, the abandonment of the liberal attitude, the flight from the reasonable solution and, indeed, from the very use of human reason to reach solutions."[5]

Although it remained outside the structure of European alliances, America shared in these violent, destructive tendencies. It joined the new imperialism and became a great power.[6] Like Europeans, Americans sought strategic security, guaranteed markets, sources of raw materials, and havens for investment. Encouraged during their war with Spain by Britain's poet laureate of imperialism, Rudyard Kipling, Americans also turned expansion into a crusade. In the Philippines and elsewhere they learned that the white man's burden involved, among other things, the suppression of Native resistance to the liberators. Defending the strenuous life against his overcivilized critics, President Theodore Roosevelt urged his countrymen to show their mettle in a severe test of the nation's manhood. If Americans were "too weak, too selfish, or too foolish" to act resolutely, then "some stronger and more manful race" would assuredly take their place:

> Resistance must be stamped out. The first and all-important work to be done is to establish the supremacy of our flag. We must put down armed resistance before we can accomplish anything else, and there should be no parleying, no faltering, in dealing with our foe. As for those in our own country who encourage the foe, we can afford contemptuously to disregard them; but it must be remembered that their utterances are not saved from being treasonable merely by the fact that they are despicable.[7]

The formation of the new empire was a continuation, an extension over seawater, of the earlier drive to assert manifest destiny across the North American continent. In the 1890s white (as well as some black) Americans were bringing to its logical, terrifyingly thorough conclusion the Native policy that is associated in world history with the moving frontier. To the school of Frederick Jackson Turner, who as an assistant professor gave his famous paper at the meeting of the American Historical Association in Chicago in 1893, the frontier was not primarily military in nature. Propelled by economic causes, it was a largely impersonal force that influenced American society and character.[8] In the Turnerite version of American history there are not many Indians about: Apparently the frontier moved through virgin lands. As in the writings of Edward Gibbon Wakefield, the English economist and propagandist whose ideas had become so popular in Great Britain during the mid-nineteenth century when the British were systematically colonizing Australia and New Zealand, the Natives had mysteriously vanished.

The Native policy of the United States presented the Indians a stark choice between physical removal and segregation (in Native reservations, like the Bantustans of South Africa) or extermination. The struggle for the American West belongs to the most brutal type of conflict in the history of warfare. Its stakes were land, grass, minerals, and water. It was a war, in the word that Adolf Hitler made famous, for *Lebensraum.* It was justified, in the transparently self-serving Social Darwinist language of the time, as the survival of the fittest. There was remarkably little pretense that the result would be "good for the Indians." They were in the way, and they had to be removed.

Indeed the language of the period was literally true. The contest for the Wild West *was* Darwinian. The unfit did not survive. Indians were considered innately suited not for manual labor but for extermination. American attitudes and behavior can most usefully be compared not to South Africa's Native policy – for the Africans there have survived and multiplied – but to Australia's. The history of the American Indians, as Booker T. Washington frequently reminded his audiences, must be the fate of a people unable or unwilling to accommodate to the irresistible demands of a capitalist society and an imperialist state.[9]

Although it is hardly this book's purpose to provide an apology for the highest stage of white supremacy, the broad context of American history and of Western civilization in general throws the origins of segregation into a perspective very different from those to which we are accustomed. Indeed, different kinds of questions push themselves forward. What made blacks different from Indians? The fact that there were more of them? Or that they were the useful and even essential bedrock of the Southern and some of the Northern economy? Was the racism that George

Fredrickson and others have analyzed significantly less virulent than, say, the anti-Semitism that the young Adolf Hitler was imbibing in Vienna around the turn of the century? If the economic and political circumstances of America had been different, would American racism have been sufficient to support a holocaust? The fact is that it did support a similar action toward Indians. Fortunately the question cannot be answered. As Hannah Arendt argues in her superb study of totalitarianism, in the twentieth century – with its highly developed technology for mobilizing and controlling public opinion – all things are possible.[10]

In the context of the nasty intellectual and political tendencies that were characteristic of American and Western civilization in the decades around the turn of the century, far worse things than segregation are imaginable. Far worse things could and did take place. Segregation was by no means the harshest of the solutions to the Negro Question that Southern whites were considering. For instance, there was simple exclusion. It stood to reason that if there were no schools beyond the primary grades, no services, no facilities that would enable blacks to rise above their station, then there would be no problem. Inadequate and inferior though they were, however, *some* facilities and services were provided. The black man's place was subordinate, humiliating, and exceedingly dangerous. It was also profoundly ambiguous, for he was not quite excluded. At least under segregation not *all* the doors were closed.

In the Southern cities, where the practice of residential and other forms of segregation developed most rapidly during Reconstruction and its aftermath, Howard Rabinowitz argues, those who urged that separate facilities be made available to blacks were not unreconstructed Conservatives or Democrats.[11] Typically they were Northerners, Republicans, or even blacks. If they had not persisted there would have been no facilities for blacks at all. In the late-nineteenth-century South, Rabinowitz concludes, the practical alternative to separation was not open participation, much less racial integration, but exclusion. The segregated Negro colleges and industrial schools that were founded comparatively frequently during this period, for instance, were not the result of diabolical plots hatched by Southern politicians to keep education for blacks inferior. They were financed and developed almost entirely by Northern philanthropists against strenuous local opposition or, at best, grudging acquiescence. Even when legislatures did provide support, it never matched the blacks' own contributions to state revenues from direct and indirect taxation.

My own more limited research supports Rabinowitz's conclusions. As an ideology of race relations, segregation was not synonymous with extreme racism, although it would become so in time. Even after 1890 the word "segregation" continued to inhabit the language of moderates and even that of the black man's "best friends." It was not on every tongue, however. Indeed, the best-known racial fanatics of the period – Ben Tillman of South Carolina, James Vardaman of Mississippi, Furnifold Simmons of North Carolina – seem to have used it very infrequently. It occurs rarely if at all, for instance, in the four thick volumes that were eventually published from the Alabama disfranchisement convention of 1900.[12] Segregationists were usually racists, but not all racists were segregationists. The language and therefore the ideology of segregation, composed of layer upon layer of mystification and obfuscation, took some time to come together. The precise chronology of this process remains obscure. A systematic content analysis of the huge volume of pertinent literature – especially of speeches in the U.S. *Congressional Record* and of newspaper reports of state legislative proceedings – would probably confirm the conclusion that the highest stage of white supremacy became synonymous with segregation perhaps even as late as the 1920s.

In the spectrum of white Southern and American attitudes toward the Negro Question, segregation came to cover a very broad range of attitudes to the left of exclusion. Its very softness, its very lack of precise definition, would become one of its greatest strengths. One of its most important components was what South Africans would later call separate development, a concept that has also come to have mainly negative connotations. But in the late nineteenth and early twentieth centuries it was a positive notion that was under sharp attack from the right.

Opening the Negro State Fair at Raleigh, North Carolina, in 1901, for example, Furnifold Simmons's milder, Progressive colleague Governor Charles B. Aycock developed the mystique of separate development with some finesse. (The fact that he agreed to speak to a black audience at all is perhaps significant; so is the fact that he thought separate development would be acceptable to them.) Aycock hoped that "recent events," presumably the virtually total disfranchisement of the adult male members of his audience, would not unduly excite his listeners: "Remember that your best friends are those who live in your State." Although it has not been recorded that he asked them, the governor well understood what they wished and needed: "the establishment among yourselves of a society founded upon culture, intelligence and virtue, and in no wise dependent upon those of a different race."

Whereas separation of the races might or might not be in vogue elsewhere, it was the settled system of the South, and "its violation would be to your destruction as well as to the injury of the Whites." The words "destruction" and "injury" conveyed a threat that was skillfully veiled in segregationist rhetoric, much of which – though not quite all – might have been delivered by Booker T. Washington:

> No thoughtful, conservative, and upright Southerner has for your race aught but the kindest feelings, and we are willing and anxious to see you grow into the highest citizenship of which you are capable, and we are willing to give you our energies and best thought to aid you in the great work necessary to make you what you are capable of, and to assist you in that elevation of character and of virtue which tends to the strengthening of the State. But to do this it is absolutely necessary that each race should remain distinct, and have a society of its own. Inside of your own race you can grow as large and broad and high as God permits . . . But all of them in the South will insist that you shall accomplish this high end without social intermingling.[13]

It would not be difficult to convict Aycock of racism: One need only point to his notion that the only upright Southerners were white. As the biographers of Vardaman and Tillman make clear, however, those men had nothing but contempt for such pious platitudes, which they delighted in puncturing. They did not favor development, separate or otherwise. They wanted nothing so ambiguous or so complicated as segregation. One may well be skeptical about whether a moderate like Aycock was sincerely "anxious to see you grow into the highest citizenship of which you are capable." Only the year before, after all, he had run for governor on a disfranchisement platform, and his campaign manager had been Furnifold Simmons.

The extremists left no room for ambiguity. In speech after speech they proclaimed their harsh, violent, nasty views.[14] God had placed blacks only a little higher than the apes – and there was apparently some doubt about that. Intending them for servility, He had marked them with His curse. Anything that might raise blacks from their naturally inferior status they denounced and, when in office, vetoed. Anything the white man might do (including lynching in cases of suspected rape) to defend his supremacy and especially the purity of his women was fully justified.

There can surely be no quarrel with Woodward's thesis that the violent, abusive, inflammatory language of politicians was a powerfully destructive force in its own right. On occasion its dangerous potential bothered even the politicians themselves. "It is a glorious victory we have won," Charles Aycock wrote in November 1898, just after a campaign during which Furnifold Simmons's Red Shirts had been unusually imaginative in devising methods of intimidating black voters in the eastern part of the state, "and the extent of it frightens me." A few days later a white mob shot up the black districts of the seaport of Wilmington, ran a black newspaper editor out of town, and drove the lawfully elected municipal government from office. A future state supreme court judge reflected that "the politicians have stirred the minds of the people more than they intended."[15] The state government in Raleigh did nothing, the leader of the insurrection was widely hailed as a hero, and his revolutionary regime remained in control.

Although the details of the Wilmington insurrection were not typical, they did demonstrate the logic of the situation. As politician after politician made quite explicit during the disfranchisement campaigns, the alternative to white supremacy, which in fact meant the power of the Democratic Party, was nothing less than a complete breakdown of the rule of law itself. Blacks, indeed, might be forgiven for thinking that any close resemblance

pt: not a
Radical movement
(vs Woodward
sos)
but a reaction
movement that
may have improved
the [law/black]
life the loss,
it was a new
ideology that
came from ~
modernity elite
so woodward's
idea of a
new system, just
right, just
not modern

between the political system they lived under and the language of the American Constitution had already disintegrated. The large number of riots and lynchings of this period faithfully reflected the tactics of deliberate polarization. If the leaders were intent on pushing the situation as close to the brink as possible, it is not surprising that others frequently went over it. Across the South elections were being held in an atmosphere that must bring to mind the latter days of Germany's Weimar Republic.

The logical conclusion of the politicians' mounting rhetoric went well beyond disfranchisement and discrimination. There seems no useful purpose in quoting extensively from this venomous material, for example the speeches of the U.S. Senator from Mississippi Theodore Bilbo. It perhaps bears repeating that it is hard to imagine actions against black people so extreme that the vituperative racist culture would not have provided sufficient sanction for them. As the moderate Alabama minister Edgar Gardner Murphy explained, the "more radical spokesmen" had evolved "from the contention that no negro shall vote, to the contention that no negro shall learn, that no negro shall labor, and (by implication) that no negro shall live."[16] It is hard to disagree with scholars who have called the late nineteenth and early twentieth centuries the nadir of American race relations. Even a student like myself, who came to this literature after several years of work in the sources on South and Central Africa during the same period, must record his sense of shock.

In the decades on either side of 1900, then, as the racism of the South, of the American nation, and indeed of the Western world was reaching a stridently hysterical crescendo, segregation was not the harshest version of white supremacy that was either conceivable or possible. The language of segregation ranged from disfranchisement and what South Africans call the petty apartheid of Jim Crow to the deceptively positive promises of separate development. It was a skillfully fabricated maze in which the simplest, most straightforward issues of discrimination and deprivation could be made to seem incredibly complicated and practically insoluble, a prime example of what Marxists call mystification.

The ideology of segregation was not the contribution of the most fanatical, ignorant, unbending racists of the period. It was developed and articulated by moderate men, who spoke in softer, more modulated voices. In a world of conflict they sought civility, peace, and harmony. In a frightening atmosphere of widening extremes and apparent social disintegration they sought the middle ground of sanity and compromise. Where others spoke in negatives, they stressed the positive.

Many white Southerners minced no words. They intended to "keep the niggers down" for all time and in every conceivable way, and that was that. These people, whom Rabinowitz calls exclusionists, were probably in the majority. The segregationists urged instead, although always with the proviso that there must be no social intermingling, that doors should be open. Schools, jobs, and opportunities – even perhaps the vote for a few black men of the right type – should be available. In their own way, at their own pace, under their own leadership, blacks should be encouraged to build their own society and culture to their highest potential. As they did – as they ceased as much as possible to compete with whites, bending their thoughts and energies instead toward the separate development of their race's own condition and character – blacks could hope in time for the whites' respect and even their qualified acceptance.

Segregationists urged a lessening of tension. They sought to build bridges of understanding across the color bar. They worked for conciliation, coexistence, and collaboration. The word collaboration is used advisedly. Those who tried to stand upon the high but shifting ground of segregation were black as well as white.

Who were these moderates who sought in segregation a basis for sanity, compromise, and collaboration? What were their interests, motives, and tactics? What was their relationship to the consolidating Southern power elite and to what, in fact, was going on? To such questions, which would require extensive investigation into the 1920s and beyond, this essay on the origins of segregation can give no definitive answers. The available literature, however, does provide some interesting and plausible suggestions.

THE ROLE OF THE NEW SOUTH MOVEMENT

From Paul Gaston's excellent book it is clear that segregation first gained prominence as an organic component of the New South creed.[17] The separate-but-equal formula, which – in *Plessy* v. *Ferguson* (1896), among many U.S. Supreme Court decisions – was to become the centerpiece of the national compromise on the Negro Question, began to appear in the speeches of Henry Grady as early as 1883. Not surprisingly, he used the phrase most frequently in addressing Northern audiences. By 1885, in an essay in *Century Magazine,* the Atlanta editor's argument was fully developed.[18]

The U.S. Constitution, Grady contended, "holds that there should be equal accommodation for the two races, but separate . . . In every theater," he added, "there should be a space set apart for the colored people, with precisely the same accommodations that are given to white people for the same price." Moreover "the same rule should be observed in railroads, schools, and elsewhere." As long as facilities were equal, absolutely no hardship would be imposed on blacks. After all, had not they themselves voluntarily withdrawn from white churches? Obviously blacks preferred their own society.

The New South movement contained considerable variations. Gaston identifies Grady with the conservative wing, who believed strongly in complete white ascendancy and innate black inferiority. For Walter Hines Page, a North Carolinian who became a New York publisher, segregation had to be accepted as a necessary evil given the political climate of the time. Eventually, he hoped, two trends would make possible a gradual relaxation of restrictions: first, the education of poor whites, whose ignorance in his view was the fundamental cause of the South's backwardness in general and of the surge in racism in particular; and second, the material advancement of the blacks.[19] On the whole, however, the New South publicists were agreed. By pursuing the goal of separate-but-equal accommodations they would best serve the interests of the white South, of the blacks themselves, and of the nation.

From the beginning of the movement, Gaston argues, "the new world of progress was tied . . . to a relatively small group of merchants, industrialists, and planters"; that is, to the three components of the mercantile, industrial, and agrarian power elite who, according to the revisionist interpretation, were opting for the so-called Prussian route to modernization. Supported by the rhetoric of Grady and others, "this new ruling class . . . forged what it supposed was a mutually advantageous partnership with Northern capitalists and fastened its control over the region's destiny in the 1880s."[20]

As we have seen, the New South movement developed a catch-up strategy based on maintaining the low-class wage of workers in agriculture and industry alike. That was one precondition for economic growth. A second prerequisite was political: home rule. The South's development, the New South spokesmen argued, had been severely retarded by the extravagant, irresponsible, un-intelligent regimes of carpetbaggers, scalawags, and blacks during Reconstruction. As long as the white man's country was in such mortal danger, all patriotic Southerners were naturally preoccupied with saving it. The South's economy had therefore stagnated. During Reconstruction the region had not been a profitable field of investment.

After about 1876, however, according to the New South version of the recent past, this depressing tale had been reversed dramatically. At last realizing its error, the North had withdrawn its troops. Capital investment had begun to flow southward, where it was met by a burst of creative energy from local entrepreneurs. It was thus no accident that the South's industrial revolution had begun in the 1880s. Home rule was absolutely essential for the success of capitalism in the South. It was also necessary if the region were to be successfully reintegrated into the political life of the American nation.

Segregation was an important, integral, and probably even essential part of the New South movement's ideology. Somehow, in the face of mounting lynching statistics and increasingly militant protests from blacks, Northern opinion had to be mollified. It had to be persuaded that the "best elements" of the South had the Negro Question well in hand. Good race relations, argued Grady and his cohorts, depended on the South's being left alone to solve the problem at its own pace and in its own way. Otherwise the tense divisiveness of the era of Reconstruction might return. As it turned out, the separate-but-equal formula of the emerging segregationist ideology performed its function admirably. Written into presidential addresses and Supreme Court decisions, it formed the basis for a national reunion of whites.

THE ROLE OF THE SOUTHERN EDUCATION BOARD

If the New South movement first brought the ideology of segregation to national prominence, reformers helped to make its doctrine credible and its practice viable. To say this is to repeat what has become a cliché of radical historiography: If the power and hegemony of a ruling class are to be based on acceptance and consent, as well as on force, then the system must be capable, and on occasion must be seen to be capable, of some benefits for the powerless, of some hope for improvement. Worse alternatives must be both conceivable and possible. Those who choose to work within a structure of authority for its improvement, instead of attacking it from outside, necessarily contribute to its stability and longevity. To say this is not necessarily to cast aspersions on the sincerity of particular individuals who choose to work for item-by-item reform. They may, after all, be right in presuming that despite its many inequities and imperfections an oppressive but stable fabric of law and order is preferable to anarchy or violent revolution. They may be right as well in predicting that gradual alterations in degree may form in time a change in kind.

Apart from politics the best hope for Afro-Americans in the era after slavery was, as it remains, education. Of that, at least, black people themselves were in no doubt. After Emancipation ex-masters frequently learned that slaves had betrayed their trust by secretly learning to read, an offense for which the penalty had usually been death. During Reconstruction and beyond the freedmen's thirst for knowledge, for the keys that would unlock the gates to the white man's mastery and power, was as unquenchable as missionaries have found it to be among Africans. Blacks welcomed Northern schoolmarms and often protected them against local whites. Their churches became schoolrooms. As a rule, despite their deep poverty, they found ways to con-

tribute funds to supplement the meager and often virtually non-existent levels of state support. In this tale of the Afro-American struggle against the fearful bondage of illiteracy and ignorance educators may find the ultimate justification of their calling.[21]

Until after 1900 debilitating ignorance was an affair of class as well as of race. Education for poor whites had not of course been illegal; it had just not been available, particularly in mountain or rural areas. In the Old South poor whites had remained on the fringes of the agrarian economy, whose ruling class had seen no point in educating them. Reconstruction governments tended to be more concerned, but funds remained short and progress was painfully slow. Because students of industrialization argue persuasively that functional literacy is an often overlooked but extremely important component of the infrastructure – England's Industrial Revolution, for example, was not made by illiterate workers – the very slow growth of public education must have been a handicap even in the comparatively low-skilled industries on which the Southern Piedmont was concentrating.[22]

The main impetus for reform, however, came from the politics of disfranchisement. As we have seen, most of the opposition came from the representatives of illiterate and semiliterate whites who feared with good reason that the laws were aimed in part at them. For the disfranchisers were operating on the assumption that there were limits beyond which, in providing safeguards against the possibility of a return to Negro rule, they could not go. As long as the Fifteenth Amendment remained on the books, moderates warned, they must proceed very cautiously. Presumably the Supreme Court would overturn voting regulations that were too blatantly discriminatory. (In fact the Court's decisions consistently invalidated this assumption, severely undercutting the moderates' position.[23]) Disfranchisement laws therefore avoided the language of explicit race discrimination. Ordinarily, prospective voters had to demonstrate they could read or understand a portion of the state constitution to the satisfaction of a registrar.

Access to the Southern franchise therefore came to depend on one's educational qualification and often on payment of the poll tax. Both devices threatened poor whites. The disfranchisers tried to buy them off with grandfather or Confederate soldier clauses, correctly predicting – or so Kousser argues – that very few would take advantage of them. In any case the grandsons of the voters of 1860 or the boys in gray would die one day. The loopholes would eventually be closed. Many poor whites would be as effectively excluded from political participation as blacks.

Artificially reducing the size of the electorate, Kousser maintains, was precisely the objective of the disfranchisers. But they had a problem: They had to push the new regulations through legislatures that had been elected under the old ones. In most states, particularly in black-belt areas, the Democratic Party was sufficiently in control of the voting process to have already used fraud and intimidation to reduce the electorate well below the danger point. Even so, in Alabama for example, the disfranchisers often resorted to specially elected conventions that could be manipulated still more easily.

In North Carolina, however, the Democratic ascendancy was far from secure. As late as the 1890s the U.S. Congressman from the state's second district, a black-belt area, was not Furnifold Simmons of New Bern, who had held the office briefly, but George White, a black man who had run on a fusionist ticket.[24] North Carolina Democrats had hardly been squeamish about employing intimidation and fraud; the trouble was that those methods had not succeeded. In 1896, however, it was whites, voting Populist and Republican, who elected a fusionist legislature and a Republican governor. Among the most significant measures of the new session was a law abolishing county control of local government and voter registration, centering the power instead in the capital in Raleigh. If that law were to remain on the books, eastern North Carolina Democrats contended with some justification, white supremacy would not just be threatened in their region. It would be dead.

That was the background for the reign of terror during and after the election of 1898, when Simmons's at least protofascist Red Shirts and the appearance of Ben Tillman from South Carolina helped secure a Democratic victory. The new legislature promptly repealed the local government act, returning power over registration to the counties. But that was only a temporary remedy. A more permanent safeguard of disfranchisement had become absolutely essential for Democratic ascendancy.

First, however, the Democrats had to win the election of 1900, which unfortunately had to be conducted under the old rules. Aycock and Simmons therefore thought it necessary to pledge that not a single white voter would be disfranchised. As it turned out, once they were in office, that rash promise could not be honored. According to the lawyers, the new law could not frankly discriminate on grounds of race or else the Supreme Court would declare it unconstitutional. Moreover, as Simmons explained frankly in a statement already quoted at length, since all the whites could not be trusted to stand together, the state might still return to Negro rule. The constitutional amendment that was put before the voters in a referendum in 1901 therefore specified that all exceptions to the rules disqualifying illiterates would cease as of 1908. Then the clock would run out.

Since the outcome of the referendum was far from a foregone conclusion, the Democrats needed to wage as persuasive a campaign as possible. The way out of the dilemma was obvious: Only a strong program of public education would prevent large numbers of whites from being permanently disfranchised. Although there is some reason to think that the disfranchising and Progressive Governor Aycock meant it, he became a fervent educationist. The state in which the Democratic ascendancy was least secure was also the one where education became a crusade. Aycock sought support and found powerful friends − in the Southern Education Board.

Founded in 1901, the Southern Education Board was an alliance of Northern philanthropists and what its secretary Edgar Gardner Murphy, a former Alabama minister and a champion of child-labor reform, called the Best South. Its progressive program rested on the intriguing premise that, as Murphy put it, the fundamental interests of the black and white South were not in conflict. For both races the first priority was law and order. Ever since the Civil War white Southerners had made it abundantly clear that black political participation had been a constant source of discord, corruption, and lawlessness. From this chain of reasoning it somehow followed that blacks should withdraw: "White supremacy at this period in the development of the South is a necessity to the preservation of those conditions upon which the progress of the negro is itself dependent." Disfranchisement,

Murphy declared, had been singularly misunderstood, for "it bore in its origin only the slightest animus against either the negro or his fortunes,"[25] an evaluation that would be hard to substantiate, for example, on the basis of the proceedings of the disfranchisement convention in Murphy's own state of Alabama. The black people's best and, under the circumstances, only hope was to seek the protection of their friends. The Best South was a small "minority powerful enough to restrain if not always to accomplish." It was constantly on the defensive against the rising tide of poor-white racism that was being fueled by irresponsibly radical politicians.

In North Carolina the Southern Education Board evolved a tacit but effective alliance with Aycock. "The philanthropists acquiesced in disfranchisement and Jim Crow laws and undertook to promote acquiescence in the North," writes Louis Harlan in his thorough study, "while Aycock pledged publicly that the schools of the disfranchised Negroes would have protection from hostile state legislation."[26] Specifically Aycock promised to resist the disbursement of school funds in proportion to each race's direct contribution to the state revenue. That promise he kept, apparently going so far as to threaten resignation – North Carolina governors have no veto power – should the legislature pass such a bill.

With some justification the Best South and its Northern allies could claim a significant victory. In Mississippi under James Vardaman and elsewhere, precisely such proportional funding laws went on the books. Consistently the Best South warned that the Supreme Court would intervene. Consistently the Best South was wrong. It would be a long time before the defensive position of Southern moderates – fighting a series of rearguard actions in a political climate where no concessions to principles of justice and equality could be taken for granted, where the power of state and even federal government was ordinarily arrayed against them – would be wholly without substance.

Across the South, Harlan demonstrates, the Southern Education Board acquiesced in systematic, wholesale discrimination against education for blacks. Between 1901 and 1915, state financial support for black schools everywhere declined substantially in proportion to that for whites. In some cases it was reduced absolutely. The record of the Best South and its Northern allies was one long compromise with injustice. The board claimed to be pursuing the formula of separate but equal. In fact, they settled for far less.

In his famous essay published in *The Souls of Black* (1903), the founder of the National Association for the Advancement of Colored People had the lack of grace to say so.[27] The supposed friends of blacks, W. E. B. Du Bois charged, were helping to block their only escape route. Not only were they acquiescing in grossly unequal treatment by the states. In the probably forlorn hope of gaining support from Southern whites for black education, they were insisting that the very sparse funds that were being contributed from the North should go primarily to institutions of the right type, that is, to those that specialized in the agricultural and industrial training programs usually associated with Booker T. Washington. For once Du Bois would have agreed with Edgar Gardner Murphy, who in 1901 had praised the president of the Southern Education Board, Robert C. Ogden. "More than any other man," the Alabama minister wrote glowingly, Ogden "has changed the attitude of the North toward the vexed problem of Negro education, and has brought the aid of the North . . . to that kind of education which increases the practical value of the negro not only to himself but to the South." The compromise, Du Bois charged, was dangerous and damaging. It had about it the pungent smell of a sell-out.

For decades Du Bois waged a verbal war against "Mr. Booker T. Washington and Others," including the Southern Education Board, the Phelps-Stokes Foundation, and especially the secretary of the latter, Dr. Thomas Jesse Jones. By no means limited to the American South, the conflict resounded in South and tropical Africa.[28] Everywhere the clash of educational strategies had deep political and philosophical implications. It went to the heart of the ultimate issue: whether the black people's destiny rested with integration (which inevitably would involve some submergence of their cultural identity) or with separate development (which even in black man's countries such as Nigeria ran the risk of closing doors of opportunity in European government or firms). In Africa as in the American South the positions of various interests – missionaries, advocates of black power, proponents of indirect rule – were neither simple nor predictable. The debate about the right type of education for Africans and Afro-Americans was complex, heated, and protracted. It rages still.

Of course education should be practical, Du Bois agreed. Many blacks were farmers, who needed to be exposed to the most efficient, most scientific methods available. The black artisan, of whom Du Bois made a special study, was severely threatened not only by the job-reservation system but by the wide adoption of standardized measurement in building. Blacks needed not less industrial training, but more. So, for that matter, did whites. But to single out the blacks for peculiar treatment because of their political status, to say that this and not that was the right type of education, to support only those institutions that would prepare black people for lives as manual laborers, was particularly insidious. Black people needed all kinds of education, in preparation for all kinds of positions and careers. Nor was it proper to insist that the race must progress together, that all must be educated to the same level and in the same way. The race needed leaders. What Du Bois called the talented tenth must be urged forward as rapidly as possible.

The most crucial part of this long debate on education has been waged among black people themselves. The argument has been central to their attempts to evolve effective modes of dealing with the awesome fact of white power. That subject I shall try to analyze in a later chapter. Here my concern is with white moderates, not with Mr. Booker T. Washington but with the "Others."

The Southern Education Board or the Phelps-Stokes Foundation could argue that Du Bois's attack ignored or oversimplified the economic and political realities. Most blacks were agricultural and industrial workers. And so they would remain, for a long time to come. There would of course be exceptions. But the first priority must be to help blacks make a living and survive. The prospects of a white backlash against education that prepared blacks to compete or become uppity were not imaginary. They were terribly real. To urge militant, unyielding resistance to white supremacy in New York was rather different from doing so in Alabama. Surely the most realistic strategy was not to attack segregated education per se but to accept it and work for its improvement.

Even discrimination in favor of white education, continued the defense of Southern moderates, might not be all bad. If ignorance were the primary cause of racism, then preferential support for the schools of poor whites might well be the best hope of solving the Negro Question. In time, through friendly persuasion rather than ceaseless and immoderate criticism, the Best South would be enlarged. The formula of separate but equal would come increasingly closer to being achieved.

The strategy of moderate segregationists – accepting and promoting segregation as the most hopeful alternative available under the circumstances, working within existing institutions to achieve limited short-term gains, defending the South against attacks from Northern critics, hoping that time would be on their side – was not wholly without validity. Gradually, much too gradually, although support for black education did not approach equality – a level it still has not reached – it did increase. Although the most important forces that would ultimately overthrow segregation were gathering not within the South, but outside it, moderates did become somewhat more influential. Gradually extreme racism was forced on the defensive. The most decisive proof of this is the fact that, from its original position on the left of the Southern political spectrum in the 1890s, by the 1920s or 1930s segregation had become identified with the extreme right, with the most unyielding of white supremacists, with the most fanatical of racists.

Between moderate segregationists and extreme racists a complex, symbiotic relationship existed. Sometimes, as in the case of Governor Charles Aycock and his campaign manager Furnifold Simmons, the working relationship was close enough to suggest deliberate conspiracy, like that between salesman and controller in a used-car dealership. More often there was a bit more distance, as in the case of the Montgomery Conference of 1900, organized by Edgar Gardner Murphy, where all points of view about the repeal of the Fifteenth Amendment were represented – which meant hearing the leader of the Wilmington, North Carolina, insurrection but relegating black spectators to silence in their separate-but-equal gallery.[29] Moderates and extremists shared the same racist culture. Their arguments about tactics and degree were overshadowed by their broad general agreement on the principle of white supremacy. Moreover, without the extremists, the moderate segregationists would have lacked credibility. The fanatical racists enabled them to say, with clear consciences and with some justification in fact, that if they didn't regulate the South's order of race relations, others would. And then it would be worse.

Without the moderates, however, the extremists would also have been weakened. As all colonial powers have discovered, "keeping the niggers down" can be an expensive, difficult operation. Some sort of fabric of collaboration, to which large numbers of blacks at least tacitly conformed or accommodated, and which in part they enforced themselves, was badly needed, especially in the cities, if white supremacy were to be secure. Such a system could not possibly have been built or maintained on the basis of the unyielding fanaticism of a Tillman or a Vardaman. If radical extremists like them had been the only ones present, nothing but permanent race war could have been the outcome. The collaboration that underlay the highest stage of white supremacy required a softer, more flexible, more intelligent racism.

white sup. system needs moderate men to keep in control.

new racism – needs to work with society to keep moderates there

pt: something new: legalized segregation: dialectically, it was an improvement, was not new, but was new by change form, an ideological level w/ Modernization, power elite, and moderates

pt: even to continue status quo segregation would require a systematic change in ideology.

8. South Africa makes segregation

Analyzing within one book the origins and early development of segregation in South Africa and the American South is more than an interesting academic exercise. For the two cases of modernizing race and class relations were historically connected. As we saw in Chapter 2, contemporary observers – including the English ambassador Lord Bryce, the white South African Maurice Evans, and the Afro-American missionaries Henry Turner and Levi Coppin – understood this.

The evolution of segregation in South Africa ran a decade or so behind that in America. South Africans of all races watched the American case closely and made it a germane, though not a determining, part of their own discussion. Bryce's *American Commonwealth* remained the standard account of race relations in the Republic. But several English-speaking South Africans, notably Howard Pim, Evans, and Charles Loram, traveled in America, studied the extensive American literature on the subject, and tried to learn from American experience. So did such influential members of the British high commissioner Sir Alfred Milner's "kindergarten" as Lionel Curtis and Philip Kerr, who tried to reconstruct the former Afrikaner republics after the Boer War. Because they were ordinarily less well educated, Afrikaners were not so widely engaged in this comparative analysis. The young Jan Smuts's study of Walt Whitman and his admiration for Abraham Lincoln made him a significant exception. (Smuts's support for the unitary rather than the federal model when he was drafting the South African constitution was to some extent the result of his reflections on the causes of the American Civil

War. In his view the outstanding lesson was that states' rights should be very sharply curbed.)[1]

Numerous Africans, many of whom were to play important roles in African politics, were educated at American Negro colleges. Some of them were indoctrinated with the mixture of accommodationism and economic self-sufficiency associated with Booker T. Washington, others with the more advanced ideas of Henry Turner or W. E. B. Du Bois. In either case the experience reinforced the importance of self-reliance and organization. In South Africa as well as in West Africa the Congress model in particular owed much to Afro-American influence. Indeed, whites found the need to check the spread of the potentially inflammatory ideas of American blacks the most persuasive argument in favor of state support for an institution that would make it unnecessary for Africans to seek education abroad: the Native College at Fort Hare.[2]

Their observations of the American South taught white South Africans important lessons. White Americans might say that blacks were backward. But white South Africans were impressed with the pace at which an African people, albeit one with the "advantage" of having been schooled in slavery, might become useful, disciplined workers and consumers in an expanding and increasingly sophisticated economy. In the cotton-manufacturing industry they saw a white working class whose low wages enabled them to withstand the economic competition of an inferior race. If only that could be achieved in their own country, then the grave dangers they foresaw of dependency on black labor might be avoided. The Great Republic inspired white South Africans. Against fearful and tremendous odds, their own grand effort of preserving a white man's country in the southern part of the Dark Continent might yet succeed.

Yet most of the lessons seemed to be negative. White South Africans were appalled by the chronic, explosive violence of the American scene. Frequent lynchings and race riots, political corruption, unspeakable crimes against white women: America was full of examples of what must be avoided. The American South, to borrow R. H. Tawney's famous metaphor of the magic mirror, was an enchanted glass in which South African whites might glimpse fleeting images of their own future. Some of the distorted reflections were hopeful and comforting; others were ugly and frightening. All of them were fascinating.

It was already too late for America, white South Africans usually concluded. At the root of the South's stormy troubles was competition. At every conceivable level of relations – agricultural, industrial, commercial, political, and therefore social and even sexual – the two races were locked in an intense struggle from which neither could apparently be extracted. As long as this deadly rivalry continued, tension and violence would assuredly persist and accelerate. But even competition was not the most dangerous characteristic of American race relations. On the contrary it was their ambiguity. A white South African such as Maurice Evans could not avoid being struck by how frequently the races worked side by side. As long as white and black maintained such close contacts in their daily lives, the white man's unpardonable sin of miscegenation would be stamped on the ever-lightening faces of Afro-Americans.

Those faces foretold the impending doom of the white man's country in southern America. The awful fate of mongrelization awaited those whites who, allowing themselves to be beguiled by short-term profits, permitted their society to build its economic institutions on the treacherous ground of the cheap labor of an inferior race. In the long run the only way to avoid disaster was physical, territorial separation. To some extent that might be happening in America. By moving into the lower South, where the hotter climate better suited their racial instincts, Bryce and others suggested, blacks might be achieving some separation themselves. From this observation, however, white South Africans could draw small comfort. In the American South the ratio of white to black was roughly 2 to 1. In South Africa it was no better than 1 to 3. In America the proposition that voluntary territorial segregation would succeed was dubious at best. In South Africa, except in the western Cape, where Bantu-speaking Africans had never settled in large numbers, it was absolutely impossible. If territorial segregation were to happen, it must be made to happen.

The apparent failure of segregation in America might conceivably have led white South Africans to conclude that the problem of race relations in their country might require a fresh approach after all. Not surprisingly, in view of their history and attitudes, they concluded otherwise. They thought the South had not begun soon enough. Its segregation had not been sufficiently thorough. Most significant, segregation had developed there only after the catastrophic experiment of Reconstruction had tried to lead Southern society in the opposite direction of racial equality. Like the posture of French philosophes toward despotism in the eighteenth century, the prescription of white South Africans for remedying the faults of segregation was ordinarily more segregation.

Since the sheer facts of demography would obviously make South Africa's own problems so much more severe, it seemed to follow that its brand of white supremacy must be all the more rigorous and complete. Yet without an expanding economy, no white working class could be attracted or retained. Unless the country developed, unless it built up mining and white agriculture, unless it improved its transportation facilities, unless it industrialized, the frail transplanted seedling of Western civilization would wither and die. Here was a severely vexing dilemma. Were not these two objectives incompatible? Would not economic development, which would inevitably draw Africans out of the protective shell of tribal backwardness, itself prove dangerous to whites? Would it not severely increase competition? Either way, it seemed, the white man's country must be placed in jeopardy.

The risk must be run. To control the pace of social change, white South African experts on the Native Question set as a goal economic development coupled with the maintenance and reinforcement of white supremacy. Their country would build capitalism. It would also maintain racial stratification. Segregation became both their strategy and their ideology.

The stakes were high. If segregation should fail, then in their view the last hope of preserving white civilization anywhere in Africa south of the Sahara must fail with it. Their beloved white man's country would inevitably degenerate into a mongrelized society like Brazil or Portuguese East Africa just next door. In the hostile African environment, degeneracy once in motion would surely be an irreversible, terminal cancer. Like the famous stone ruins of Great Zimbabwe in Rhodesia, but on an infinitely larger and more tragic scale, their cities would be left as empty shells, curious symbols of the white race's brilliant achievements, of a glorious past that could never be recaptured. At the last "little brown children," as General Smuts used to say, "would play in the ruins of Johannesburg."[3]

THE SOUTH AFRICAN NATIVE AFFAIRS COMMISSION

At the national level the debate on the shape and texture of South Africa's Native policy began with Sir Alfred Milner's appointment of the prestigious South African Native Affairs Commission (SANAC, 1903–5), under the chairmanship of the former native commissioner of Basutoland, Sir Godfrey Lagden. Its assignment was to hammer out a compromise from the diverse policies of the four South African colonies, a task that seemed an essential precondition for union. Not least because some of its members were well-known Negrophiles, the commission's recommendations were to be extremely significant in the evolution of South Africa's version of segregation. Again and again they would be quoted. One by one most of them would be enacted into law. They therefore need to be analyzed in some detail.

Land. At the heart of any such discussion was necessarily the land issue. The SANAC recommended territorial separation, a clear division of the country into white and African areas. Fortunately, it seemed to the commissioners as they surveyed the map of southern Africa, white settlement had left largely intact traditional homelands for the larger tribal groups: Zululand, Basutoland, and the homeland of the Xhosa in the Transkei and Ciskei regions of the eastern Cape. The smaller, more divided groups, such as the Tswana of the northern Transvaal or the numerous non-Zulu Africans of Natal, detribalized peoples such as the Mfengu of the Cape, who had been made refugees by the Zulu Mfecane (or holocaust) of the early nineteenth century, not to mention Asians or the Cape Coloured People, would of course be much more difficult to place. Nevertheless, the basis for a great deal of natural separation was happily already at hand. As a first step the existing reserves should therefore be surveyed, gazetted, and thus protected against further white encroachment. More land could be added later on.

In retrospect it might seem that even as early as 1905, a group of reasonably competent investigators would have been able to reach no other conclusion than that the reserves would soon prove woefully insufficient to sustain more than a fraction of the large and growing African population. But the SANAC's perspective was very different. Demographic estimates, of course, were little more than guesses. Over the last quarter of the nineteenth century, it now seems probable, the rapid spread across Africa of human and animal diseases, the demands of the expanding labor market, and the last push of pacification had resulted in a decline of twenty-five percent or even more of the African population. Indeed, until after World War I, the concern of Africanists was with underpopulation.[4] Moreover, the dogma of Social Darwinists that Africans as an inferior race were likely to follow the Australian aborigines and the American Indians toward extinction was still fashionable.

Even more significant, the commission was meeting in the atmosphere of an intense labor crisis. Africans in large numbers were refusing to come out to work at wages that experts seemed to think were reasonable and that in any case were all "the country" could afford. By keeping themselves off the labor market Africans were severely jeopardizing Sir Alfred Milner's plans for postwar reconstruction and for massive British immigration, both of which required an expanding economy. The reserves were thus providing Africans with the means of bringing white South Africa to its knees. The problem that confronted the commissioners in 1903–5 was therefore not the poverty of Africans but their prosperity. They possessed not too little land but too much.

Yet the apparent self-sufficiency of the reserves was not the only source of the labor crisis. Even more dangerous in the long run was the growing pressure of African peasants on landholdings in "traditionally white" areas. In parts of Natal and the Transvaal, the commissioners learned, the problem was already becoming acute. At the worst, either directly or indirectly through white intermediaries, such as missionaries, Africans were buying land. That at least, the commissioners concluded, should be prohibited. But renting, sharecropping, or squatting – in which farmers permitted African families to live on their land and cultivate small plots in exchange for part-time labor – were only a little less objectionable. All of these were forms of Kaffir farming, a practice that "fills up with Natives land which would otherwise be better utilized and developed" by whites. More than economic results were involved. Semi-independent peasants living permanently outside the reserves were cut off from the supervision of their tribal authorities, causing "the absence of due control over them."[5]

If this substantial and increasing migration of African families into white areas were left unchecked, the commissioners continued, then the natural basis for territorial separation of the races would be destroyed, perhaps forever. The purchase of land by members of either group outside their own traditional areas should therefore be outlawed as rapidly as possible. (The commissioners did not pause to reflect that what they called the traditional division of the country into white and black areas usually reflected the military balance of power of the previous half-century or less.) Because the interests of white employers were involved in Kaffir farming – often it was the most efficient and profitable use to which they could put their land – renting, sharecropping, and squatting must be investigated very carefully. All of these practices, however, should probably be eliminated or at least strongly discouraged. The control of population movement was by no means a merely economic question. The future safety of the country required that South Africa's de facto separation into white and African areas should be legislatively frozen.

Labor. Did territorial separation in fact mean that interchange of population between the sections of the country would not be permitted? Of course not. In white areas African laborers would still be essential. But their movement and settlement should no longer be left to the capricious laws of a laissez-faire market system. Therefore Native locations should be established near all the major labor centers. There alone would the workers who were required by mines or industries be permitted to live. Pass laws, which fortunately were already on the books of all four colonies, would satisfactorily regulate the influx. In white areas the economic needs of whites would naturally be considered paramount. The locations "should not be a refuge for surplus or idle Natives for whose labour there is no local demand." These redundant folk would be returned to the reserves. In white areas, if the commission's recommendations were put into effect, all Africans would be bona fide laborers. They would be landless, temporary, and overwhelmingly male.

For any population of peasants, as well as for pastoralists and subsistence agriculturalists who were evolving into peasants, such as the Bantu-speaking Africans of the early twentieth century, the problems of land and labor were peculiarly interconnected. As in any migration, to be sure, both "push" and "pull" factors were responsible for the hundreds of thousands of temporary workers who annually left the reserves for jobs in white areas, or who streamed down from Central and East Africa. In African economies the means of obtaining cash for taxes or for manufactured goods were extremely limited. Young men who had seen the bright lights of the wide world acquired prestige. But the lights apparently shone more brightly at greater distances. The gold mines in particular, with their high death rates, the Transvaal Labour Commission learned in 1903, had acquired a bad reputation. Among local Africans "push" factors were therefore far more significant. If a sufficiently large and regular migration from the reserves were to be ensured, then the delicate equation between land and labor was obviously the key. The balance had to be right. Up to a point African families needed to be able to support themselves. If they were truly self-sufficient, however, they would not come out to work.

The SANAC understood this close relationship between land and labor. Nevertheless it considered the two topics separately. Two reasons for this artificial separation come to mind. One is bureaucratic inertia. Throughout the nineteenth century land and labor had always been two separate items under the general heading of Native affairs. The second reason is that by maintaining the distinction, the commissioners were able to present their recommendations in a less transparently exploitationist form. The division of the country into white and Native areas, which ultimately had the effect of making it absolutely impossible for most African families to survive unless most of their men worked away from home for whites, would in fact be the long-term solution to the labor problem. Never again would the South African economy be so vulnerable to a wholesale withdrawal of labor such as the one that took place after the Boer War. But that solution could be discussed as though the crucial land component were an entirely separate subject. It could be presented as the territorial separation that so many missionaries and other Negrophiles favored as a means of protecting the African's interests and way of life.

In 1903, after an exhaustive, industry-by-industry investigation of the whole labor situation, the Transvaal Labour Commission concluded that South Africa's mines, farms, and industries were some 300,000 workers short of their requirements.[6] That, the SANAC agreed, was probably a reasonable figure. What could be done to improve the situation? Unfortunately – apart from their sweeping recommendations regarding land, which the commissioners were not discussing in this labor section of their report – not much. Direct compulsion – for instance, the quota system that had been so scandalous a feature of King Leopold's Congo – must be ruled out as morally repugnant. But indirect means – for example, what Cecil Rhodes had called the gentle stimulus of a tax on idle Africans – were only a little less reprehensible.[7] Besides, all of the available evidence from the Glen Grey district of the Cape, where Rhodes had tested his gentle stimulus, as well as elsewhere, indicated that if the tax were in fact restricted to the chronically idle, its effect would be negligible.

The reason, explained the SANAC, pausing to demolish one of the white settler's favorite stereotypes, was simple. For himself and his family, if not for the whites, the African was already at work. The notion that he was innately lazy, that if he were not at work for the white man he was therefore unemployed, was a myth. To be sure, like members of other preindustrial societies, like Europeans before the nineteenth century for example, Africans ordinarily worked at an irregular, comparatively undisciplined pace. They had an entirely different conception of time. Granted too that women usually worked harder and more continuously than men. There was nothing surprising or peculiarly African about that either. Anthropologists had demonstrated that such an unequal division of labor within the family was common throughout the primitive world. (The commissioners, who were all men, did not seem to notice that not all that much had changed with civilization.) As the market system penetrated more deeply into African society, males would alter their attitudes toward work. When the plow replaced the hoe as the basic tool of agriculture, the men would move with their animals into the fields.

The African male was neither innately nor even especially lazy. He was capable of learning the dignity of labor. Notwithstanding his very recent entry into the labor market, he was already the country's most valuable economic asset. Just who did his critics suppose had been working the farms, digging the mines, or laying the rails? The African must be given time to adjust to the discpline of modern economic life. Time and patience alone would solve South Africa's chronic labor shortage.

Might higher wages stimulate the labor supply? The answer seemed so obvious that the divided commissioners examined the question with some care. The minority presumed that like any rational economic man the African would come out to work once he found the rewards for doing so sufficiently attractive. The majority demurred. Laws of supply and demand might be realistic enough in advanced societies, but the tribal economy was an extremely complex mechanism, delicate and fragile. A sudden influx of money might damage it beyond repair. To Westerners the Native mind was absolutely baffling. Attuned to different values, it functioned according to its own peculiar but quite consistent rules. Europeans who would understand tribal economic life must try to adopt the African cultural perspective, leaving their own "rational" preconceptions behind. In the African world the apparently self-evident laws of Adam Smith did not hold.

Raising wages precipitously would be dangerous. Nor would it do much to correct the labor shortage. For what some economists now call the backward-sloping curve seemed to be at work.[8] Primitive man would exert himself only to achieve immediate, tangible objectives. Once he had his gun, his bicycle, his roof, or the money for his tax, he would stop. Among a small minority the work ethic was beginning to develop. But the raw African simply had no conception of working steadily to improve his standard of living in the future, let alone that of his children. In time that too would come. Meanwhile, concluded the majority of the SANAC, higher wages would merely shorten the African's temporary sojourn in white areas.

There was probably some truth in all that. Africans, like other preindustrial peoples, did have different work habits and economic attitudes. When the means of saving are not available, people tend not to save. The fact is, however, that in 1903–5, as the SANAC was holding its hearings throughout the colonies, Africans in effect were rather successfully engaging in what after all is a very simple form of collective bargaining: the strike. Employers had set rates of wages that they thought they could afford and that they deemed appropriate for the degree of skill involved in the work to be done, as well as for the level of civilization of the workers. By organizational means that remain obscure, Africans were withholding their labor in the hope of raising those wages. By a learned and circuitous route the SANAC was recommending that the strike should be resisted. Not for the first time, or the last, anthropology was being put to work as an instrument of self-interested propaganda.[9]

Underlying the SANAC's discussions of the labor question was a curious contradiction. Notwithstanding the substantial evidence, which the commissioners themselves took some pains to accumulate and emphasize, that the African was steadily adopting the attitudes and disciplined habits appropriate to a complex, advanced economy, the commissioners assumed throughout that the African would always remain a marginal participant. He would continue to be a voluntarily migrant worker. He would stay in white areas only for short periods. The basis of his family's existence would continue to be in the reserves. The African would therefore never become a true proletarian, capable of surviving at the subsistence level only by the sale of his labor.[10] His wages would continue to be determined not by how much his family needed, nor by collective bargaining, nor even by calculations of the rates particular industries could afford relative to profits. Instead the average wage, which would vary remarkably little from industry to industry, would be determined by how much "the country," including the least efficient sectors of the white economy, thought it could afford.

On the whole, the majority report concluded, it would be best to continue the present system, permitting wages to seek their own level in a free market. In the context of a report that had recommended legislation against African peasants in white areas, as well as recommending the use of pass laws to regulate the influx of prospective workers into Native locations, this was curious language indeed. As one of its members, the future leader of the Labour Party Frederick Cresswell, remarked, an economy that imported hundreds of thousands of Portuguese East African and Chinese workers for the express purpose of keeping both white and African wages low could hardly be called free. To raise wages in those industries that might afford them, such as the more profitable of the gold mines, the majority report continued, would merely increase competition among agricultural and industrial employers and bring about a general rise all round. Rapidly increasing the amount of money in the hands of Africans would increase their individual independence. The dreadful process called detribalization would accelerate. Thus, despite the doubts of some of its members, the SANAC threw its considerable weight behind the class color bar.

Education. If Africans were to take their places as efficient workers in a modern, industrial economy, then they had to be educated. On this controversial question the SANAC, which included several missionaries who had devoted their lives to African education, was in no doubt. Indignantly the commissioners refuted a common white stereotype. What was often scornfully referred to as literary education did not spoil the African. No doubt unfortunate examples of uppity Natives could be found. But basic facts must be recognized. First, literacy must be the foundation of any scheme of education, no matter how practical its goal might be. Second, beyond the very early primary stages, the basic language of instruction should be English. It would be a very long time indeed before more than a handful of books could be translated into African vernacular languages. Why should students be permanently denied access to the world's culture simply because they were African? Third, there could be no doubt about the immense benefits of African education for the white economy. The illiterate worker was of very limited utility. As the educated Africans' wants increased, so would their incentive and efficiency as workers. Education multiplied their value both as producers and as consumers.

Yet, the SANAC admitted, the critics of African education had a point. All education, for whatever race, should be practical, taking full account of the child's needs and background. That, indeed, was a truism. But given the severely limited resources that were available, given the awesome task of schooling an almost entirely illiterate people, African education must be especially practical. Mission schools had perhaps not been sufficiently flexible. Their curricula and methods, usually imported from England or Scotland, were sometimes unsuited to the specific circumstances in which they had to function. Literary education should not be abandoned in the vain attempt to pacify critics whose real objective was to keep Africans ignorant and backward. But agricultural and what was called industrial training, following as closely as possible the admirable educational philosophy of Booker T. Washington, would be "of particular advantage to the Native in fitting him for his position in life." That position, of course, would be governed not merely by the quality and availability of education but by other recommendations concerning land, labor, and political representation. This point the commissioners ignored. As usual, the habit of carving out artificially distinct categories was very convenient.

Government should increase support for mission schools, which at present were being financed entirely from abroad, concluded the commission, as well as encourage Africans who were able and prepared to pay. But, at least for the present, it was unrealistic to expect more. Compulsory education would be both premature and prohibitively expensive. Finally, higher education should be available locally to Africans who could pay for it, not least as a means of checking the dangerous flow of advanced ideas from America.

Political representation and control. As Lord Bryce and others had pointed out, the government of mixed dependencies composed of different races, at varying levels of civilization and possessing different cultures and degrees of political sophistication, was always peculiarly difficult. For the white section of the community representative or democratic institutions were appropriate. For the other section, an authoritarian regime seemed to be in order. Ideally, perhaps, the two political systems should be kept separate and distinct. But that was hard to achieve. For the institutions of representative government had powerful and ultimately irresistible claims to legitimacy. Inevitably they sought totalitarian domination over the decision-making power of their whole society to the end of its natural limits. Maintaining boundaries between the polities of what are now called plural societies was difficult enough while they remained in transition as dependent colonies. Once they became autonomous states, as South Africa presumably would very soon, the task became impossible. The SANAC had come to the core of the Native Question, to the fundamental issue that had remained unspoken in its discussions of land, labor, and education. The subject was power.

As long as it remained healthy and functional, the commission believed, the African tribe, with its marvelous "unbroken chain of responsibility," could hardly be improved upon.[11] Orders could be transmitted to the chief and his council; those authorities possessed potent means of enforcing them; in case of disobedience the group could be punished collectively. Through their tribal institutions the opinions and interests of ordinary Africans, as distinguished from the self-appointed and numerically insignificant educated elite, who spoke mainly for themselves, could be fairly and effectively represented. In the tribe the authentic African voice could be heard.

In those parts of southern Africa where tribalism remained more or less intact, for instance in the High Commission Territory of Basutoland, the mountainous region that the brilliant nineteenth-century chief Mosheshoe had so astutely governed and protected from encroachment by white settlers, Africans were contented and prosperous.[12] Sir Godfrey Lagden, the chairman of the commission and the former native commissioner of Basutoland, was particularly anxious to refute the common charge that the inhabitants of Basutoland were merely stagnating. On the contrary the Sotho were unusually industrious, thrifty, progressive, and thirsty for education. They came out to work in satisfactorily large numbers. They were known to be uncommonly steady and reliable. In Basutoland the tribal system was like a self-correcting governor on a finely tuned machine. The traditional political system had not stopped the process of culture contact. Instead, with admirable efficiency and at little or no expense to the government, it regulated the pace and impact of social change to degrees that Africans could comfortably absorb.

In Basutoland, even in the admittedly more backward protectorate of Bechuanaland under the legendary chief Khama, tribalism was gradually weakening. Elsewhere, for example, in the eastern Cape among the Xhosa, who had been exposed to continuous white contact for more than a century, the system had broken down almost entirely. Large numbers of Africans were already detribalized. In the long run, it must be presumed, traditional institutions that had evolved to serve the needs of a primitive and relatively isolated society would be unable to survive the challenge of contact with a higher race. Despite its unquestionable advantages, both for Africans and for those who intended to control them, the tribal system would surely continue to disintegrate: rapidly in some areas, more gradually in others. Increasingly it would become anachronistic. It deserved study and respect, but not the sort of reverence that was properly reserved for treasures in a museum.

Since Native policy was always in transition, it must be highly flexible, based on the most current anthropological research. Strengthening of the tribal system, wherever a realistic chance existed, should certainly be attempted, perhaps by making its authorities responsible for local concerns such as public works, perhaps by giving them limited control over a portion of their people's tax contributions. To assist Africans in maintaining their own institutions was an admirable and profoundly important objective.

Native policy should be intelligently conservative but not doctrinaire, according to the SANAC. The decay of tribalism might be delayed, but it could not be halted entirely. Inevitably the point would come when new institutions, representing a more advanced, more politically sophisticated African voice, would need to be created. Avoiding unnecessary disruption of African family life, the transition should be as smooth as possible. Fortunately, in the Transkei district of the eastern Cape, a progressive administration widely respected in other parts of British Africa was developing a promising model for this delicate stage. Native councils had been formed there, composed not merely of appointed chiefs but of representatives elected by the Africans themselves. Gradually those councils were adding to their responsibilities and increasing their prestige.

In the transitional phase, continued the SANAC, it was essential that the Native councils not remain purely symbolic. Unless they were functional, unless they were seen to be functional, they would have no vitality. Under sympathetic white supervision, which in due course might somewhat decrease, councils should be put in charge of local affairs – schools, roads – that were crucial in the lives of ordinary people.

Indeed, the SANAC had a point. In its basic mechanisms as well as in its language, the Native administration of southern Africa had much more in common than is usually recognized with the famous system of indirect rule that Sir Frederick Lugard was developing in this very period in Northern Nigeria. Both regimes at bottom were attempts to control conquered people. Both were short of men and money. Both therefore had to develop effective means of collaboration with Africans. The most obvious available mechanisms for collaboration were existing African institutions. Where these were in reasonably good working order – in Basutoland or Zululand in southern Africa, in Northern Nigeria or the kingdom of Buganda in Uganda – the regimes tried to use them. Where the tribe had broken down, or where as in Kenya or among the Ibo people of Southern Nigeria it had never developed in the first place, the white rulers tried to manufacture substitutes by appointing chiefs or instituting Native councils. So that these inventions might acquire some legitimacy, they had to be given something to do. Too much prestige, however, was also dangerous. For mechanisms of collaboration might easily become centers of resistance.

In the long run these two systems that evolved side by side – segregation or separate development in southern Africa, indirect rule in British tropical Africa – would work out very differently. Indirect rule would lead to self-government and independence, segregation to the perpetuation and hardening of inequality. For this there are two basic reasons. The cosmopolitan and liberalizing power of Great Britain maintained control over the colonies of tropical Africa, whereas South Africa's Native policy was decided by local whites. The second reason is more fundamental: Indirect rule was put into effect where white settlers did not intrude in significant numbers, where – except for divisions among Africans themselves – societies were not mixed.

In the early twentieth century, however, at the time of their simultaneous consolidation, the characteristic policies of South Africa and of the British in their colonies in the north had strikingly similar goals and assumptions. Both spoke the language of trusteeship, which Lugard was to put in its classic form in the *Dual Mandate:* The rule of dependent peoples served both the interests of the civilized world and of the backward races themselves. Both systems professed to have devised means of hearing the authentic African voice. Both excluded the educated elite as much as possible. Both were based on the presumption that the African racial genius was innately distinctive. Both claimed to be protecting African tradition against becoming pseudo-European. Both aimed to guide the evolution of Africans on their own lines.[13]

Tribalism, the SANAC report explained patiently, thereby demolishing yet another mythical white stereotype, was not necessarily or even typically despotic. Even the extremely authoritarian, warlike Zulu under Cetewayo or the legendary, terrible Shaka had possessed a council of lieutenants, called the *indaba.* Although the contrary notion that their traditional system had been an ideal type of democratic "Kaffir socialism" was also mistaken, Africans were accustomed to far more political discussion and representation than Europeans ordinarily supposed. They were fully capable of participating in local institutions on their own lines.

Nothing in their tradition, however, in any way prepared them to participate in European institutions. As much as possible, the SANAC recommended, the politics of white and black should therefore be kept separate and distinct. Three of the colonies – the Transvaal, the Orange Free State, and Natal – already fully accepted this principle. The Cape Colony was the exception. Under its color-blind franchise, which was based on educational and property qualifications alone, the African vote had so far remained small. But it was increasing steadily. As more and more Africans rose into the middle and artisan classes, the number of voters would accelerate. Theoretically there was no limit whatever.

In the SANAC's view the long-range prospects were frightening. Already African participation was creating unhealthy rivalry among white politicians. The more unscrupulous of them were trading promises in return for black votes. The day could even be foreseen when, by means of their concentration in certain electoral districts, African voters would be able to decide elections or the formation of ministries. The government would then be under the effective control of the most ignorant, the least morally advanced sections of the community. Surely the American experiment of open political participation during Reconstruction demonstrated conclusively the catastrophic consequences that must result from such misguided altruism. Even a generation after the nightmare had ended, as Lord Bryce and other observers of the American scene agreed, the South's political system had still not recovered from the rampant corruption to which whites had understandably been driven in order to maintain their supremacy.

With good reason, the SANAC concluded, white South Africans were frightened. Would the Cape liberals themselves want to see their system carried to its logical conclusion of African majority rule? Surely not! Even if the other three colonies were to agree to it, which they emphatically would not, the Cape's model should not be adopted in the coming constitution. Mixing up the black and white political systems was probably wrong in principle. And it would certainly make the Union of South Africa an utter impossibility.

"Provided this can be done without conferring on them political power in any aggressive sense, or weakening in any way the unchallenged supremacy and power of the ruling race," the African voice ought to be heard respectfully in the highest parliaments and councils of the land. How could such a delicate balance between representation and safety be achieved? There was no reason why South Africans' thinking should be provincial. As members of the British Empire they could draw on a long, unparalleled experience of the government of backward races in mixed societies, a laboratory rich with models. Perhaps the likeliest possibility, thought the SANAC, was the separate roll that had been established for Maori voters in New Zealand, a colony renowned for good race relations. Africans might be allowed to choose a fixed number of Europeans to represent their interests in the parliament of the proposed Union, "the number not to be more than sufficient to provide an adequate means for the expression of Native views and the ventilation of their grievances, if any, and not to be regulated by the numerical strength of the Native vote."[14]

THE IDEOLOGICAL CRYSTALLIZATION OF SEGREGATION

From a later perspective the South African Native Affairs Commission may appear to have been unambiguously exploitationist. Its recommendations and assumptions were all thoroughly consistent with the developing system and ideology that would be called successively segregation, apartheid, and separate development. Indeed, it is difficult to read its report without calling to mind laws that reached the statute books after 1948: the Group Areas Act, the Representation of Natives Act, or the Bantu Education Act.

But this was no reactionary commission. For its time and place it was moderate to liberal. It was heavily dominated by English-speaking whites. Some of its members were missionaries and Native administrators who had worked with and for Africans over long periods. As a whole their questions do not strike a modern reader as naïve. Given the anthropological information and concepts that were available in the early twentieth century, their grasp of their complex subject was both sophisticated and up-to-date. Working hard at their job, they traveled throughout the black and white areas of southern Africa. They took particular pains to gather testimony from many points of view, including the perspectives of educated Africans as well as those of "raw" ones. They demolished several current white stereotypes: tribal despotism, the innately lazy Native, the spoiling effect of literary education.

Products of a racist culture, the commissioners were racists themselves. But they were not fanatics. In an intelligent and even scientific manner they sought to gather information and to base their conclusions on it. Their interest was clear: a compromise that would enable the divided white community at the end of a long and bitter war to unify, modernize, and survive as a white man's country. The SANAC was the surprisingly well-informed base from which the evolution of South Africa's modern Native policy began.

The truly remarkable thing about the SANAC, however, is the language it did *not* employ. The word "segregation" does not appear in the index or in the report of the SANAC, nor (as far as I have been able to determine) in the thousands and thousands of words in five large, closely printed volumes of proceedings and testimony. The general philosophy of white supremacy, as well as all or most of the parts of the new order, are certainly there. But they had not yet been combined into a coherent ideological whole, into a package that could be both compressed into election slogans and extended into a sophisticated, seductively attractive theory, according to which the relationship of black and white could be so organized that they need not conflict, enabling each group to develop on its own lines. To be sure, the next step would be a small one. The omission of the word "segregation" from the report and proceedings of the SANAC indicates that that step had not yet been taken. Since the seventeenth century, white South Africans had been white supremacists. As late as 1903–5, however, they were still groping for a formula. The moment of intellectual consolidation, the highest stage of white supremacy, was not yet at hand.

When an ideology crystallizes – when heretofore diverse and often incoherent thought fixes dramatically upon a key word or a cluster of words, which thereafter become clichés – the precise point of the shift and the particular persons responsible for it are ordinarily difficult to identify. This is a truism of intellectual history, whose students therefore retreat to the safety of imprecise but necessary phrases such as "climate of opinion" or "spirit of the age." Newton's term "mechanical philosophy" had been bandied about for half a century before the publication of the *Principia* in 1689. So had much of Darwin's explanation of evolution by means of natural selection. Only Alfred Wallace's agreeable self-effacement saved him from being accused of plagiarism. Various parts of Marx's "historical materialism" have been traced so diligently to influences among British classical economists, German philosophers, and French socialists that the quite mistaken conclusion has sometimes been drawn that he originated nothing.

So it was with the emergence of segregation as an ideology. As late as 1905 it was just another word, and employed surprisingly infrequently. Then, within a remarkably short time, strands of thought and experience were wound together. Trying to determine which of these was first is not only impossible but pointless.

These strands can usually be identified with particular colonies. In Natal the doctrine ordinarily associated with the nineteenth-century Native administrator Sir Theophilus Shepstone emerged with new clarity during the Natal Native Affairs Commission's inquiry into the causes of the widespread tax revolt of 1906–8. Its most effective spokesmen were J. W. Shepstone, S. O. Samuelson, Maurice Evans, and, later on, its historian, Edgar Brookes.[15] The doctrine called for administrative and territorial separation in the interests of separate development. Its basis was the tribe. Within their traditional framework Africans should evolve together, on their own lines, according to their own unique racial genius.

In the Transvaal, where large Afrikaner farmers had been urging the very opposite of economic and physical separation, small groups of English-speaking businessmen and government officials formed a society, read papers to each other, and published articles in *The Star, The State,* or the *South African Quarterly.* As Martin Legassick and Paul Rich argue persuasively, such men as Lionel Curtis and Howard Pim have at least as strong a claim as the Natalians do to a place among the founding fathers of segregation.[16] In the Orange Free State General James Hertzog insisted that his colony's tradition of total prohibition of African ownership of land would form a sound basis for good race relations. Some Cape leaders did urge the constitutional convention to extend their limited African franchise throughout the country, and they insisted upon its retention in their own province. But

moderates such as John Merriman yielded to none in their sophisticated understanding of how the carefully regulated equation of growing wants and severely restricted land could make
Africans the country's most valuable economic asset. The Natives Land Act of 1913, the single most important piece of segregationist legislation, would be based primarily on precedents
from the Cape.[17]

It was in the decade after 1905 that segregation crystallized.
The strands came together. While all of them had been present
in the report of the SANAC, they had remained to some extent
in tension. The commissioners had been unable to reconcile them
under one all-embracing formula. And then the groping ended.
Suddenly – in the deliberation of the constitutional conventions
leading to Union in 1910, in party platforms hastily drafted for
the elections to the first parliament, in books and periodicals –
the formula is present. The word "segregation" became ubiquitous. No dramatic transformation of attitudes had taken place,
no sudden alteration of the mode of production or the forms of
social relations. But an intellectual breakthrough had taken place,
even though the program would take years to achieve in practice.
An organizing principle had been discovered. An ideology was
being created. White supremacy was moving into its highest
stage.

The new formula was desperately needed. There had always
been conflicting approaches to the Native Question among the
various sections of the white community – large Afrikaner farmers
with their demand for plentiful, cheap, bona fide laborers instead
of economically independent African peasants who would compete with them; mining magnates with their need for an exploitation color bar that would keep low-grade mining profitable
and even permit it to expand; insecure urban residents with their
wish to be protected from the menace of redundant Africans
hanging idly about town; even missionaries with their idealistic
hope that African life might not be disrupted too violently by
European influence. Those fundamental disagreements would
continue. The reason is simple. In a country where some two-
thirds of the population and the basic labor force were African,
the self-interests of white people were intimately involved. At
stake in what General Smuts called the sphinx problem were not

only Africans' interests but their own. Their concerns, and therefore their views of what to do about the Native, would continue to be inconsistent. It was remarkably convenient that all of these competing interests could be contained, however uneasily, under the umbrella of segregationist rhetoric.

In the early years of the Union circumstances seemed to reflect a conspiracy to split the fragile new nation apart: class war at home; the international conflict of World War I, which triggered in South Africa a rebellion by militant Afrikaners against the government of one of their own, General Louis Botha, in 1914; the divisive insurgence of Afrikaner nationalism led by General J. B. M. Hertzog; the continuing snobbery of English-speaking whites. Only segregation, and of course the powerful economic forces and the fear of being "swamped" and "mongrelized" that lay behind segregation and drove it forward, enabled the white community to carry on a common political discourse at all. The most potentially divisive issue of them all, the Native Question, could be screened off, kept artificially separate from the rest of the white man's politics. Segregation was the essential ideological base on which white South Africa was founded. As the state it made possible grew stronger, so segregation would intensify.

As in the American South, the ideology of segregation was not developed by white South Africans of limited intelligence or inferior education, isolated from a wider, more enlightened world.[18] Its most important theoreticians included Hertzog and Smuts, good lawyers trained abroad. The latter was an exceptionally gifted Renaissance man, who studied botany and Walt Whitman and who wrote an important book on the philosophy of science. The segregationists included Charles Loram, an educationist with a doctorate from the Teachers College of Columbia University, Howard Pim, a prominent Quaker accountant and philanthropist, and Edgar Brookes, a bright young historian. Brookes's later career as a senator representing African interests and as a founding leader of the multiracial (and banned) Liberal Party leaves no doubt that the Negrophile sentiments that he expressed in his pro-segregationist *History of Native Policy in South Africa* (1922) were genuine.

Typically the leading segregationists were thoughtful, reasonable men. With the possible exception of General Hertzog, who after all was the first prime minister to meet directly with Native councils and who did carry out the promises of the Land Act of 1913 by adding to the reserves, they were not racist fanatics.[19] As in America, the doctrine of segregation simply cannot be dismissed as the clumsy fabrication of second-rate minds. Had it not been reasonably sophisticated, capable of holding its own in intellectual combat, it would not have been so seductively persuasive or so successful.

In the decade after 1905 the ideology of segregation emerged and crystallized. Simultaneously, with the formation of the Union in 1910 and thus the removal of the last effective checks from British imperial control, the means for carrying out the program became available. Thereafter the power of the state and the system of segregation rose together. As Marxist historians have argued, segregation was appropriate and at least convenient for the development of South African capitalism. For the consolidation of white political power it was absolutely essential.

THE MAKING OF THE SEGREGATIONIST SYSTEM

In 1925 General Hertzog's Nationalist–Labour coalition took power, dedicated to making segregation thorough and complete. Although in retrospect his demands seem astonishingly mild – the recognition of Afrikaans as an official language, a distinct national flag, the right to decide whether to participate in Britain's wars, a revision of symbols and legal forms within the Commonwealth of Nations – much of the English-speaking community had become severely frightened of Hertzog's insurgent Afrikaner nationalism.[20] Among liberal observers, such as the historian of the University of the Witwatersrand, W. M. Macmillan, it became customary to identify Hertzog's accession to office as a turning point not only in white politics, which it was, but in the evolution of South African race relations as well.

In this interpretation, however, the liberals were probably mistaken. Important steps were indeed taken after 1925. The Colour Bar Bill (1926), which reserved certain categories of semiskilled industrial jobs for whites, the Immorality Act (1927) against mixed marriages and casual sexual intercourse among the races, and the elimination of the Cape's African franchise (1936) were far more than insignificant details. But these acts did not create the momentum of segregation. Nor did they alter in any fundamental way the structure or course of a system whose foundations had already been securely laid. The principal architect of segregation was not General Hertzog. It was General Smuts.

In the decade and a half before 1925, first under General Botha, and after his death in 1919 under Smuts, that is, under the Afrikaner leaders on whose enlightened collaboration the British counted to cement the Commonwealth relationship, the main lines of segregation were established. First, the Mines and Works Act (1911), but more important the informal understandings under which its rather unspecific provisions were implemented, created racial job classifications in mining and on the railroads. This was the legislative basis for the exploitation color bar. Second, the Natives Land Act (1913) divided the country into white and Native areas. "At a stroke," as Sol Plaatje put it in his classic account, peasants were transformed into rural proletarians. Drafted and presented with sobs and tears by a reputed Cape liberal, J. W. Sauer, the Land Act was the centerpiece of the segregationist program. Its descendant is the Group Areas Act (1950).

Third, the Native Affairs Act (1920) established a Department of Native Affairs, with the prime minister at its head, and authorized Native councils to exercise limited self-government in transitional, detribalized areas. The logical conclusion of this legislation is the recent transfer of power to supposedly independent Bantu homelands, which to this day take up thirteen percent of the country. Fourth, the Native (Urban Areas) Act (1923) enabled municipalities to create Native locations nearby, where the economically essential African migratory labor force would be temporarily housed. Pass laws would control the influx of workers, and those who became redundant could be returned to the reserves, whether they had ever visited them or not. Although Africans were unfortunately essential in white areas, they did not belong in town. (The drafters of this act could not have foreseen the huge size to which these locations would eventually grow. Soweto, the biggest location for the industrial–mining complex on the Rand, now rivals Johannesburg.)

Thus, in four central areas – industrial, territorial, administrative, and urban – the Botha–Smuts regime laid the foundation of South Africa's modern system of race relations. In comparison with the stormy atmosphere of the late twenties and after, when the Senate, for example, delayed for a decade Hertzog's proposal to abolish the Cape's African franchise, the steadily building program of segregation before 1925 created little stir either in Great Britain or among the English-speaking community in South Africa. There was always a vocal Negrophile faction – the Colensos, the Shreiners, the Ballengers – who could be counted on to protest the latest outrage. Notwithstanding the wistful search on the part of white politicians for channels through which they might hear the authentic Native voice, there was no dearth of African opinion. Africans published newspapers, held congresses, petitioned, organized demonstrations, and sent delegations to England. It was all a great pity, sympathized successive British colonial secretaries. But the Treaty of Vereeniging at the end of the Boer War, which had specified that African voting rights would not be discussed until responsible government had been granted to the defeated republics, had tied their hands.[21]

In contrast to this posture of fatalistic acceptance, Hertzog's proposals for segregation in 1925 generated sharp, prolonged controversy in Britain and among South Africa's English-speaking whites. The rising opposition even extended to the Colonial and Dominions offices. In those departments it had usually been assumed that, in keeping with Cecil Rhodes's grand vision, Britain's goal was a United States of South Africa, to include the colonies of Southern and Northern Rhodesia as well as the High Commission Protectorates of Basutoland, Swaziland, and Bechuanaland, over which the British still exercised direct jurisdiction. That the expansion of the South African state would mean an increase in the power of Afrikaners, who, after the failure of Milner's plans for large-scale immigration after the Boer War, remained a large majority of the white community, did not unduly trouble British official thinking. South African politics seemed to be firmly in the hands of safe collaborators, Botha and Smuts, men bent on achieving their country's destiny as a member of the British Commonwealth.

Gradually British policy swung away from support of South

African expansion. In the early 1920s, when Smuts tried to bring Southern Rhodesia into the Union, drawing from Hertzog the charge that he intended to dilute the white man's country in a huge black ocean, the Colonial Office was ambivalent. The largely English-speaking Rhodesian settlers decided the issue, opting in a referendum for separate dominion status. In the 1930s, when Hertzog demanded the incorporation of the High Commission Protectorates, as provided in the Act of Union of 1909, the British stalled and finally turned him down. South Africa's expansion was halted in its tracks.[22]

There are several reasons for this change in British policy. First, as I have argued elsewhere, British opinion, which earlier in the century had differed very little from that of South Africa's English-speaking whites, was becoming less racist.[23] Not long before, segregation had been a central doctrine of *Britain's* policy throughout its tropical colonies. During the 1930s, however, the system of segregation, based in South-East Africa, and the system of indirect rule, centered in the export colonies of West Africa, were rapidly drawing apart. In such standard works as Lord Hailey's *African Survey* (1938) and Keith Hancock's *Survey of British Commonwealth Affairs* (1940) the two systems could be described as being diametrically opposed, embodying different principles, working in very different ways, and aiming at entirely different goals.

Second, Hertzog's program emphasized the race rather than the class component of segregationist discrimination. Whereas the Natives Land Act of 1913 or the Urban Areas Act of 1923 had dealt mainly with economic questions involving large masses of people, Hertzog's measures – such as the Immorality Act, the elimination of the African franchise, or the Colour Bar Bill, which prohibited otherwise qualified individuals from filling certain jobs – threatened individual rights and civil liberties. But it was precisely such matters of individual freedom that the great tradition of English liberalism had dwelt upon since the seventeenth century. The collectivist tradition, holding that large classes of people such as the poor or women have rights to decent jobs, education, housing, health care, or legal representation – and that these opportunities be kept open or if need be provided by the state – was much newer and only partially incorporated into

British political philosophy. Liberal whites, who ordinarily accepted the fact of white supremacy as inevitable in the circumstances of South Africa, and who were accustomed to class discrimination, may have been struck more readily by the kind of
issues Hertzog was raising.

Third, and most persuasive, is the argument that Hertzog's
great sin was not his allegedly novel views toward Africans but
his lack of loyalty to the British Commonwealth. After all, for
the British to suddenly discover that an opponent was at fault
with respect to the Native Question was not exactly unprecedented. During the Boer War they had published in "blue books"
the very explicitly discriminatory laws of the Boer republics concerning Africans. But those propaganda tracts could easily have
been compiled from the statutes of Natal, a colony dominated
by English speakers. During World War I, having always respected the Germans' efficient, scientific management of colonial
resources, and having said very little about Germany's harsh rule
in Tanganyika and South-West Africa, the British decided that
Germany's exploitationist record made it unfit to regain its lost
colonies.[24] (Later, Prime Minister Neville Chamberlain, who at
least was evenhanded in his willingness to see Eastern Europeans
join Africans under Hitler's domination, concluded that Germany's claim for colonies was after all negotiable as an element
of appeasement.[25]) And so it was with Hertzog's claims for the
High Commission Protectorates. Once Afrikaner nationalism had
ceased to be in safely collaborationist hands, the Native Question
became a convenient stalking horse.

SEGREGATIONIST IDEOLOGY

In his great biography of General Smuts, Sir Keith Hancock includes a brief but illuminating discussion of the intellectual history of segregation. Several strands, he argues, were skillfully
woven into an ideological maze: political, territorial, industrial,
official, educational, social.[26] To some extent, as Hancock maintains, these strains possessed distinctive pedigrees, represented
different interests, and spoke to various, even conflicting constit-
uencies. But segregation was more than a haphazard collection
of miscellaneous elements. It was an intellectual system with log-

ical consistency and integrity whose parts supported and reinforced one another.

The parts were not, however, necessarily interdependent. Even
the most dedicated champions of African interests, such as the
mystical and poetic missionary Arthur S. Cripps of Rhodesia,
might couch their arguments in segregationist terms, favoring
territorial segregation, meaning partition, as the only conceivable means of preserving *An Africa for Africans*.[27] Their support
for some parts of the system weakened their opposition to other
parts, such as the Colour Bar Bill or disfranchisement. Disintegration was a danger: Once the threads of the intermeshing fabric
began to unwind, the whole system might come undone. White
paternalists might conclude with some justification that Africans
would profit most from political stability. If comparatively moderate leaders were attacked too vigorously, then extremists might
well replace them. Although the African reserves were insufficient and hopelessly overcrowded, at least they were something.
Jobs in the gold mines were low paying and dangerous. But Africans needed those jobs desperately. Segregation might be bad.
But worse was easily conceivable.

Ultimately segregation rested on the premise that important
differences existed among Europeans, Africans, Asiatics, and
Coloured People. Until well into the twentieth century those differences were ordinarily defined as innately racial characteristics.
Stereotypes of racial inferiority abounded, two thousand years
behind being a favorite round estimate of the backwardness of
raw Africans compared with whites. Segregation and racism became virtually synonymous. But the connection was neither necessary nor indissoluble. As physical and social anthropologists
demonstrated that racial assumptions were fallacious, segregationists escaped with astonishing dexterity to higher, more de-
fensible ground. Differences came to be identified primarily with
distinctiveness, explained on grounds of culture, environment,
or history, not necessarily implying racial inferiority, and bearing a superficial resemblance to the separatist rhetoric of African
nationalism. One could therefore be a segregationist without
being a racist or even a white supremacist.[28]

The ideology was flexible enough to contain considerable internal variations. One segregationist might argue that the pre-

mature closing of the cranium, unfortunately restricting the con-volutions of the brain, made the education of an African child "beyond a certain stage" absolutely pointless. Another might argue on environmental grounds, as did Dudley Kidd, that at a certain stage initiation rites and the intensely sexual preoccupation of life in the Kraal distracted the African child. Still another, such as the educationist Charles Loram, might contend that even beyond a certain stage the African child's intelligence was probably not inferior. But Loram, like spokesmen for the Hampton-Tuskegee school in the American South, argued that education must be practical, shaped according to the child's background and needs as an adult member of a society that unfortunately would remain racially discriminatory. Education must "fit the child for his station in life." A humane paternalist, who eventually became Sterling Professor of Education at Yale University, Loram welcomed Hertzog's segregationist program and helped him to draft speeches defending it. So did the historian Edgar Brookes, for similarly positive motives. As the clear-headed British expert on Kenya, the radical doctor Norman Leys, pointed out – and by the 1930s Brookes at least agreed with him – the differing degrees of prejudice and paternalism among the segregationists mattered very little. What was important was their common political assumption about the future of their students: "If a boy is going to be a king some day he has no less need to learn how to sweep the stable well. But stable sweeping should be taught as training for kingly duties."[29]

Another segregationist might support the vote for a few exceptional Africans, as long as their possession of the franchise did not lead to political power "in any aggressive sense." But he was more likely to argue that European institutions were inherently incompatible with the strange combination of chiefly despotism and Kaffir socialism that supposedly constituted the African political tradition. Or, recognizing that the truly civilized African could be equal or even superior to the average white man, he might urge the educated African elite to help their people by participating in their own institutions. Although the assumptions and the arguments somewhat differed, they led to the same conclusion.

Unlike nineteenth-century missionaries, who typically had regarded African customs and institutions as so many instances of heathen ignorance, superstitition, and evil, blocking out Christian enlightenment and therefore to be attacked by all means possible, segregationists professed for African tradition the warmest fondness and respect.[30] This exaggerated, romantic veneration for the African past was a recent phenomenon. Zulu chiefs, for example, had with good reason been feared and hated as threats to white society. As late as the aftermath of the African tax revolt of 1906–8 chief Dinuzulu had been prosecuted for conspiracy on very flimsy evidence and then exiled. By the 1930s, however, George Heaton Nicholls and others had made the Zulu royal family into a veritable cult.[31] The attachment of segregationists to African traditional institutions increased in inverse proportion to their decline in functionality.

In the tribe, which Elizabeth Colson has identified as a European stereotype, segregationists had available a ready mechanism for collaboration and control.[32] Chiefs became the paid agents of the white regime. They could be held responsible for law and order, and the group could be penalized for the transgressions of individuals. Tribalism kept Africans divided. White rulers intensified rivalry as much as possible. In the closed compounds at the mines, for example, tribes were ordinarily housed separately. Strikes could be broken up by pitting group against group. The tribe was a symbol of the distinctiveness of the unique African racial genius, of the evolution of Africans on their own lines, of the immense, unbridgeable gulf between peoples. For segregationists African institutions were like beautiful, delicate orchids, which must be sheltered and protected from the harsh winds of European influence. Detribalization was a fearful and pathetic process. It was so much better for Africans to develop in their own pace and in their own way.

Segregationists adapted their doctrine to economic facts. Their most notable contribution to theory was the so-called dual economy. For them the European capitalist and African communal economies were distinct, compartmentalized, and fundamentally incompatible. The two sectors had entirely separate histories. During the long European penetration of the South African interior they had coexisted. Gradually they had begun to interact, but the boundaries between them had largely been maintained. African labor had moved from one compartment to the other, no doubt contributing substantially to the growth of the European sector, but leaving the African traditional economy essentially unchanged.

Along with coexistence and interchange, according to this version of South African economic history, came culture contact. At first very gradually, then more rapidly after the Kaffir wars of the mid-nineteenth century and the mineral discoveries of the 1880s, the stronger, more complex economy of the Europeans impinged on the simpler, more fragile African way of life. Inevitably the world market's irresistible forces were attracting Africans. Kaffir socialism was being severely disrupted. Painfully perhaps, but in the long run providentially, Africans were adjusting to a more rigorous, more disciplined economic pace. The transition should be as gradual and as controlled as possible. If African traditional institutions were intelligently conserved instead of being thoughtlessly and ruthlessly discarded, if they were given real responsibilities and important functions, then they might provide an effective buffer.

In the period between the world wars a generation of functional anthropologists, who were mainly inspired and trained by Bronislaw Malinowski at the London School of Economics and by A. R. Radcliffe-Brown at the University of Cape Town, brought social anthropology to a new level of precision and sophistication, based on painstaking fieldwork. The institutions of primitive society, they maintained – land tenure, marriage customs, religious ceremonies, law, age–grade divisions, the rules under which chiefs and councils worked – were an interconnecting whole that might shatter to pieces under intense pressure from outside forces. Once in motion, the sequence of culture contact – impingement, attraction, disruption, adaptation, reorientation – was probably irreversible. If possible, however, it needed to be regulated and slowed down. Like their successors, these anthropologists had to have research grants, and they applied for them to the most likely sources: European colonial governments. Their later disclaimers notwithstanding, social engineering in the colonial situation became for this generation of anthropologists the rationale and justification of their profession.[33]

The segregationists of the early twentieth century, however, had anticipated the anthropologists. Like them, they professed to have the interests of Africans at heart. Like them, they professed to be facing facts. To attempt to halt the interaction of the two sectors of the dual economy would be impracticable. White areas would continue to have labor requirements, and Africans from the reserves would still need jobs. African workers would be needed in, or rather near, town. But cities were not good for Africans. Liquor, prostitution, bright lights, and advanced ideas all lay in wait for them. Too large a dose of the influence of a higher civilization would disorient, demoralize, detribalize, and ultimately even de-Africanize raw Natives, turning them into those laughable but pathetic figures the pseudo-Europeans.

So as not to destroy the African family and tribal life, General Smuts explained in 1917 to a distinguished London audience that had gathered in his honor, South Africa had decided that the African labor force would be both temporary and predominantly male. Migrant workers were therefore being housed separately in closed compounds, where they could be carefully supervised and protected. Pass laws regulated their movements. After a year or so, when they became restless or when they were no longer required, they returned to their homelands in the reserves, taking with them some of the white race's superior culture. Some – but not too much. The Africans' economic, social, and political lives remained based in their own areas. South Africa's Native policy was thus fully in tune with the ideas of the leading authorities on the proper government of backward races. It was a courageous attempt to regulate the frighteningly disruptive process of culture contact.

Quite unlike the ruthless Germans – who in Tanganyika, the Cameroons, and South-West Africa had systematically rooted out and destroyed those inefficient tribal institutions that seemed to stand in the way of the most complete exploitation possible – white South Africans had decided on a slower and much more difficult policy. They had not disdain but the profoundest respect and liking for their Africans. The policy of Smuts's country was enlightened, responsible, and humane. The British called their system trusteeship. In South Africa it was called segregation:

Instead of mixing up white and black in the old haphazard way, which instead of lifting up the black degraded the white, we are now trying to lay down a policy of keeping them apart as much as possible in our institutions. In land ownership, settlement and forms of government we are trying to keep them apart, and in that way laying down in outline a general policy which it may take a hundred years to work out.

Their principles were tentative and their means still more flexible. But the outline of the future South Africa toward which they were working was reasonably clear:

You will have . . . large areas cultivated by blacks and governed by blacks, where they will look after themselves in all their forms of living and development, while in the rest of the country you will have your white communities, which will govern themselves separately according to the accepted European principles. The natives will, of course, be free to go and work in the white areas, but as far as possible the administration of white and black areas will be separated, and such that each will be satisfied and developed according to its own proper lines.[34]

Neither General Hertzog nor even Dr. Hendrik Verwoerd ever really improved upon General Smuts's formulation of segregation. Smuts's recognition of the crucial function of the African reserves in a modern industrial economy was not of course unprecedented. The chairman of the South African Native Affairs Commission and former Native commissioner of Basutoland, Sir Godfrey Lagden, had explained it more succinctly in 1903: "A man cannot go with his wife and children and his goods and chattels on to the labour market. He must have a dumping-ground. Every rabbit must have a warren where he can live and burrow and breed, and every native must have a warren too."[35] By 1917 segregationists had become more sophisticated. They were learning to smoothe the dual economy's rougher edges and to fit it into a larger intellectual system. They were becoming extremely adept at mystification. By 1917, at least, the ideology of segregation was rapidly maturing.

As early as 1934, in a seminal analysis published in the *South African Journal of Economics,* H. M. Robertson argued persuasively, and one would have thought conclusively, that the dual economy was a myth. Ever since the spectacular failure of Jan van Riebeeck's famous hedge, planted round the first settlement at Cape Town in the 1650s and intended to segregate the settlers from the Khoikhoi, the interaction of Europeans, Asiatics, Africans, and Coloureds within a single economy had been the central, continuous theme of South African economic history. Even Robertson was not wholly original, for much of his argument had already been anticipated by W. M. Macmillan. From the late 1930s such liberal historians as Sir Keith Hancock and C. W. De Kiewiet carried on a strenuous campaign of demystification. The increasing attention of recent historians to the African side of South African history has further intensified the attack. And however much they may disagree about important matters of causation, Marxists have continued the effort. For nearly half a century the main currents of English-speaking historiography have been engaged in a campaign against the hypothesis of the dual economy.[36]

Yet the dual economy has had a long run.[37] It was, it must be emphasized, a plausible explanation of the facts. When anthropologists investigated the reserves, they found Africans living what apparently were thoroughly traditional lives, almost entirely unaffected by the progressive methods, habits, and attitudes associated with the European sector. The conclusion seemed self-evident: The cause of rural poverty was the persistence of African backwardness. The evidence of an earlier period of prosperity among a substantial minority of African peasants, which Monica and Francis Wilson and Colin Bundy have used to support their recent interpretations, lay hidden in government and missionary reports, in the written, historical materials that functional anthropologists discounted as secondhand and unreliable. Very likely, thought the advocates of the dual economy, conditions in the reserves were deteriorating. But the explanation seemed obvious. More people, employing the same conservative and increasingly obsolete methods, were attempting to subsist on the same amount of land.

Given its assumptions, given the limitations of the methods of direct anthropological investigation, the dual economy seemed indisputable. As long as one concentrated upon economic laws rather than upon the political forces that limited the land, routed the railways, located the industries, and accumulated the capital, the theory explained the facts very well.

The concern of many segregationists with the African side of the dual economy went no further than using the reserves to justify low wages, nonexistent health and retirement benefits, and the withholding of civil and political rights in white areas, all on the pretext that these were fully provided or exercised in the homelands. Others, the "good" segregationists, took things more seriously. As members of interracial organizations, advisory councils, and government commissions, such men as Howard Pim, Charles Loram, and the Lovedale missionary establishment worked hard to expose the facts and to improve conditions in the reserves.

White liberals faced a cruel dilemma. They might quite legitimately ask themselves just how much half a century of coming out to work for whites had accomplished for Africans. Would they not be better off staying at home in their own part of the dual economy? But working to improve the homelands meant to some extent accepting them. So did participating in the various channels that from time to time were set up as safety valves so that Africans might "ventilate their grievances, if any." These exercises in pacification – toy telephones as Africans came to call them, for no one was listening – might accomplish little. But was not some communication, however imperfect, better than none?

As Martin Legassick and others have argued, liberals played an active and significant role in developing and refining the ideology of segregation.[38] Noted Negrophiles were prominent members of the South African Native Affairs Commission, whose recommendations formed the basis for the evolution of Native policy in the twentieth century. Lionel Curtis, Howard Pim, and Philip Kerr (later Lord Lothian) played leading parts in the crucial discussions that culminated in the compromise on the Native Question in the Act of Union of 1909. Cape liberals drafted the Natives Land Act of 1913. Edgar Brookes wrote an influential book in which he praised segregation as a legacy from the most enlightened and successful administrators in the country's history. Charles Loram developed a theory of separate education and, as late as 1926, wrote speeches and proposals for General Hertzog. The position of all these men was one that Alabama's Edgar Gardner Murphy or North Carolina's Howard Odum would have appreciated. Segregation was not the best of all possible worlds. But it was the one they had to live in. If they did not participate in its institutions, then others would. The Native would surely be the loser.

Much of Legassick's argument about the functionality of liberals had been anticipated by Sir Keith Hancock. Certain well-meaning academics, he wrote in his *Survey of British Commonwealth Affairs* (1940) – historians, economists, especially anthropologists – had naïvely supposed that it was possible to compromise on matters of principle. They had tried to accept the broad outlines of segregation and then to work from inside the system to modify its details. Unfortunately a little segregation was like a little pregnancy. The unwary found themselves ensnared in an "entanglement of words and phrases" that obscured simple, basic facts about economic exploitation and political discrimination. Unwittingly some of the "Native's best friends" had been giving ideological aid and comfort to those who had repeatedly demonstrated "that their intense emotional awareness of colour . . . could not be appeased except by a segregation which was totalitarian and to the last degree complete."[39] In fact Edgar Brookes, whom Hancock cited in a footnote, had already courageously made the same declaration himself.

Segregation, as Hancock so aptly called it, was an entanglement of words and phrases. It was also a cluster of ideas and symbols, an economic theory, an interpretation of history, and a vision of the future. Some of it was transparently self-serving. But some of it was not. The decision that the reform of an existing system is impossible is difficult for the white liberal to make. Although the implications are appalling, the liberal will not directly suffer the consequences. Segregation existed. Any attempt at reform meant, inevitably, compromise not only on tactics but on some matters of principle. Segregation was not, however, the worst of all possible worlds. It was not entirely inflexible. It held out at least the promise of peaceful, progressive improvement. Otherwise there would have been no basis for African or liberal collaboration. Like any successful ideology, segregation did not altogether shut off all avenues of protest and opposition. Instead it channeled and absorbed them. To become entrapped in the entanglement of words and phrases has never been difficult.

9. Conclusion: Reactions to segregation

As the reader will have noticed, this book is about white people. In the comparatively recent past – in the American South after about 1890, in South Africa after about 1910 – two traditionally racist societies dedicated to maintaining white supremacy were becoming increasingly competitive. Fundamental social changes were taking place: the early stages of industrialization and urbanization, the formation of industrial elites and proletariats, the consolidation of state or, in the American case, of party systems; that is, changes in all those diverse but ultimately related areas that Marxists sweepingly label structure and superstructure. To those in power, who sought ways by which their societies might absorb such massive and explosive energy, the period was one of intense crisis. In their view the very basis of social order was being threatened severely. The primarily vertical lines of authority and deference characteristic of traditional white supremacy were breaking down. New, mainly horizontal patterns of social and political relations, mechanisms of control that had been undreamt of in the plantation and frontier histories of South Africa and the American South before the late nineteenth century, were desperately required.

To meet this crisis, the power of the state was invoked at an accelerated pace that sometimes left contemporaries on both sides of the color line gasping for breath. In the decade or so after 1890 the Southern states frequently conspired with each other to enact an impressive array of Jim Crow laws and to disfranchise black and many poor-white voters. In South Africa, newly centralized and completely autonomous after 1910, the state partitioned the country into grossly inequitable white and Native areas, established a national structure of Native administration, and devised instruments for dealing with the essentially novel problems posed by the presence of Africans in town. In both societies moderates played a leading role. Sophisticated ideologies rapidly emerged, mystifying what in fact were simple, straightforward issues of race and class discrimination in an entanglement of words and phrases. A key word, which had been employed surprisingly infrequently in the previous half-century, quickly gained currency. It was the effective beginning of segregation, the highest stage of white supremacy.

These complex processes, taking place in very different circumstances thousands of miles apart, were primarily the results of internal dynamics. South Africa did not need the example of the American South to demonstrate how a white man's country might both modernize and maintain racial stratification. But the comparison was there; it was convenient; and it was used. The American South entered the competitive phase more than a decade ahead of South Africa. By the time representatives of the four South African colonies met in 1908 to bring about white political unity, the American solution to the Negro Problem had already generated a large literature. A few strategically important individuals – Lord Bryce, Maurice Evans, Howard Pim, Lionel Curtis, General Smuts – examined American conditions and precedents closely, noting successes as well as glaring errors to be avoided. Through these men the two cases of evolving segregation were linked historically.

Neither in South Africa nor in America was segregation economically determined in any direct or mechanical way. The specific forms of race and class relations that emerged may, as Marxists say, have been appropriate to the dynamics of industrial capitalism and urbanization at a certain stage. But they were certainly not inevitable. Very different results are easily imaginable. Indeed, they *were imagined*. Town, mine, and factory might have acted as powerful disintegrative agents. They might have dissolved the irrational and apparently obsolete patterns of racial dominance and discrimination that had been inherited from the past. They might have led to the emergence of communities that were more open, more democratic, and more tolerant.

The case is sometimes made that this is precisely what has happened. In the long run, it is maintained, the economics of discrimination and the dynamics of modernization run in opposite directions. Irrational restrictions on the flow of capital and labor impediments, which are inherently incompatible with the requirements of advanced industrial capitalism, become increasingly anachronistic, expensive, and inconvenient. For some time the society may contrive to develop despite these handicaps. But eventually – by the 1960s in the American South, at some point in the (steadily receding) future in South Africa – the contradictions between economic imperatives and political artificialities become too severe to be maintained. Segregation gives way.

I agree with those who do not find the economic determinist argument persuasive. Important alterations in the American South's internal economy were taking place after World War II; most significantly, the plantation system in cotton collapsed, as its workers were both pulled away into Northern industry and pushed by the widespread adoption of machinery. Undoubtedly these changes made the terrain rather more favorable than it had been a generation earlier. The fact is, however, that the white South did not accept change easily or gracefully. In some cases resistance was massive. In others it was undertaken with subtlety and finesse. Either way the pace was forced. The alteration in the political balance of power – the growing voting strength of Northern blacks, the increasingly militant civil rights movement in the South, the intervention of the federal government – was far more important than economic forces in overthrowing the legal structure of segregation.

A few students still argue that political trends and economic imperatives must gradually come into line in South Africa, as well. Since by definition the "long run" is long, that may of course be true. But the history of the country under nationalist rule since 1948 has made such optimism increasingly less convincing. The ability to achieve both modernization and continuing racial stratification has been impressive.[1] In the nature of things, it seems, important political changes do not ordinarily come about spontaneously, merely because economic forces may point in their direction. They are imposed by power, by groups that are organized and that are therefore political.

What may be agreed is that in the short run, that is, by about the 1890s in the American South and by the first decade after the Union of 1910 in South Africa, the traditional and primarily vertical forms of white supremacy were showing signs of severe strain. In some Southern states Populists or fusionists took power. In the Cape Colony in South Africa, African and Coloured voters were increasing, and the numbers of educated, urban Africans who were potential voters were rising elsewhere. Did not history clearly show, John Merriman of the Cape grimly reflected, that eventually the class that did the work of farm and industry could not be denied a share of power?[2] What must be remembered is that contemporaries possessed many of the census figures and other data concerning land ownership, composition of labor forces, numbers of graduates, and so on, that are now consulted by historians. The politicians of the period were fully capable of projecting trends to logical and, in their view, frightening conclusions.

The early phases of modernization created a crisis for white supremacy. Swift, decisive action was required to save it. Imaginative, ingenious, and often moderate men, whose knowledge and sophistication should not be underestimated, put their minds to work. Changes in degree of such magnitude that taken together they would constitute a revolutionary change in kind were carried out. The architects of the new order did not work in a historical vacuum. Most of the procedures and devices they adopted had precedents. But they were not slavish imitators. In fact, they were boldly innovative in mystifying the relationship between past and present, in disguising their contrivances, in making what was really discontinuous appear to be organic, "normal" evolution. Their *system,* if not necessarily its individual parts, was an act of political creation. They called it segregation.

A complex, interlocking system of control that regulated the lives and to some extent the minds of millions of people on both sides of the color line, segregation was developed and imposed by men with power. They were white. Moreover, the primary targets of the segregationist fiction that peoples who in fact were living and working ever more closely together within a single economy and civilization were developing separately on their own lines were the minds and consciences of whites. If the black and brown victims also became ensnared by the promise of separate development, as they sometimes were, that was a bonus. The principal function of the segregationist ideology was to soften class and ethnic antagonisms among whites, subordinating internal conflicts to the unifying conception of race.

Segregation was a world white people made. But it was not, and in the nature of things could not have been, merely imposed from above by fiat on so many inert lumps of clay. The black and brown peoples of South Africa and the American South were hardly helpless, passive nonparticipants. In this book I have argued that segregation emerged as part of the larger systemic change of modernization, associated with the early phases of urbanization and industrialization. That argument, of course, is oversimplified and depersonalized. It was the economically necessary and irreversible movement of black and brown people into towns and industries, their increasingly effective political participation, their growing uppityness as they became educated or left their place on plantations or on tribal lands that created the crisis of white supremacy in the first place. If they were not for a time strong enough to be a decisive part of the solution, then, as Frederick Douglass used to say, at least they were the problem.

Their role did not stop there. Like any system of control, segregation was a continually evolving process of negotiation and bargaining. The scales of power were extremely uneven. Until perhaps the 1950s in the American South, and even later in South Africa, whites kept the political initiative. The process was mainly white action and black–brown reaction. Yet in any such system, in periods of apparently placid stability as well as in times of crisis, the limits of tolerance are being tested and renegotiated. What was at stake was not only what the dominant group wished to impose but how much the oppressed were willing to accept for the time being.

All of which brings us to some very complex and controversial questions. What is it like to be exposed, continually and relentlessly, to the double jeopardy of race and class discrimination in a segregated society? Through what processes, mechanisms, or support systems do the oppressed manage to cope? At least some outward conformity to the regimented etiquette of deference is virtually essential for survival. To what extent is the external ritual of self-effacement necessarily internalized? With what kinds of effects on personality, family, or community?

MODELS AND SUGGESTIONS

Among American historians the discussion of the impact of white supremacy has centered on Stanley Elkins's controversial interpretation of the slave personality.[3] Basing his argument on the analogy and literature of the Nazi concentration camps, Elkins describes the large plantation of the antebellum South as a closed-behavior system, where significant-other role models were successfully denied and where the range of behavior was regulated within a very narrow range. Submissive behavior was a requirement for survival. Indeed, lest a rebellious interior be betrayed by a careless glance or gesture, a thoroughly submissive personality was necessary as well.

Slaves who survived supposedly became incomplete, dependent persons. Like the Jewish survivors of the concentration camps, Elkins argues, slaves became childish, docile, and imitative. Irrelevant and dangerous, their rich and varied African heritage was suppressed and all but forgotten. In the two centruies and more of their enslavement Afro-Americans became a remarkably homogeneous and severely stunted people. To a large extent they accepted the values and outlook of their oppressors, including the masters' denigration of them. Expected to behave immaturely, and punished severely if they acted otherwise, on the whole they conformed. The white stereotype of Sambo was therefore fact as well as fiction.

According to the Elkins interpretation the slave family and community were likewise creatures of the closed-behavior system, irresistibly molded into instruments of submissive conformity in a severely restricted environment over which the slaves had little or no control. Families were frequently broken up, and slaves were bred like horses. As cooks, "mammies," or concubines, women were sometimes capable of gaining somewhat higher status, somewhat more secure positions as members of the "plantation family." Their own families were therefore weakened and distorted. During slavery and beyond the typical black family became matriarchal. The father, if he did not desert, suffered from an acute castration complex. As for the institutions of the slave community, especially religion, they mainly reinforced the submissive behavior of individuals and families.

The closed-behavior system aimed to produce creatures psychologically incapable of organized, sustained resistance. In that, at least, the plantation, like the concentration camp, succeeded. For, in Elkins's view, the most remarkable fact about slavery in the southern United States, in sharp contrast to the more tumultuous histories of the Caribbean or Brazil, was the infrequency and conspicuous lack of success of slave revolts. The psychological impact of slavery was pathological, catastrophic, and enduring, continuing to maim the slaves' descendants unto the third and fourth generations.

Written in the 1950s, in the wake of the *Brown* decision but before the civil rights movement or the explosive urban riots of the mid-sixties, both of which overturned so many white assumptions about Afro-American character and history, the Elkins interpretation of slavery was part of the American liberalism of the postwar era. It helped to shape, and no doubt in turn was influenced by, contemporary studies by psychologists and sociologists of the impact of segregation. Under segregation, though obviously not so rigidly as during slavery, a closed-behavior system had supposedly continued. And, especially in the South, black people on the whole had continued to submit to it.

In the South at least the slave personality of Sambo still lived. Blacks continued to bear the mark of oppression. Their personalities continued to be warped by the acceptance of a color complex that made them hate whites but that also made them despise and reject themselves. They were "abnormal." Typically their family system remained matriarchal, with black women being forced into domineering roles that psychologically castrated their husbands or drove them away, that prolonged into manhood the anal stage of their sons, leading them in turn into unhealthy, violent habits of indirect aggression. In the racist outlook that had pervaded the era when segregation originated, high crime rates, low IQs, and numerous broken families had been ascribed to inherited racial traits. In the later environmentalist interpretation these traits were attributed to the endurance of the stunted personality and institutions that had been imposed upon black people under slavery and that had largely continued under segregation.[4]

Ultimately, of course, the reason for black apathy was white racism. The vast majority of blacks remained poor, ignorant, and powerless, ill-equipped to engage in a struggle for the rights that the Supreme Court had decided must be conceded to them. Somehow the focus was no longer the system but the victims. Somehow they were responsible for their own hapless, pathetic condition.

More than two decades of research and often heated debate have surrounded the Elkins interpretation of the slave personality and the closely related analyses of the impact of segregation. Clearly the concentration-camp analogy was forced and overstated. Even large plantations did not really function like Auschwitz. For in such agricultural factories slaves had far more room for maneuver, far more significant-other role models than Elkins presumed. Their life expectancy and value to their masters were comparatively high. The environment of American slavery was not that closely circumscribed. For all its undoubted cruelty and oppression, the plantation was not primarily a device for forming a particular kind of stunted personality. It was a rational and, on the whole, a profitable system of production. It possessed and employed potent means of coercion. But it did not gas or torture to death most of its inhabitants. In the nooks and crannies, in what Eugene Genovese calls the interstices, in the very ambiguities and contradictions that enabled the plantation to function as a system of production, resourceful slaves found ways of asserting psychological autonomy and dignity. American slavery was a continual process of negotiation, even of reciprocity. It was a world the slaves as well as the slaveholders made.[5]

Although black families, like those of other poor and oppressed peoples, often had absent fathers, they have never typically been matriarchal, a word with connotations of power that is singularly inappropriate when women are exposed to the triple jeopardy of race, class, and sex.[6] Slave families were indeed broken up. But masters often recognized the family's usefulness as an instrument of coercion and a basis of stability, as a way of decreasing the number of runaways. Although they were unrecognized in law, slave marriages were surprisingly permanent. The numerous examples of freedmen and -women tramping sometimes hundreds of miles in search of kin who might have been separated for decades eloquently testify to the black family's strength.[7] After Emancipation, and with every economic gain, that family has become increasingly more "normal." During the "great migration" to the north and west, like the families of European peasants, it became a sophisticated chain, passing money and people back and forth over hundreds or thousands of miles, housing new arrivals and helping them to find jobs. Both in nuclear and extended forms the black family has not been a fragile reed, but a powerful and enduring mechanism of support.

The psychological effects of segregation, recent students have argued, were not so debilitating as might have been supposed. Although oppression does shape the personalities of its victims, it also makes them develop internal strength. Black children were no doubt harmed by negative color identifications, but they did not wallow in them. Afro-Americans lived in a tough, cruel world to which they reacted in perfectly normal ways. They were neither warped nor maimed. Otherwise, comes the clinching argument, the black movement and even the riots would have been impossible.

The institutions of the slave community, especially religion, were also powerful means of support. They could, and did, facilitate both docility and resistance, both self-effacement and dignity. The infrequency and lack of success of slave revolts on the North American mainland, compared with the far more numerous risings elsewhere in the hemisphere, remains a problem to those who have not sufficiently considered the implications of the extremely unfavorable ratio of black to white in the South. Even where blacks were in the majority, overwhelming white power was always within easy riding distance. Sustained rebellion was hopeless. But slaves resisted in many ways, including flight, theft, slowdowns, and sabotage.[8]

As a description of the realities of North American slavery, and by extension of the impact of segregation, the concentration-camp analogy must therefore be used cautiously if at all. It would be still more absurd, however, to argue that those who are exposed to an institution within the very broad genre of closed-behavior systems – which range from concentration camps and prisons to armies and the English public school – experience *no* important psychological effects. Of course slaves were damaged by the necessity of being submissive. The huge literature of Afro-American autobiography, fiction, and social science, extending back over more than a century, eloquently explains what it means to be black in America, refuting any notion that the victims of the several stages of white supremacy have not undergone a searing and psychologically damaging experience. Some of that literature of survival, indeed, seems to confirm something like the Sambo stereotype. But the support is only superficial. Whereas the Elkins school has emphasized the legacy of the slave personality after Emancipation, Afro-American writers have stressed the need to react defensively to white racism in modern America.

The moment of discovery, when the black personality first comes to full recognition of the realities of life under white supremacy, is a constant topic of Afro-American autobiography. If the person were fortunate, like the novelist and anthropologist Zora Hurston, who grew up in a black town in Eatonville, Florida, the confrontation with self and society might come as late as the identity crisis of young adulthood. More often the moment of realization came early. It was usually violent and traumatic. The earliest memory of Benjamin Mays, a distinguished scholar of his people's religion and president of Morehouse College in Atlanta, was of the Phoenix riot of 1898 in Greenwood and surrounding counties of rural South Carolina. Hundreds of blacks were lynched or shot down. Mays was not yet five:

> I remember a crowd of white men who rode up on horseback
> with rifles on their shoulders. I was with my father when
> they rode up, and I remember starting to cry. They cursed
> my father, drew their guns and made him salute, made him
> take off his hat and bow to them several times. Then they
> rode away.[9]

Walter White, secretary of the NAACP, whose blue eyes and blond hair enabled him to pass for white when he risked his life to investigate lynchings, had his moment of full discovery during the Atlanta race riot of 1906. His father, a postal worker for the federal government, was a particular target of the mob, and their house was attacked.[10] Ellen Tarry, who could also pass, was the daughter of a relatively prosperous Birmingham barber. Her moment came when she was a teenager. In front of their house policemen beat a black man into unconsciousness; as she ran to help him they drove off laughing. That incident brought to mind a Klan march during her childhood:

> I remembered how Mama took me out of bed and carried me to the parlor where I saw Papa, in his old-fashioned night shirt, standing by the front window. He was as still as a statue and his fists were clenched . . . As the reflection from the burning cross lighted up our room, it glistened against the steel of the revolver in his hand. Mama tightened her grip on my arm but I broke away and pressed my nose against the windowpane, the better to see the men who rode white horses and carried fiery crosses. After the last clop-clop died away there was a long stillness.[11]

Such examples – in some cases involving violence and extreme danger, in others a particularly insulting remark or situation – must be typical. In any case, black parents had to teach their children "the art of how to get along with white people."[12] By an incredibly early age – even two or three – writes the white psychoanalyst Robert Coles, black children have already begun to be socialized into "the indirection, the guile needed for survival." Already they have begun to wear the mask. "It's like that with cars and knives," a mother told him:

> You have to teach your children to know what's dangerous and how to stay away from it, or else they sure won't live long. So if you want your kids to live long, they have to grow up scared of whites; and the way they get scared is through us; and that's why I don't let my kids get fresh about the white man even in their own house. If I do there's liable to be trouble to pay. They'll forget, and they'll say something outside, and that'll be it for them, and us too. So I make them store it in the bones, way inside, and then no one sees it . . . The colored man, I think has to hide what he really feels even from himself. Otherwise there would be too much pain – too much.[13]

Parents and teachers faced a cruel dilemma. Should the harsh facts of life be spelled out in early childhood? That was certainly the safer course. Or, lest the child's spirit be damaged before it had formed, should the moment of full realization be postponed as long as possible? Some parents insisted that their children fight back if white kids attacked, because doing so was usually safe enough. During puberty, when African boys, for instance, become men in initiation rites, the youngsters would have to be taught to back away. There were some things that all parents must have warned against. For sons it was white women: One would be better off picking up a rattlesnake. For daughters it was white men as well as black. Jim Crow cars were dangerous places, and domestic service was full of opportunities for sexual harassment.[14]

The psychological impact of such a socialization process, of learning to place constraints upon the expression and therefore upon the sense of self, of making self-effacement so instinctual that true feelings are stored in the bones, is not easy for those who have not undergone it to understand. But the children's drawings collected by Robert Coles, in which black people are typically stunted or disfigured, whereas white figures are drawn larger and more boldly, demonstrate graphically and unforgettably what denigration of self can mean to a bright, alert child.[15]

Even those who have experienced the pressure find it difficult to explain its impact. Benjamin Mays was "not wise enough to say categorically" what white supremacy "did to Negroes in Greenwood County." Simple fear made the system work. "It certainly 'put the rabbit' in many Negroes. They were poor, inadequately trained, and dependent on the white man for work. Few dared to stand up to a white man. When one did, he got the worst of it." The responses varied: "Most Negroes grinned, cringed, and kowtowed in the presence of white people." Some, like Mays himself, went north for jobs or education. "There were others who, though they could not get away, never quite accepted in their minds the role they had to play." If they wanted to live, however, they played the role anyway. Mays observed his father's deference to whites: "Did this mean that my father mentally accepted or emotionally approved this cringing behavior? I doubt it. It was a technique of survival. But I have always wondered how long one can do a thing without eventually accepting it."[16]

In the passage just quoted, Mays was explaining the impact of white supremacy in a rural area. His autobiography, indeed, drives home the point that race relations in South Carolina amounted to a chronic state of war. But even Mays found a difference in what I have called a segregated society when he went to teach at Morehouse College in 1921. In his childhood, as well as during his first year of higher education at the black college of Virginia Union in Richmond, he had had very little contact with whites. At Bates College in Maine, and then at the University of Chicago, he was a black man in an overwhelmingly white world, which ranged from pleasant to not too bad. In Atlanta he was "entering a new world in Negro–white relations." There "I was to see the race problem in greater depth, and observe and experience it in larger dimensions . . . I was to find that the cruel tentacles of race prejudice reached out to invade and distort every aspect of Southern life. The picture was not pretty."[17] For Zora Hurston the black town of Eatonville, Florida, had been separate but not segregated. It was "Jacksonsville [that] made me know that I was a little colored girl. Things were all about the town to point this out to me."[18] Blacks in town had somewhat better opportunities for education and for economic security. But they lived in a world that was far more complex and ambiguous. Whether urban segregation had a more or less severe impact than rural white supremacy must remain a moot point.

Black people survived in America. But they paid a high price. Segregation was less of a closed-behavior system than slavery, let alone a concentration camp. It was nonetheless powerfully constraining and inhibiting. It was not characterized, however, by a simple, unilinear path that had to be followed with no permissible deviations whatever. That, after all, might have been psychologically easier. Instead the dominant motif of segregation was ambiguity. When white people were present, one wore the mask of deference; in his novel *Invisible Man,* Ralph Ellison describes the college president stopping in front of a mirror to "put on his face" before meeting a white trustee whom he controls. But whites were not always present. With a dexterity that had to become instinctive, blacks switched roles and manners quickly.

As Richard Wright explains in the first volume of his autobiography, covering his youth in Memphis, Tennessee, and Jackson, Mississippi, he could never get it right. Half-enviously he watched others "play the nigger" and wondered how they managed it. One look into his eyes, or the way he carried himself, one careless phrase of forthrightness, one assertion not even of aggressiveness but merely of ordinary humanity: Somehow white folks always knew. He must, and did, leave the South. But in Chicago, Wright says in his second autobiographical volume, he found that he had internalized the habit of self-effacement – what Ellison called being invisible – more than he had realized. Months and even years passed. Wright finally went to France. In America he had never been able to relax and be himself.[19]

The psychological pressure of living under a system of discrimination that is not quite total, that leaves open some if not many avenues for self-expression, that is not only oppressive but ambiguous, is intense. But psychologists have been unable to isolate discrimination from physical hardship, malnutrition, wretched housing, and extreme poverty. Statistics enumerating disturbed or antisocial behavior are plentiful. Blacks have high incidences of crime, most of it domestic or contained within the black community, of drunkenness, and of drug use. Most blacks are not criminals, although the reader of Richard Wright's *Native Son* may wonder why not. Not all blacks are schizophrenic, although rates of mental illness are significantly higher. Psychologists have seriously questioned why schizophrenia is not a universal condition among black males; in fact, the rate among black females is even higher.[20] Nor do all blacks suffer from hypertension, though it would not be surprising if they did.[21] Although the black sociologist Kenneth Clark recognized that the community life of Harlem contained strength and hope as well as disintegration and despair, he described the "dark ghetto" as "institutionalized pathology; it is chronic, self-perpetuating pathology . . ."[22]

In South Africa too there is a growing and also eloquent literature of autobiography and fiction by black and brown writers.[23] Since writing is itself a subversive, self-assertive activity, most of what we possess comes from people now dead, banned, or in exile. Like Afro-Americans, South African writers describe the socialization process for children and for new arrivals in the locations or on white farms, the dexterity with which the mask of deference is worn in the presence of the dangerous white "baas," the inability of the few who leave the country to realize at first that the pressure of the system is really gone. In South Africa too the impact of discrimination is impossible to isolate from other related factors. Statistics of drunkenness, of ubiquitous gangsterism and crime, again the vast majority of it being black against black, are high. The figures for Coloured People, all of whom live in white areas, most of whom speak Afrikaans, and whose lives are even more ambiguous than those of Africans, are still higher.[24] Rural and especially urban Africans live in conditions of institutionalized pathology. Periodically the dark ghettos explode in violent rage.

The South African psychological literature is markedly one-sided. The vast majority of it deals with the incidence and nature of prejudice among whites, concentrating on such questions as whether Afrikaners are more prejudiced than the English, whether there are sex or generational differences, whether racism can be correlated with an authoritarian personality.[25] Material on the psychology of nonwhites is very thin indeed: here a study of a few "future autobiographies" of students, which not surprisingly turn out to be highly politicized; there an analysis of hallucinations in a couple of dozen dreams. There are two interesting but slim volumes by the one African psychologist I have found, who concentrates on "body images" as reflections of the extent to which Africans may internalize the self-denigration of the white color complex.[26] Although Steve Biko and the black consciousness literature have made many perceptive comments about the desperate need for blacks to stop thinking of themselves as nonwhites, South Africa has yet to produce a Frantz Fanon.[27] What is strikingly unavailable is any South African counterpart to Robert Coles's *Children of Crisis,* a psychoanalytic work based on the ability of a white doctor to make himself the trusted confidant of normal people who are oppressed and intimidated because they "happen to be black."

According to Peter Lambley, whose recent *Psychology of Apartheid* has much material on the psychology of whites, has some account of the consequences of ambivalence among Coloured patients in Cape Town, but presents no systematically documented analysis of the psychology of Africans, there is a conspiracy of silence. There is certainly silence! African mental patients, he writes, are tested inadequately, and they are commonly diagnosed as having illnesses that by definition are incurable rather than conditions that can be treated. Drugs or electric shock treatment are overwhelmingly preferred to psychotherapy. Since this seems to be true of state mental hospitals in America and elsewhere, the charge may well be valid. Lambley's further contention that mental hospitals are systematically employed by the security police to "stabilize" the personalities of blacks who are politically dangerous is probably true as well – that too is not unheard of in Europe and America – though the extent is obviously impossible to verify.[28]

Part of the reason for the conspiracy of silence lies in the nature and preoccupations of South African medicine and social science over the past half-century. Doctors who treat Africans have concentrated on malnutrition and physical disease. Most anthropologists have been social rather than cultural specialists. They have written many excellent studies of Africans in both rural and urban areas, but they have concentrated on social mobility, family patterns, and elite formation rather than on psychology. Until recently, at least, most psychologists probably assumed that so-called primitive peoples develop few if any mental illnesses that can be diagnosed in clinical psychiatric terms. Indeed, the incidence and nature of madness across social classes, cultures, and time remain open and controversial questions.[29] The conclusion to be drawn from M. J. Field's remarkably well-documented study of patients at shrines in rural Ghana, however, is that all peoples have more or less the same kinds of mental disorders, which they interpret and treat very differently.[30] The occurrence of these disorders undoubtedly increases under stress, such as the influenza epidemic of 1918 or later collapses of the cocoa market in Ghana, or the overcrowding of reserves and urban apartheid in South Africa.

A book such as Field's, based on the patients of so-called witchdoctors in rural South Africa, would be an extremely important addition to an already distinguished anthropological literature. An urban study would have to take into account the fact that many Africans use both traditional and Western medicine. Yet the fact that Africans in white areas do have high rates of mental disorders is not in dispute. They are treated by the thousands in state hospitals. White psychiatrists – a few years ago, at least, there was no qualified African psychiatrist in practice – treat African patients. But they do not write about them.

A second and related group of questions touches a turbulent and apparently endless ocean of complexity, which such students as E. P. Thompson, Eugene Genovese, and Barrington Moore have begun to chart: the extremely flexible and amazingly broad limits of human tolerance to pain and suffering.[31] Segregated peoples were and are brutally oppressed and victimized. Why then have they not always been in revolt? Why, over long periods, did they remain largely quiescent? The obvious answer – that the white man's power was too strong – is both true and insufficient. For even in the most unfavorable circumstances, there was always some resistance. Moreover, in both South Africa and the American South, this resistance was cumulatively effective. Although whites continued to hold the balance of political and military power, the point was reached – in the South by the 1930s, in South Africa by the 1950s – when they lost their moral hegemony, their arrogant assumption that their will would necessarily be deferred to.

In a celebrated gaffe during his tour of America in 1930, General Smuts declared that the black man's patience was one of the world's marvels, second only to the ass's. Observers much more sympathetic than he frequently remarked on the race's ability to turn the other cheek. There was, however, nothing unique about their behavior. During the twentieth century it has become increasingly clear that people can and do submit to just about anything.[32] Sometimes they do – sometimes they don't. But how in specific circumstances are boundaries drawn between what must be endured and what, despite the cost, must be resisted? Why is intolerable injustice in one situation interpreted in another as "hard times" that are inevitable, bearable, and therefore acceptable? Or, as Richard Wright put it: "Injustice which lasts for three long centuries and which exists among millions of people over thousands of square miles of territory, is injustice no longer; it is an accomplished fact of life. Men adjust themselves."[33] Why men and women do not revolt is at least as complicated as why they do.

To pose such problems about the long hegemony of white supremacy in its several phases does not mean that I expect to resolve them satisfactorily. To do so would require a totally different book, which I am neither qualified nor equipped to write. Moreover, particularly on the South African side, much of the essential psychological evidence does not yet exist. Such complex and controversial questions do, however, provide a useful perspective from which to think about the ways black and brown peoples in two segregated societies have reacted to the world white power made.

THE QUESTION OF COMPARABILITY

First we must face again a question that has recurred throughout this book. Are the situations in South Africa and the American South really comparable? The differences between them are considerable. The African, Coloured, and Asian (mostly Indian) peoples were and are a large majority of South Africa's population, now more than seventy-five percent. By 1900 blacks were about one-third of the American South's population and less than one-fifth of the nation's. By that date Africans had only recently been conquered or disarmed. Although millions of them lived and worked in white areas, the majority lived in tribal reserves that were truly separated from whites. Politically and linguistically Africans were divided from each other, and they were separated culturally and racially from Indians and Coloureds as well as from whites. American blacks were extremely homogeneous and, despite important links with their African past, they were not culturally autonomous. Their distinctiveness was mainly the result of their long experience of oppression in America. Although miscegenation declined as Afro-Americans became better able to protect their women, most blacks had some "white blood." In America mulattoes were Negroes; in South Africa they were Coloured.[34]

Important political and economic differences affected particular strategies of accommodation and resistance. Although debt and crop-lien laws, sheriffs, and white mobs often blocked their ways, Afro-Americans could leave – if not for Africa, then for the North and West. In large and growing numbers, which accelerated during and after both world wars, they did so. Outside the South blacks could hope for a higher standard of living and the full enjoyment of their rights as citizens. In the North, however, they experienced racism in many forms: riots, informal discrimination in schools, jobs, housing, mistreatment by police and other public authorities. In the North they were, and are, more physically separated from whites than they had been in the South. Through migration, however, blacks could escape the totalitarian legal structure of segregation. Moving north they enlarged the scale of the Negro Question. By 1942, when draft boards once more invited them to fight and die in segregated units for the country that had persistently denied their humanity, most of the world's largest urban concentrations of black people (apart from São Paulo, Brazil) were in New York, Chicago, Philadelphia, and Washington. The problem was no longer peculiarly the South's.

Africans could also migrate, either from the reserves or from the white farms that had often been their traditional homes. But their only destination was the white areas of their own country. They could not escape the tightening web of segregation. Instead of assisting emigration, as they did in the American South, economic forces effectively blocked it. As whites never ceased to inform them, Africans in South Africa enjoyed the highest living standard of any black people on the continent. Capitalism was a magnet with immense powers of attraction, drawing workers south by hundreds of thousands. To the north, economies were underdeveloped and stagnant. Emigration overseas was therefore the only possible escape route. And it was open only to a few.

Strategies of reaction to segregation were also affected by the nature of the two constitutional systems. In the American federal model, powers were separated horizontally among the executive, legislative, and judicial branches of government as well as vertically between national and state units. The South African system was parliamentary and unitary, with the provincial authorities expressly subordinated to the central government and with power effectively concentrated in the majority party of the

House of Assembly. Ultimately the contrast between the two systems became significant. A federal model would have made the totalitarian uniformity of apartheid somewhat more difficult to achieve.[35] In the early twentieth century, however, both systems were working very effectively against blacks.

In the American South, state governments, as they conspired in friendly competition with each other to build the walls of segregation still higher and thicker, were having things very much their own way. The checks that had once been used against them during Reconstruction remained in abeyance. Again and again moderates urged caution. This straw, they warned, might just prove to be the last. Again and again the Supreme Court proved them wrong. Could blacks be sure that any discrimination would be declared illegal? As long as the Fourteenth and Fifteenth Amendments remained on the books, however, the constitutional situation remained ambiguous. Based on that ambiguity the NAACP developed a strategy of challenging segregation in the courts, case by case.

In the United States, Gunnar Myrdal contended during World War II, the democratic philosophy on which the nation had been founded and built contained an irresistible and irreversible momentum. Ultimately America would be driven to resolve the Negro Question by extending full freedom and equality.[36] There was some truth in Myrdal's statement. Yet the value system of white Americans had managed for the better part of a century and a half to contain the contradiction between the facts of racial oppression and the philosophy of the Declaration of Independence. The "American dilemma," whose external manifestations Myrdal examined so exhaustively, was not centered in the hearts and minds of white people, nor even in their political rhetoric. Most of them would probably have been quite content to see de jure segregation in the South and de facto segregation in the North continue more or less indefinitely. Myrdal was too optimistic. The American democratic ethos did not create the Negro Question. Through their own struggle against tremendous odds, black people did.

Within the American political system, however, a profound constitutional ambiguity did exist, and Afro-Americans exploited it. Even the Black Muslim Malcolm X, who distinguished between the South African wolf and the more cunning but equally vicious American fox, recognized its usefulness. "Whenever you're going after something that belongs to you," he explained to youthful Southern blacks in 1965, shortly before his own assassination, "anyone who's depriving you of the right to have it is a criminal. Understand that." Whatever his audience might think of the "cracker politicians" in Washington, in which he included the administration of Lyndon Johnson of Texas, which later that year would pass the Civil Rights Act, the law and therefore an important moral initiative belonged to the insurgents. The fact was that the Supreme Court had declared segregation unconstitutional: "Which means a segregationist is a criminal. You can't label him as anything other than that. And when you demonstrate against segregation, the law is on your side. The Supreme Court is on your side."[37]

Black and brown peoples in South Africa also tried to exploit constitutional ambiguity, most of which emerged out of their country's membership in the British Commonwealth. Britain had neither the inclination nor the power to enforce the entrenched clauses of the South African constitution, embodied in the South Africa Act of 1909. Certain kinds of class legislation, however, would be clearly illegal unless the act were amended, which required a two-thirds majority of both houses in joint sitting. Until 1936 a few Africans voted on the common rolls of the Cape. The Senate, with its four Europeans representing African interests, could delay measures. Thus General Hertzog's legislation respecting land and the franchise, first proposed in 1925, was blocked until the Hertzog–Smuts coalition finally passed it in 1936. In individual cases, most notably the famous Treason Trials of the 1950s, the courts sometimes protected the rights of those engaged in extraparliamentary opposition, though not before the long and expensive process of imprisonment and litigation had already performed its disruptive function. But such interventions were rare. As the security police candidly explained at the inquest into the death in custody of Steve Biko in 1977, they do not "work under statutory authority."[38] South Africa's political system contained some ambiguities, but no internal contradiction comparable to the American dilemma. The power of the state was neither divided nor irresolute.

Despite such substantial differences, these two cases of reaction to evolving white supremacy are surely comparable. Set against attempts to arrive at a common anatomy of revolution or a typology of internal war, for instance, the comparative study of race relations in South Africa and the American South appears remarkably tidy.[39] The time frame is common. Both countries had long histories of racial oppression and antagonism, and they consolidated segregation little more than a decade apart. Subsequently the two systems evolved within a common context of world politics: the two world wars, the Depression of the 1930s, and the revolt against colonialism in Asia, the Middle East, and Africa. Moreover, the problems that confront liberation movements that must build from below, that must operate in societies whose governments do not obligingly collapse, as Russia's did in 1917, but instead remain strong and viable, do have much in common. Again, as was the case with connections between the white creators of segregation, the comparison between these two cases of reaction to oppression is more than an interesting academic exercise. On both sides of the Atlantic important black and brown actors perceived relationships between the two movements and forged important historical linkages.

Like other victims of organized and for the time being irresistible oppression, Afro-Americans and Africans evolved a variety of mechanisms – personal, social, political, cultural – that enabled most of them to survive by absorbing relentless physical intimidation and psychological pressure. Through these mechanisms they submitted and collaborated. Both peoples also developed mechanisms of resistance. There were as many mechanisms on one side as on the other. Both collaboration and resistance ran through black society, from the individual personality to the family, to community organizations such as church, school, fraternal association, or tribal council, to overtly political movements and strategies. "Sambo was real," writes Barrington Moore about the slave personality controversy, "and so was the slave who slit the master's throat in the night. They might be the same person. Which was mask and which was real?"[40] Between modes of resistance and modes of collaboration the relationships were often subtly interwoven. Sometimes mechanisms were separate and distinct. More often they worked in both directions, closely connected or even the same.

Collaboration and resistance were not so much contradictory

approaches as they were two poles of an extremely broad spectrum of possible responses to white power.[41] Total resistance meant outlawry, imprisonment, exile, or death. As an emotional reflex against attack or pressure that had become unbearable, individual and group violence occurred frequently. In the lives of many individuals there came a point, as the character Josh exclaims in Charles Chesnutt's novel based on the Wilmington, North Carolina, insurrection of 1898, when a man or a women would "ruther be a dead nigger dan a live dog!"[42] Less frequent was conscious, symbolic martyrdom: "Strike a blow and die," as the white abolitionist John Brown said at Harper's Ferry, and as John Chilembwe, the American-educated leader of an African rising, is supposed to have repeated in the British Central African colony of Nyasaland in 1915.[43] But as Lenin argued in his pamphlet *What Is to Be Done?* total resistance against a well-organized state can be sustained only by a few, who as professional revolutionaries do nothing else, and even then only with great difficulty.

Yet neither the American South nor even South Africa ever demanded total passivity. Neither regime ever possessed the means to enforce it completely. Both systems of segregation presumed and relied upon some acceptance and collaboration. And collaborators were always available. But the coin of accommodation had a reverse side. As long as courageous individuals were present – and again, they always were – some means of opposition short of deliberate or automatic suicide was possible. The problem was to discover the means.

Most individuals, as well as most institutions, movements, and strategies, therefore fell between the poles of collaboration and resistance, combining elements of both in complex, shifting ways. Through collaboration, or so its advocates from Booker T. Washington to Chief Buthelezi of KwaZulu (a homeland) have hoped, positions of power might be consolidated. On the other hand, by helping through trial and error to define the boundaries of practical opposition, as well as by providing the justification for strengthening the state coercive machinery, resistance itself might be functional, feeding back into the system and legitimizing it. Those who tried to work with, or against, segregation inhabited a world that was as confusing as it was dangerous.

GANDHI IN SOUTH AFRICA

The complex interaction between collaboration and resistance in an insurgent movement that must operate within a strong state is well illustrated by one of the most famous strategies of them all, that of South Africa's Indian community under the leadership of Mohandas K. Gandhi.[44] As Gandhi himself explains in his autobiography, from 1893 until his return to India two decades later, South Africa was the arena where the lawyer-saint faced and eventually overcame an acute personal identity crisis that came to include the destiny of his people and country. Segregation was a laboratory where he developed and refined the philosophy and tactics of nonviolent resistance. Gandhi called this form of insurgence Satyagraha. For this was not, he insisted, mere passive resistance forced for want of an alternative upon the defenseless weak. It was soul force, chosen deliberately by the morally strong.

Like the man himself – and when Gandhi died Albert Einstein would declare that future generations would marvel that such a mortal as this had once walked upon the earth – Satyagraha combined tradition and modernity in a baffling amalgam of ancient Hindu thought, Theosophy, and the pacifism of Tolstoy. But Satyagraha was made in South Africa. Day by day, in Natal and then in the Transvaal, where he confronted General Smuts, another English-trained lawyer with a philosophic bent, Gandhi evolved and modified the strategy. After 1915 he would graft it onto the thicker trunk of Indian nationalism. In British India, where its founder would face problems unknown and unimagined in the South African years, Satyagraha would continue to grow and change. In South Africa itself it would remain the principal approach of the Indian Congress movement, which Gandhi had founded. It would influence the important passive resistance campaign of the African National Congress in 1952. Across the Atlantic it would become a factor in the thought and action of Martin Luther King, Jr.

Satyagraha was a classic combination of collaboration and resistance. The precise mixture of the ingredients varied – to some extent according to the phase of Gandhi's own evolution, to some extent according to the circumstances. As long as the British imperial factor remained in control in southern Africa, Gandhi sought with some success to ally himself with it. Never, he later declared, had the Crown possessed a more loyal subject than himself. He sent petitions and led deputations to London. Despite some sympathy with the Boers, he organized an ambulance corps to aid British troops during the South African war. During 1906–8, in what observers as various as Winston Churchill and General Smuts agreed was an unnecessarily ruthless suppression of a reluctant rebellion by Africans, Gandhi even offered his services to the government of Natal. Collaboration worked! British humanitarians such as the Aborigines Protection Society, at times the British government, and most important the government of India, who found that support for Indian claims in South or East Africa was a cheap and painless way to mollify nationalist opinion in India, were all drawn into the struggle.

After 1907, when the Transvaal received responsible government, and especially after 1910, when the Union became an autonomous state, the politics of collaboration grew a good deal trickier. When the Transvaal enacted severe restrictions (including fingerprinting) against Indian immigration, Gandhi led a small movement – after all, fewer than 10,000 Indians lived there – in a campaign of militant resistance. The participants pledged "not to submit" and "to suffer all the penalties attaching to such nonsubmission."[45] Those two phrases, "not to submit" and "to suffer," were the keys to Satyagraha.

Whether Gandhi was primarily reformer or revolutionary remains a central problem in the historiography of Indian nationalism. As he explained at one point, a dynamic law of progression was axiomatic to Satyagraha. One campaign must always lead to the next. And since "the minimum is also the maximum, and as it is the irreducible minimum, there is no question of retreat, and the only movement possible is an advance."[46] Gandhi's long-term goals – in South Africa the attainment of "partnership with the white people of the country"; in India full freedom, or *swaraj* – were therefore open ended. Opponents charged him with duplicity and cunning. His campaigns in India drew thousands of followers, growing to a size that could not possibly remain disciplined, and thus contained explosive potential for violence. Was he not responsible for the consequences? In another conundrum Gandhi claimed for Indians the right to bear arms; otherwise the deliberate choice to renounce them would be meaningless. At times, as in the Non-Cooperation campaign of 1920–1 and again in the Quit India resolution of 1942, he virtually closed the door on collaboration.

More often the door remained ajar. For long periods during the 1920s and 1930s Gandhi carried on protracted roundtable discussions with the British. As far as the government of India was concerned, the object of these talks was unambiguous. It was delay for the purpose of delay. As the nationalist movement grew frustrated and fragmented at the lack of movement, some of his followers wondered whether delay might not be his object too. Apparently he was more concerned with the moral sanctity of the search for truth than with the pragmatic goal of political independence.

In India, where a mass following set a pace he had to match because, as Gandhi once said with humorous self-mockery, he was their leader, the dynamic revolutionary side of Satyagraha outweighed if it did not entirely erase the tendency toward collaboration. In South Africa, where the small numbers of Indians was a disadvantage in terms of weight but an advantage for maintaining cohesive discipline over the course of a long campaign, the balance tipped the other way. Gandhi therefore kept his demands limited and tried to settle conflicts quickly. He did not seek victory. And he did not achieve it. The celebrated, but in the long run unfulfilled, compromise of 1914 with Smuts on the immigration issue was a small return for two decades of intense organization and agitation.

Compared with Africans Gandhi enjoyed important short-term advantages. He could draw on the support of the government of India, an overseas state with a vested interest in his campaign. Africans, as they learned very painfully, could not. He could also restrict the level of his demands. Like Gandhi after his return to India, the leaders of a movement striving to represent a majority must work toward complete victory to maintain legitimacy. Thus, although Gandhi dismissed the argument that Satyagraha was imposed on the weak by the logic of the situation, there was a good deal of truth to this. For the very reason that other options were obviously available to them, including violent revolt, Africans could not successfully employ his tactics. It is not that

Satyagraha was too sophisticated for primitive or semicivilized Africans. It is far too subtle for most of us. The fact is that Indians did not threaten the supremacy, let alone the survival, of the white man's country. Africans did, and do.

AFRO-AMERICAN STRATEGIES

In the American South after 1890, and more gradually in South Africa after the Boer War, Afro-Americans and Africans faced situations that they perceived to be rapidly deteriorating. The forces of white supremacy that were arrayed against them were becoming more concentrated, better organized, and more powerful. They themselves were being weakened and disarmed. Their allies were falling away. For black and brown peoples who experienced the consolidation of segregation, it was a time of monumental problems and severely narrowing options.

The previous experiences of these peoples had not been easy. In the American South the struggle for freedom had been terrible and violent, waged against fearful economic and political odds. Southern mythology notwithstanding, blacks had never dominated politics, even during Reconstruction. In that period, however, Northern troops and the Freedmen's Bureau had sometimes intervened on their side. Frequently becoming chummy with planters or railway magnates, they had sometimes enforced inequitable contracts or had served informally as labor recruiters. At least during Reconstruction blacks had not had to face Southern whites alone. Some checks against state oppression had operated. Even after the South achieved home rule in the 1870s the pattern of comparatively open participation by blacks and poor whites often continued. All parties sought black support. The significance of the franchise was therefore more than symbolic. Wherever they could possibly do so, blacks used the weapon effectively. That was why it had to be eliminated.

Disfranchisement, along with the impressive panoply of Jim Crow laws, was not a gradual process. Taking place over little more than a decade in the South as a whole, and still more rapidly in some states, it was breathtakingly swift. Times had been bad before. Now they were worse.

What, in the face of this deep and protracted crisis, were Afro-

Americans to do? Though it would be extraordinarily difficult to achieve, the long-term objective was obvious. It must be the building of a mass movement, composed of politically conscious and unintimidated members, acting under effective and disciplined leadership, possessing economic and political weight. The American political system was and remains a contest among power blocs, some of which are economic and others ethnic, whose demands are heard to the extent that they are backed by muscle. Both the means and the goal of the struggle were therefore clear. They revolved around the concept, broadly defined, of black power.

The question was how best to pursue that general and largely agreed-upon objective. What should the priorities be? Should the apex of the movement, what W. E. B. Du Bois called the talented tenth, be emphasized? Or the base? Should blacks concentrate on political goals, on the presumption that economic gains would follow? Or the reverse? Ought they to come forward during wartime, for instance, on the theory that loyal sacrifice would be rewarded? Or presuming that only in a country whose social structure was radically altered would blacks be able to achieve equality, should they try to polarize the situation? Should they try to integrate themselves into the cultural mainstream of American society? Or should they reject white America, building instead a distinctive, separate, identifiably African culture of their own? There has been remarkably little disagreement about the long-range goal of black power, again broadly defined. But the debate among Afro-Americans about how best to achieve that end, especially in the short run, has been vigorous, heated, and protracted.

Three main approaches characterize the thought and actions of Afro-Americans in the crisis of the late nineteenth and early twentieth centuries: accommodation, associated with Booker T. Washington; militant confrontation within the American political system, associated with W. E. B. Du Bois; and separatism, associated with Marcus Garvey.[47] These strategies were all implicit in the situation. All of them had begun much earlier, with ample precedents before as well as after Emancipation. All of them continue to compete and interact in the far-from-concluded struggle for freedom and equality. None of them was simple or organically consistent. All were eclectic and ambiguous. All were, or could be, either the tactics of collaboration or resistance or, even more typically, of both simultaneously. None of them worked. All of them did.

The literature of Afro-American history is full of such paradoxes. The standard biography and the admirably edited correspondence of Booker T. Washington, for instance, make the point repeatedly.[48] There is no doubt about it: Washington, very consciously and deliberately, made himself a collaborator of the "right type," played a role largely defined by whites, and raised accommodation to a high art. He told white audiences what they wished to hear, including racial jokes, and he repeatedly insisted against all available evidence that the prejudices of Southern whites were abating. Seeking an alliance with planter patricians, he urged his race to remain in agriculture. His Jeffersonian economic views, stressing the self-sufficiency of blacks in rural areas and small towns, were curiously out of date in this the monopoly stage of American capitalism. His often-repeated remark that the dollar knows no color line was singularly ill-founded.

Washington had effective control over several important black newspapers, which he used to try to silence black critics. Especially during the presidency of Theodore Roosevelt, who consulted him on patronage, including white appointments, the Tuskegee machine had considerable power. In the main Washington employed it to further his own interests and those of his school. As Du Bois charged, his advocacy of industrial education – and, as it turned out, there would be precious little of that, too – was a blind behind which whites could systematically undermine all black education. Washington counseled submission, patience, and the acceptance of social segregation, as though the boundaries between what was social and what was not could be clearly and fairly drawn. After all, the phrase that best sums up the life and program of Booker T. Washington is "separate development."

Yet Washington led a complex double life. Sometimes openly, more often secretly, he opposed the segregationist orthodoxy to which he contributed. He joined and gave financial support to test cases against Jim Crow laws. Though he usually ignored it, he sometimes denounced lynching. He tried to influence legislators and delegates at disfranchisement conventions, urging qualifications based on property and education but not on race. At considerable risk to himself and his school he harbored a fugitive from a lynch mob. Would a more forthright, more outspoken strategy have accomplished more in Alabama? It seems likely that it would have achieved less.

The fact is that although they often paid lip service to Washington's ideas about separate development, most Southern white people were not in favor of that approach. Washington was not terribly popular with them. As one delegate to the Alabama disfranchisement convention put it with customary delicacy, Tuskegee, like any institution where blacks were being educated, was a nest of snakes. Any black man with Washington's power, any institution not directly and thoroughly under the control of whites, was a potential threat to white supremacy. For the same reason Marcus Garvey, numerous African students, and more recently Stokely Carmichael all saw in the blackness of Tuskegee both a symbol and a force.[49] Separate development could point in very contradictory directions.

The second figure in the trilogy, W. E. B. Du Bois, was even more complex. During his long, distinguished, and unique career his genius covered virtually the whole spectrum of the Afro-American and worldwide struggle against what, in a famous essay of 1903, he called the twentieth century's most pressing problem: that of the color line.[50] His tactics ranged from the calm intellectual persuasion of his early books and essays to the bombastic journalism of The Crisis; from deliberate collaboration during World War I to continual, militant confrontation within the American constitutional and legal system, the main strategy of the NAACP; to extremist opposition in his last years as a member of the Communist Party and declared friend of the Soviet Union. For most of his life his goal was racial integration. But unlike Marcus Garvey, who advocated large-scale emigration, Du Bois went to live and die in Africa. A brilliant and tenacious organizer, he founded both the NAACP and the Pan African Congress.

Such a man cannot be neatly categorized. Moreover, although they represented very different backgrounds, styles, personalities, and sections of America, although the gulfs between them were intense and profound, the simple dichotomy that is some-times drawn between Du Bois the militant resister and Washing-ton the abject accommodationist is misleading. The two men and the two approaches they personified had much in common. Du Bois, too, as I shall argue in the concluding section of this chap-ter, found that separate development was one of the few realistic strategies left open to blacks under segregation. Imperfect and at least partially self-defeating, it could not be the only strategy. But it had to be pursued.

The third approach of the period was the back-to-Africa movement associated with Marcus Garvey and the Universal Negro Improvement Association, which exploded in New York and other Northern cities in the aftermath of World War I.[51] A movement from but not *in* the Caribbean, Garveyism stood the whites' color prejudice on its head. Black – not white, and not the light brown of the mulatto – was beautiful. The movement stressed political, emotional, and physical reunion with the fa-therland. The basic message was an old one, urged by Martin Delany among others and, as we saw in Chapter 2, by Bishop Henry M. Turner. But the force of Garvey's personal charisma combined with the extreme tension of postwar America to inject the old idea of black nationalism with explosive, contagious en-ergy. Neither Africa nor the diaspora in the New World had ever seen anything like it. By the late 1920s, discredited by financial scandal, its leader deported by the American government, Gar-veyism crumbled as an organized movement. But it reverberated outward, especially to the colonies of English-speaking Africa, and onward. Malcolm X's father, for instance, had been a Gar-veyite.

Even Garveyism, its opponents such as Du Bois charged, was collaborationist – in effect if not in intention. Why, critics asked, had such white racists as Thomas Jefferson and Abraham Lincoln looked upon African colonization schemes so warmly? "Back to Africa" might be thrilling, but it was practically impossible. The continent happened to be controlled by whites; poor, underde-veloped colonial economies were hardly equipped to take in large numbers of immigrants; it was unthinkable that the American government would finance the operation, let alone pay compen-sation for the property that would have to be abandoned; Afro-

Americans who went to Africa would face a formidable cultural gap; and so on. The Garveyites, Du Bois admitted, had shown how a mass movement could be built in an amazingly short time. But the struggle of blacks must be fought in their own country. Did not a strategy that was escapist and that could not work play into the hands of the opponents?[52]

The spectrum from cringing accommodation to militant resistance was extremely broad. At one pole, for instance, was the chancellor of the Georgia Normal College (for Negroes) at Albany, Joseph W. Holley. Reared in the same part of rural South Carolina as Benjamin Mays, where he too must have witnessed the Phoenix riot and other atrocities, Holley also went north for his education. There the similarity ended. Mr. Holley based his career on the conviction that "we colored people can get what we want, if it is within reason, from a white man if we approach him in the right way." The right way, his father had taught him, was "never to go to a white man for a favor just before a meal and never go to his front door. Wait until the meal is over and he has had time to get his pipe or cigar, and then go to the kitchen." Convinced that, in their hearts, Southern whites were black people's best friends, Holley singled out for specific praise such well-known benefactors of his race as Ben Tillman of South Carolina and Eugene Talmadge of Georgia. In 1935, in a speech at Statesboro, Georgia, before a white audience, Holley argued that

> the educational requirements of the people who are only a few hundred years out of the jungle are not the same as those of people who have had thousands of years of civilization back of them. Their future prospects are not the same . . . It is not fair for the State to force my boy to fit himself for service in a field where the door is closed. Train my boy in a field where there is a prospect of his getting work.[53]

Published in 1946, Mr. Holley's autobiography argues against federal antilynching legislation, the Fair Employment Practices Commission, anti-poll tax legislation, and the forced mixing of the races in education. It would be hard to argue that his career contained even the slightest hint of resistance. Yet his autobiography records that when he came south to teach before World

War I, he was inspired not only by Booker T. Washington, whom he out-Bookered with a vengeance, but by the author of *Souls of Black Folk,* W. E. B. Du Bois.

At the other pole, it would be hard to discover collaboration in A. Philip Randolph's Union of Railway Porters or the Southern Tenant Farmers Union of the late 1930s. Yet the sharecropper union's platform can be quoted word for word from the speeches of Booker T. Washington and his disciples. William J. Edwards, for instance, who records his arrival at Tuskegee as a cripple from the Alabama black belt who did not know how to use a toothbrush, went home to become principal of Snow Hill Institute. Among his works was the Black Belt Improvement Society, a friendly society, which worked for temperance and against gambling and sought "to eliminate the credit system from our social fabric; to stimulate in all members the desire to raise, as far as possible, all their food supplies at home, and pay cash for whatever may be purchased at the stores." Where supplies could not be raised at home, the society tried "to bring about a system of co-operation," thus attacking the basis of the furnishing merchant's power.[54]

The three main strands of accommodationism, confrontation, and separatism that pervaded Afro-American thought and action were not so much distinct schools as they were philosophies in a state of continual tension, interaction, and adaptation. The variations and combinations were virtually endless. By no means did they exhaust the strategies and tactics that were employed in their struggle for survival by a resourceful people. Using a broad model, such as that developed by Thomas Hodgkin in his classic study of African nationalism, any organized activity of an oppressed or intimidated people is or may become a facet of the struggle.[55] That would include all sorts of voluntary associations, such as churches, lodges, secret societies, and neighborhood groups, or cooperatives and cultural movements, such as jazz and the Harlem renaissance. All of these were support mechanisms. Most of them were eclectic and ambiguous, looking toward collaboration or resistance or both.

The black-town movement, to take a case on which a great deal of research remains to be done, was a widespread phenomenon involving thousands of people.[56] Some towns, such as

Mound Bayou, Mississippi, are comparatively well known. Others, unincorporated as well as incorporated, were established mainly in the 1870s and 1880s and can be found throughout the black-belt and Piedmont regions of the South. The general idea took something from all three main currents of Afro-American thought: separatism, confrontation, and accommodation. Such settlements, separate but not segregated, could be mechanisms of support for either collaboration or resistance. The town fathers might – indeed must – arrive at informal working agreements with sheriffs and other white authorities, gaining a measure of autonomy in return for a share of responsibility in enforcing the white man's law. How – and one searches the literature in vain for an answer – did such informal understandings work? The black town was also a power base, where residents might mass their shotguns to repel lynch mobs. Children might grow up a bit more securely; their parents might postpone the awful moment of full recognition of what it meant to live under white supremacy. The black town was a means of survival and struggle in a cruel and hostile land.

AFRICAN RESPONSES TO SEGREGATION

For Africans the late nineteenth century had been an era of crushing military defeat. For most of them the moving frontier had been a recent experience. Even in the eastern Cape, where the Xhosa fought their last Kaffir war in the 1870s, the test of strength against Boer or Briton went back little more than a century. Until the technological gap widened so enormously after about 1860, Africans had fought on comparatively even terms, their numbers nearly compensating for the whites' superior fire power. Africans continued to fight bravely, their most notable victory coming in 1879, when the Zulu wiped out a British regiment at Isandhlwana, but they lost the wars. To the victors went the spoils. Vast tracts of territory, much of which had been used from time to time by Africans and their herds for centuries, were taken over by whites. The grossly inequitable division under the Natives Land Act of 1913 would reflect not the boundaries of the traditional homelands, nor even the effects of the forced migration of the Mfecane that accompanied the consolidation of the Zulu kingdom in the 1820s and 1830s, but the status quo that had been achieved by the military campaigns of the late nineteenth century.[57]

Pacification was neither sudden nor complete. Still to come was the tax revolt of 1906–8 by the Zulu and other Africans in Natal. By the 1890s, however, the center of the white man's frontier in southern Africa had passed on to the north, to the land its conquerors called Rhodesia. Within South Africa itself the lines were stabilizing. The era when Africans could realistically hope to defend themselves through their traditional institutions, the phase of primary resistance, was over. Secondary resistance, which is undertaken by a people who are conquered and at least partially incorporated into an economic and political structure controlled by the victors, would require all the creative inventiveness of which a brave people were capable. New forms of organization transcending tribal divisions, new leadership, and new tactics would be needed.

White supremacy was an accomplished and, for the time being, an irreversible fact. From the perspective of the small but growing minority of Westernized Africans, however – that is, of the very people who would have to lead the struggle in its modern phase – the results of white contact had been mixed. To the educated elite, products of mission schools and in some cases of overseas universities, the future looked hopeful. The world's culture and the keys to the whites' mastery over nature had become accessible. So had Christianity. Within established missions, as well as within separatist churches under their own control, this Westernized elite was transforming the white people's faith into an African religion. In the Cape, where a few of them could vote, they were organized into an articulate party under the leadership of Dr. Tengo Jabavu.

By 1900 a Westernized elite, a black bourgeoisie, one of the essential preconditions of modern politics and of African nationalism, was on the make.[58] But its members were not alone. As we have seen, large numbers of tribesmen, many of whom were associated with Christian missions, were taking advantage of expanding market opportunities. They were peasants. Already they were competing effectively with white agriculture. Most African workers on the railroads, on the docks, and in the mines were temporary migrants who soon returned to the homelands. But some of them were not. Although they were still comparatively rare, Africans living permanently in town were increasing. In short, both components, the elite and the masses, to which its students have traced the origins of nationalism in West Africa, for example, were developing rapidly. Political consciousness and secondary resistance in South Africa would be neither slow nor backward. But the struggle, which had to be waged in a colony of white settlement rather than in an exploitation colony under the control of a cosmopolitan power represented on the spot by a handful of Europeans, would be immeasurably more difficult.

Closely paralleling developments in West Africa in the first decade of the twentieth century, educated Africans favored not resistance but collaboration as loyal subjects of the Crown.[59] The Empire, to be sure, had not done much for them lately. But the color-blind franchise, imposed on the Cape Colony half a century ago by the Colonial Office, embodied an ideal of racial inclusiveness and tolerance. In the Aborigines Protection Society, in British and local missionary societies, among some members of Parliament, Africans had strong supporters. In a sense, because so many of the English-speaking whites who waved the Union Jack so jingoistically in fact opposed a strong role for London in the domestic politics of southern Africa – that, for example, was the view of Cecil Rhodes – educated Africans were the only true imperialists.

The African elite viewed the fact of conquest with ambivalence. No black man could completely disregard the sobering implications of white supremacy. Yet the tribal authorities who had been humbled were also their enemies, whom they saw as conservative obstacles in the way of progress. Under British protection, educated Africans looked forward to the material improvement and growing participation of their people in an enlightened, increasingly tolerant Christian country. The famous formula of Rhodes, "equal rights for all civilized men" – he had substituted "civilized" for "white" in order to appease Coloured voters in the Cape – was a stern test of African ability. They were ready and anxious to meet it.

After the Boer War (1899–1902) alliances shifted with incredible rapidity. Africans had been encouraged to view the conflict as a direct clash between two fundamentally opposing traditions: that of the Afrikaners, which was narrow, provincial, intolerant, and stubbornly exclusive, and that of the British, which was cosmopolitan, tolerant, and inclusive. Peace, however, did not entrench "liberal" British values. Instead, beginning with the Treaty of Vereeniging, which pledged that an African franchise would not be a necessary condition for full self-government in the Afrikaner republics, it compromised them. Peace meant not increased protection and a widening role for loyal Africans but appeasement of the rebellious Afrikaners. This extraordinary turn of events was very similar, again, to the alliance Sir Frederick Lugard was forming at the time with conservative Muslim emirates in Northern Nigeria, after having conquered them with encouragement from educated Africans in the South.

Although the situation was confusing, educated Africans were not slow to perceive what was happening to them. As early as 1903, when the British colonial secretary Joseph Chamberlain visited the country, he was greeted by a statement from the South African Native Congress, which had been founded the year before. Charging that Afrikaners and the anti-African faction among the local English were in collusion, the document called on Britain to uphold the principle of that great statesman Cecil Rhodes: "equal rights for all civilized men." In measured, sophisticated language the Congress examined the labor question: the lack of tact, to say the least, in severely reducing wages while simultaneously demanding a huge increase in the supply of workers, the virtual absence of administrative control over the notoriously greedy magnates of the Rand. As they saw it the problem was universal: "The capitalist demands cheap labour. The labouring man has not, in this or any other country, had a satisfactory interpretation of the term." And it was just beginning. "It is not a race question," the statement concluded, but a much more basic contradiction: "The attempts to reconcile low wages with high living" would plague "the country long after the present generation has departed."[60]

After the Liberal victory in the British election of 1906 the pattern of appeasement accelerated. The Transvaal and the Orange Free State gained responsible government. The Closer Union movement grew apace. Unrepresented in the constitutional convention, which refused to extend the Cape franchise to the rest of the country, the South African Native Congress sent a deputation to London in 1909 to urge rejection of the Act of Union. Four years later another deputation arrived, this time to plead that the Crown's assent be withheld from the Natives Land Act, only to be told to seek redress from the duly constituted authorities of their own country. This latter deputation bore the credentials of a new organization, formed in 1912, with a distinguished career ahead of it: the African National Congress.[61]

Educated Africans have been criticized for pursuing a futile strategy based on British intervention during this crucial period, when white and particularly Afrikaner power remained comparatively weak. Instead, it is maintained, they should have concentrated on building their own movement on the basis of tangible economic issues possessing mass appeal. That, however, could only have been a long-term strategy. Meanwhile the futility of appealing to the Imperial conscience could not be certain until it had been tried. Until 1909, after all, Great Britain did have the power. Parliament had never ratified the Treaty of Vereeniging; the appeasement of Afrikaners had been carried out entirely by administrative order. The Act of Union could have been rejected. The Natives Land Act could have been declared class legislation that was in violation of the South Africa Act. Even after 1910 the precise extent of South Africa's constitutional autonomy remained somewhat ambiguous. General Hertzog, at least, thought so. Nor is it apparent what other short-term strategy was available. Violent confrontation failed disastrously in Natal from 1906 to 1908. So did the African economic boycott, by about 1907. Building and sustaining an effective mass movement in any African country would require decades of hard work.

Indeed, at a pace unmatched by any other African people, the African National Congress (ANC) did broaden and strengthen its base. Abstract issues such as the franchise and civil rights, symbolically significant but of direct interest only to the comparatively privileged few, were prominent in the ANC demands. So were issues with broader appeal, such as wages, pass laws, working conditions, and above all land. Nor was it all talk. In 1913, and again in 1919, demonstrators led by the ANC burned their passes. In 1920, according to police reports, outside agitators from the ANC were active in the well-organized but unsuccessful strike by African miners.[62]

Violent unrest was ubiquitous all over the world in these tense times after World War I, the Russian Revolution, and the influenza epidemic of 1918. In India there was General Dyer's massacre in the Punjab and Gandhi's Non-Cooperation campaign; in Turkey and Egypt, revolution; in every important British port, race riots; in Ireland, civil war; in the United States, the Red Scare, the Garvey movement, a race riot in Chicago, and a wave of lynchings across the South. The world seemed to be on the verge of explosion. In South Africa bloody clashes between police and Africans took place at Bloemfontein, Port Elizabeth, and elsewhere. Africans were massacred at Bulhoek and at Bondelswarts in South-West Africa. The growing insecurity and tension among white workers, which culminated in the Rand Revolution of 1922, was matched among Africans.

Some of this unrest was closely related to the thought and action of the African elite, but much of it was not. As was also the case in West Africa and America, the gulf between the black bourgeoisie and the rural and urban masses was considerable. Like ordinary West Africans, for instance, who mounted on their own initiative tax and wage strikes and, in the case of cocoa farmers in the Gold Coast in the 1930s, sophisticated boycotts of world markets, the African masses were often ahead of their leaders.

The Industrial and Commercial Union (ICU), which was founded in 1921 by the remarkable Nyasalander Clements Kadalie, was by far the most potent mass organization among Africans of any country until after World War II. At its height it boasted, no doubt a bit enthusiastically, a membership of a quarter of a million.[63] Like the Garvey movement in the United States, the ICU produced ambivalent and even hostile reactions among the elite. The potential of an effective mass movement was exciting. But was not an organization composed entirely of semiliterate clerks and illiterate workers dangerous and premature? Using it as an excuse, the government would no doubt crush them all. The ANC leaders tried to remain aloof and, when Kadalie invaded their annual meeting, fought off his challenge.[64] Like the Garvey movement, the ICU was weakened by financial mismanagement and by the deportation of its leaders. By the late 1920s it had collapsed. The ANC's fear of government retaliation had been justified.

Nevertheless an opportunity had been missed. By the 1930s, paralleling the chronology of the Afro-American struggle, a comparative lull had set in. Moderates and Communists competed, and the ANC was split into factions. During and after World War II, once more in step with American and West African developments, the movement would surge forward in a distinctly different phase: that of mature African nationalism.

Although they at least matched the energy and sophistication of movements elsewhere in Africa south of the Sahara, the growing consciousness, organization, and audacity of Africans could not keep pace with the even more rapid consolidation of white power. The South African regime's principal concern in the interwar period was not the gradually mounting challenge from Africans but the far more politically potent threat of Afrikaner nationalism. By 1925, as we have seen, General Hertzog's Nationalist Party in coalition with Labour had taken power. But Hertzog's achievements – including very substantial state subsidies for white agriculture, the Colour Bar Bill, and the Statute of Westminster of 1931, which recognized the dominions as fully sovereign states within the Commonwealth – were insufficient to stem the tide. During the Depression Hertzog went into coalition with Smuts; in 1939 Smuts took South Africa into war again. Although he resigned in protest, Hertzog was discredited in Afrikaner eyes; in any case he soon died. Under Dr. D. F. Malan a new generation of Purified Nationalists, many of whom had close ties with Nazi Germany, was emerging. During the war Afrikaner nationalism would surge forward toward its historic victory in the pivotal election of 1948.

It was this force, the rise of militant Afrikaner nationalism, that would make South Africa's postwar evolution fundamentally different from that of the American South. In the United States white supremacy remained strong in the South. But the South was not an autonomous country, and elsewhere it was weakening. In South Africa the balance of power was tilting toward radical reaction. In 1942, in a speech before the South African Institute of Race Relations, the wartime prime minister

General Smuts declared that segregation had failed and that it must be replaced by trusteeship, something that sounded vaguely like a more open, freer, and more tolerant society.[65] As Smuts himself made clear in 1946, when he brutally suppressed a general strike by African miners, that was not to be. After 1948 the Nationalist Party would further harden segregation into apartheid. The highest stage of white supremacy would be prolonged – apparently indefinitely.

The freedom fighters who most concerned the Smuts–Hertzog regime were white. Africans had long been a "problem." In the long run their threat to the white man's country was real enough. But the structure and ideology of segregation were being driven forward primarily by dynamics working from within white society. With its gaze continually fastened on its vulnerable right flank, the Smuts–Hertzog regime in the main acted, while Africans reacted.

As in America, three broad strategies were implicit in the situation: collaboration, confrontation, and separation. Africans tried them all. Encouraged both by black American missionaries and by the attendance of many African leaders at American Negro colleges, African approaches were influenced by Afro-American precedents. Disciples of Booker T. Washington, such as Rev. John L. Dube and Dr. D. D. T. Jabavu, son of Dr. Tengo Jabavu, favored cooperation, gentle persuasion, and economic uplift.[66] The ideas and organizations created by W. E. B. Du Bois, the NAACP, and the Pan African Congress influenced Pixley Seme as well as the Pan Africanist Congress of Robert Sobukwe and others in the 1950s. The Garveyites had a counterpart in the Ethiopian Church movement, whose slogan was also "Africa for the Africans." In none of these, of course, was the Afro-American influence a controlling one. The Ethiopian Church, for example, had begun as early as the 1890s. Instead, both movements contributed to the idea of closer association between Africa and its diaspora and drew moral support from it.

At least until the great watershed after World War II, the white segregationists kept the initiative. The merging African opposition remained largely defensive and reactive. In 1919, for example, the ANC's manifesto was a document of nineteen pages, demanding the repeal of specifically enumerated discriminatory acts. (It was already a rather long list.) By 1952 the manifesto had shrunk to three pages: The organization was dedicated to the freedom of colored peoples and to a true democracy based on one-man–one-vote. The document had much to say about the character of the nationalist regime and apartheid, that is, about the causes of discrimination. There was no longer a list.

The segregationists maintained the initiative because they had the power, not because their ideology was attractive to Africans. Very rarely, notably in 1914 when John Dube, president of the ANC, declared that he had no quarrel with the principle of separation as long as it was equitably applied, as it had not been in the recent Natives Land Act, Africans tried to use the segregationist language. The reply was predictable: Prime Minister Louis Botha was glad to learn of the acceptance of segregation in principle; one must expect, in the case of a law laying down fundamental principles, a certain amount of hardship; and that was that.[67] By the 1920s even the conservative Dr. Jabavu, known to whites as a moderate of the right type, was attacking the segregationist fallacy.[68] More successfully than white liberals, educated Africans generally avoided the trap of accepting a little segregation.

The primary strength of segregation as a system of control lay not so much in its ability to mystify or persuade its victims as in the awesome force and intimidation at its disposal. Chiefs were paid government officials. If they were not loyal they ceased to be chiefs, and others replaced them. Troublemakers at the mines or in urban locations were banned, returned to the reserves, or imprisoned. Gradually an African urban elite, with a substantial economic stake in the system of segregation, was developing. As in America, they would be placed in a profoundly ambivalent position.

The white regime – and it really made no difference whether it was being led by General Botha, General Smuts, or General Hertzog – responded to the potential of African resistance as though revolution were already an accomplished fact. Repeatedly, habitually, the government overreacted, treating nonviolence as violence. Africans tried to collaborate. The regime made it increasingly impossible. Not until the 1950s, after more than half a century of overwhelmingly peaceful protest, did the African National Congress at last conclude that the white man would have no change of heart.

The sophisticated machinery of the modern police state – the numerous informers, 180-day detentions, Riotous Assembly and Suppression of Communism Acts, the long list of African leaders who were imprisoned or who died in detention – did not exist before World War II. Neither did the organized resistance to white supremacy. Albeit with increasing difficulty, segregation still worked, deflecting, channeling, and absorbing opposition by holding out some promise of improvement. At least it seemed so. Although by later standards it was comparatively undeveloped, white reaction ran far ahead of African action. Already the strategy of the ANC, relying primarily on peaceful protest and persuasion, was becoming obsolete. The country had already reached the point where, as "Mary Russell" declared in a letter to the *Cape Times* in 1933, "any attempt to inform natives of the causes of their sufferings, any attempt to organise them into bodies by which they may bring about the removal of those causes will undoubtedly lead to banishment, prison or detention." It was already "impossible to achieve reform within the framework of South African constitutional and criminal law."[69] Educated Africans had not yet accepted the awful implications of this analysis. The day would come when they would.[70]

The ambiguities and complexities of the black struggle against segregation are well illustrated by the second of W. E. B. Du Bois's three autobiographies, *Dusk of Dawn,* written in the late 1930s.[71] There, in simple, coldly analytical prose he explained what segregation was like, what it meant to be treated as a member of an inferior caste. He briefly recounted his youth in western Massachusetts, his education at Fisk, Harvard, and Berlin, and his early years at Atlanta University. He had been imbued with the belief that the sheer weight of accumulating knowledge would crush the irrationality of ignorant prejudice. He had withdrawn into an ivory tower. His research had been prolific and worthwhile. Presumably he would have continued his career of scholarship, more or less indefinitely. Except that one day they lynched Sam Hose and, at a store on a neighboring street in Atlanta, put up his bones for sale.

The result, which would be repeated thousands of times in the lives of many, was catharsis. Although this man had already written a study of the *Negro in Philadelphia* that has still not been superseded, the Negro Problem forced itself upon him with sudden, dreadful clarity. To reverse Richard Wright's sequence, it was no longer a fact, it was injustice. And he must do something. Not to resist injustice, as he once advised a Southern white liberal correspondent, was to abdicate from the human race: "That is the reason we are on earth." [72]

Leaving Atlanta for New York, for the NAACP, and for *The Crisis,* Du Bois continued to publish powerful essays and novels. Not until the 1930s, when he resigned under pressure from the NAACP, would he publish another work of serious scholarship: his monumental and still neglected *Black Reconstruction.*

His first serious mistake, Du Bois reflected, had been to conceive that racism would fall before science. For racism, he had learned from Freud, grew out of primordial impulses located deep within the unconscious. From Marx he had learned that it became embedded within the fundamental institutions and structures of society. From his travels and his study of international history he had come increasingly to perceive close connections between racism in America and imperialism abroad. The dilemma of Afro-Americans was not unique. The colored races of the world were also the politically powerless and the economically exploited.

He had made his second serious mistake during World War I, when he had supposed that by supporting the national crusade, American blacks would gain acceptance. Instead, in return for their brave sacrifice in France, the North had greeted them with violent hostility and the South with the fury of a pogrom. Gradually the lynching statistics had declined. But economically black people had suffered catastrophically. The relative prosperity of the war years had been brief indeed. Blacks had never really been part of the boom of the twenties. In the thirties things had gone from bad to worse, with unemployment rates at fifty percent or higher. Politically, though Du Bois's own efforts and those of thousands of others had never ceased, the black movement remained weak and fragmented. How little, as he looked back on four decades of struggle, had been achieved.

None of the strategies that had been suggested so far had succeeded, his own included. His "talented tenth," the educated elite,
had been insufficiently concerned with the plight of the masses.
Booker T. Washington's advocacy of black capitalism had been
equally unrealistic. How could blacks hope to achieve economic
self-sufficiency as long as whites held all the cards? There had
been nothing intrinsically wrong with Washington's support for
industrial education – blacks needed more of that, not less – but
the race's need for educated leadership at all levels remained as
desperate as ever. Marcus Garvey's movement had demonstrated
how to build a mass following, something that Du Bois himself
had never accomplished. But the wholesale emigration of some
ten million poor people was totally impractical, even supposing
that they wished to go or that white America would let them.

During the twenties and thirties Du Bois had increasingly
adopted an independent Marxist perspective. Yet he reserved
some of his most scornful prose for the American Communist
Party. He was quite uninterested in achieving some sort of Hegelian theoretical perfection, he wrote. For Du Bois, Marxism
was a useful tool. But the system of discrimination that faced
Afro-Americans was a dialectic not of class but of race. The party's strategy seemed to be based on the assumption that blacks
would be useful cannon fodder in the attempt to undermine
American capitalism. For black people, black interests must come
first. The Scottsboro boys of Alabama would be free today, he
reflected bitterly, if the NAACP had been permitted to follow its
customary strategy of working closely with local white lawyers.

Violent revolution against the colossal American state must be
ruled out. The only result would be the slaughter of large numbers of blacks, running perhaps into the millions. Did that seem
incredible? Who even ten years before would have predicted the
fate of the prosperous and apparently well-assimilated Jews of
Germany?

No conceivable strategy, then, would *work*. The problems that
blacks faced in America, and that colored peoples confronted the
world over, would not be solved. The prospect was that segregation would remain in force for many years, perhaps a century
or even longer. On the eve of World War II, which was to do so
much to alter the balance of power in America and throughout

the world, this great scholar, with his unique perspective, had no inkling of what would happen in the next quarter of a century.

What was to be done? First, blacks must continue to agitate and protest against injustice, not so much because they would necessarily succeed but because they must do so to remain human. Second, they should be more intelligent about pursuing their own self-interest. Why should they rush to serve in the next national crusade? Finally, they should put as much of their resources as possible into building the economic self-sufficiency of their own community. This was a strategy not so much of resistance as of survival. They could not hope to bring American capitalism to its knees. But they could have an appreciable effect on their own lives. "Buying black" – hiring black artisans whenever possible, forming cooperatives, organizing the production of their own consumer goods – instead of having their labor support the prosperity of their white oppressors, might not solve the problem. But it was the best, indeed the only practical, strategy available. Segregated schools were an abomination. But they were all they had, and black parents must use them to educate their children.

This was not, Du Bois insisted, support for segregation. After all, however, there was a good deal of Booker T. Washington in it. On eminently practical grounds Du Bois had ruled out violent confrontation. By no means naïvely, but from a perspective made possible by a combination of knowledge and experience of racism that has probably never been matched, he had taken the only road the white man had apparently left open to him. Stripped to its essentials, it was a strategy of separate development, the "positive" face of segregation. Depending on the context, it might lead to accommodation or to black power. Even Du Bois, fully conscious as he was of the trap, could not avoid it. The ambiguity of his analysis was a testimony to the sophisticated, flexible system of the highest stage of white supremacy.

Notes

1. THE PROBLEM OF SEGREGATION

1 Maynard Swanson, "The Sanitation Syndrome: Bubonic Plague and Urban Native Policy in the Cape Colony, 1900–1909," *Journal of African History* 18 (1977):387–410. Only in its most recent supplement does the *OED* give the definition of segregation used in this book.

2 Raymond Williams, *Culture and Society, 1780–1950* (London: Chatto & Windus, 1958), and *Keywords: A Vocabulary of Culture and Society* (New York: Oxford University Press, 1976).

3 Marc Bloch, *Feudal Society,* 2 vols. (Chicago: Phoenix, 1964), 1:xiv.

4 See Winthrop D. Jordan, *White over Black: American Attitudes toward the Negro, 1550–1812* (Chapel Hill: University of North Carolina Press, 1968).

5 See Francis Jennings, *The Invasion of America: Indians, Colonialism, and the Cant of Conquest* (Chapel Hill: University of North Carolina Press, 1968).

6 Robert E. Park, *Race and Culture* (Glencoe, Ill.: Free Press, 1950), pp. 138, 167.

7 Gunnar Myrdal, *An American Dilemma: The Negro Problem and American Democracy* (New York: Harper, 1944).

8 See the admirably compressed statement by Leonard M. Thompson, "The South African Dilemma," in Louis Hartz (ed.), *The Founding of New Societies* (New York: Harcourt, Brace & World, 1964), pp. 178–218.

9 William Keith Hancock, *Survey of British Commonwealth Affairs,* 2 vols. (London: Oxford University Press, 1937–41), 2(pt. 2):42.

10 See Jeffrey Butler, Robert I. Rotberg, and John Adams, *The Black Homelands of South Africa: The Political and Economic Development of Bophuthatswana and KwaZulu* (Berkeley: University of California Press, 1977).

11 Leonard M. Thompson, *Politics in the Republic of South Africa* (Boston: Little, Brown, 1966). The best recent survey is Robert I. Rotberg, *Suffer the Future: Policy Choices in Southern Africa* (Cambridge, Mass.: Harvard University Press, 1980).

12 Pierre L. Van den Berghe, *Race and Racism* (New York: Wiley, 1967); See also his *Race and Ethnicity: Essays in Comparative Sociology* (New York: Basic Books, 1970). In the vast literature on comparative race relations I have found the following particularly stimulating: H. Hoetinck, *The Two Variants in Caribbean Race Relations* (London: Oxford University Press, 1967); Philip Mason, *Prospero's Magic: Some Thoughts on Class and Race* (London: Oxford University Press, 1962); Leo Kuper, *Race, Class, and Power: Ideology and Revolutionary Change in Plural Societies* (Chicago: Aldine, 1975); and Oliver C. Cox, *Caste, Class and Race* (New York: Doubleday, 1948).

13 See Kenneth P. Vickery, " 'Herrenvolk' Democracy and Egalitarianism in South Africa and the U.S. South," *Comparative Studies in Society and History* 16 (1974):309–28.

14 Stanley M. Elkins, *Slavery: A Problem in American Institutional and Intellectual Life,* 3rd. ed. (1959; Chicago: University of Chicago Press, 1976).

15 "All in all," wrote the founder of the black consciousness movement, who was killed by "persons undetermined" while in police custody in 1977, "the black man has become a shell, a shadow of man, completely defeated, drowning in his own misery, a slave, an ox bearing the yoke of oppression with sheepish timidity . . . The first step is therefore to make the black man come to himself; to pump back life into his empty shell; to infuse him with pride and dignity; to remind him of his complicity in the crime of allowing himself to be misused and therefore letting evil reign supreme in the country of his birth." Steve Biko, *I Write What I Like,* ed. Aelred Stubbs (San Francisco: Harper & Row, 1978), p. 29.

16 Frantz Fanon, *The Wretched of the Earth* (New York: Grove Press, 1963).

17 Edward P. Thompson, *The Making of the English Working Class* (New York: Random House/Vintage Books, 1966), pp. 9–10.

18 Alain Locke, *Race Contacts and Inter-Racial Relations* (Washington: Privately printed, 1916). I owe this reference to Jeffrey Stewart of Tufts University. See also Alain Locke and Bernhard J. Stern (eds.), *When Peoples Meet: A Study in Race and Culture Contacts* (New York: Progressive Education Association, 1942).

19 It is a truism of African colonial history that the lack of color consciousness was an important factor in the slowness with which Af-

ricans often perceived the European threat. See particularly Hilda Kuper, "Colour, Categories, and Colonialism: The Swazi Case," in Lewis Gann and Peter Duignan (eds.), *Colonialism in Africa 1870–1960,* 5 vols. (Cambridge: Cambridge University Press, 1969–), 3:286–309.

20 Fanon, *Wretched of the Earth,* p. 22.

21 See Joel Kovel, *White Racism: A Psychohistory* (New York: Pantheon Books, 1970).

22 "The Government's policy," said Dr. Hendrik Verwoerd in 1961, "is not based on people being inferior but being different." Quoted by Nic J. Rhoodie, *Apartheid and Racial Partnership in Southern Africa* (Cape Town: Academica, 1969), p. 76. Heribert Adam calls the dissociation between segregation and racism "racialism without racism." "The South African Power-Elite," in Adam (ed.), *South Africa: Sociological Perspectives* (London: Oxford University Press, 1971), p. 79. Mr. Adam does not intend to imply that racism has been entirely removed from South Africa.

23 On Gramsci see particularly Quinten Hoare and Geoffrey Smith (eds.), *Selections from the Prison Notebooks* (New York: International Publishers, 1971); John C. Cammett, *Antonio Gramsci and the Origins of Italian Communism* (Stanford: Stanford University Press, 1967); Gwyn Williams, "Concept of Egemonia in the Thought of Antonio Gramsci: Some Notes on Interpretation," *Journal of the History of Ideas* 21 (1960):586–99.

24 See William H. Chafe, *Civilities and Civil Rights: Greensboro, North Carolina, and the Black Struggle for Freedom* (New York: Oxford University Press, 1980).

25 Marc Bloch, *The Historian's Craft* (Manchester: Manchester University Press, 1954).

26 See the opening section of Bloch's *Feudal Society.*

2. CONTEMPORARY PERSPECTIVES

1 James Bryce, *The American Commonwealth,* 2 vols., 3rd ed. rev. (New York: Macmillan, 1910), 2:491. See also Bryce's *The Relations of the Advanced and Backward Races of Mankind* (Oxford: Oxford University Press/Clarendon Press, 1902) and *Race Sentiment as a Factor in History* (London: University of London Press, 1915).

2 Bryce, *American Commonwealth,* 2:524–6.

3 Ibid., p. 547.

4 Ibid., pp. 563–4.

5 James Bryce, *Impressions of South Africa* (London: Macmillan, 1899), p. 347.

6 Ibid., p. 367.

7 C. Vann Woodward, *The Strange Career of Jim Crow*, 3rd ed. (1955; New York: Oxford University Press, 1974), pp. 111–12.

8 See Gustav Spiller, (ed.), *Papers on Inter-Racial Problems Communicated to the First Universal Races Congress* (London: King, 1911).

9 Harry H. Johnston, *The Negro in the New World* (London: Methuen, 1910).

10 Maurice S. Evans, *Black and White in the Southern States: A Study of the Race Problem in the United States from a South African Point of View* (London: Longman, Green, 1915), p. 15.

11 Maurice S. Evans, *Black and White in South East Africa* (London: Longman, 1911), p. 15.

12 Shula Marks, *Reluctant Rebellion: The 1906–8 Disturbances in Natal* (Oxford: Oxford University Press/Clarendon Press, 1970).

13 Evans, *Black and White in South East Africa*, p. 278.

14 Evans, *Black and White in the Southern States*.

15 This was Turner's third visit to the continent, the first two having been to West Africa. See Edwin S. Redkey, *Black Exodus: Black Nationalist and Back-to-Africa Movements, 1890–1910* (New Haven: Yale University Press, 1969). For the larger context of American blacks in South Africa see Clement T. Keto, "Black Americans and South Africa, 1890–1910," *Current Bibliography of African Affairs* 5 (1972): 383–406; Willard B. Gatewood, "Black Americans and the Boer War, 1899–1902," *South Atlantic Quarterly* 75 (1976):226–44; and Harold R. Isaacs, *The New World of Negro Americans* (New York: John Day, 1963). Sylvia M. Jacobs, *The African Nexus: Black American Perspectives on the European Partitioning of Africa, 1880–1920* (Westport, Conn.: Greenwood Press, 1981), p. 143, states mistakenly that Turner went to South Africa in 1892.

16 On the Ethiopian Church see particularly Bengt M. Sundkler, *Bantu Prophets in South Africa*, 2nd ed. (1948; London: Oxford University Press, 1961).

17 On Booth see George Shepperson and Thomas Price, *Independent African: John Chilembwe and the Origins, Setting and Significance of the Nyasaland Native Rising of 1915* (Edinburgh: Edinburgh University Press, 1958), a fascinating and amazingly detailed study of the interaction between Africans and Afro-Americans. See also Martin L. Kilson and Robert I. Rotberg (eds.), *The African Diaspora: Interpretive Essays* (Cambridge, Mass.: Harvard University Press, 1976).

18 *The Voice of Missions*, 1 February 1898.

19 Henry M. Turner, "Will it be Possible for the Negro to Attain, in this Country, unto the American Type of Civilization?" in A. Cromwell Hill and Martin L. Kilson (eds.), *Apropos of Africa: Sentiments of Negro American Leaders on Africa from the 1800s to the 1950s* (London: Frank Cass, 1969), pp. 44–7.

20 *The Voice of Missions,* 1 March 1898.

21 Ibid., 15 April 1898.

22 Levi J. Coppin, *Observations of Persons and Things in South Africa, 1900–1904* (n.p., n.d.).

23 Maynard W. Swanson, "The Sanitation Syndrome: Bubonic Plague and Urban Native Policy in the Cape Colony, 1900–1909," *Journal of African History* 18 (1977):387–410.

24 Coppin, *Observations,* pp. 95–102.

25 Ibid., pp. 44–6.

26 Ibid., pp. 59–60.

27 Peter Walshe, *The Rise of African Nationalism in South Africa* (London: Hurst, 1970), pp. 12–15. See also Walshe's "Black American Thought and African Political Attitudes in South Africa," *Review of Politics* 32 (1970):51–77.

28 Coppin, *Observations,* pp. 189–91.

29 Harry Dean with Sterling North, *The Pedro Gorino: The Adventures of a Negro Sea-Captain in Africa and on the Seven Seas in His Attempts to Found an Ethiopian Empire* (Boston: Houghton Mifflin, 1929).

30 South African Native Affairs Commission (1903–5), 5 vols. (Cape Town: Cape Times, 1904–5), 2:215–30.

31 Ibid., Q. 2667.

32 *The Voice of Missions,* 1 June 1899.

3. RECENT INTERPRETATIONS OF THE ORIGINS OF SEGREGATION IN SOUTH AFRICA

1 The argument that the labor shortage was really a strike is made persuasively by Donald Denoon, "The Transvaal Labour Crisis, 1901–6," *Journal of African History* 7 (1967):481–94.

2 Transvaal Labour Commission, Great Britain, Parliamentary Papers, 1904 [Cd. 1896], 39:501–7.

3 See Stanley Trapido, "Landlord and Tenant in a Colonial Economy: The Transvaal, 1890–1910," *Journal of Southern African Studies* 5 (1978):26–58, and "Reflections on Land, Office and Wealth in the South African Republic," Shula Marks and Anthony Atmore (eds.), *Economy and Society in Pre-Industrial Africa* (London: Longman, 1978).

4 David Welsh, *The Roots of Segregation: Native Policy in Natal, 1845–1910* (Cape Town: Oxford University Press, 1971).

5 See Shula Marks, *Reluctant Rebellion: The 1906–8 Disturbances in Natal* (Oxford: Oxford University Press/Clarendon Press, 1970).

6 Welsh, *Roots of Segregation,* pp. 232–3.

7 Shula Marks, "Natal, the Zulu Royal Family and the Ideology of Segregation," *Journal of Southern African Studies* 4 (1978):172–94.

8 Welsh, *Roots of Segregation,* pp. 208–9.

9 For a very useful, though inevitably already dated, survey of South African historiography see Harrison M. Wright, *The Burden of the Present: Liberal–Radical Controversy over South African History* (London: Phillip, 1977).

10 Martin Legassick, "British Hegemony and the Origins of South Africa, 1901–1914," unpublished seminar paper, Institute of Commonwealth Studies, University of London, 1970; Donald Denoon, " 'Capitalist Influences' and the Transvaal Government during the Crown Colony Period, 1900–1906," *Historical Journal* 2 (1968):301–31.

11 Cornelius W. De Kiewiet, *A History of South Africa, Social & Economic* (Oxford: Oxford University Press/Clarendon Press, 1941).

12 Sir William Molesworth, Minute of 1854, quoted in John W. Cell, "British Colonial Policy in the 1850s," unpublished Ph.D. dissertation, Duke University, 1965, pp. 205–6.

13 John S. Galbraith, *Reluctant Empire: British Policy on the South African Frontier, 1834–1854* (Berkeley: University of California Press, 1963).

14 [Jan Christian Smuts], *A Century of Wrong* (London: Review of Reviews, [1900]).

15 Robert V. Kubicek, *Economic Imperialism in Theory and Practice: The Case of South African Gold Mining Finance, 1886–1914* (Durham, N.C.: Duke University Press, 1979).

16 See Donald Denoon, *A Grand Illusion: The Failure of Imperial Policy in the Transvaal Colony during the Period of Reconstruction, 1900–1905* (London: Longman, 1973).

17 The standard work is Leonard M. Thompson, *The Unification of South Africa, 1902–1910* (Oxford: Oxford University Press/Clarendon Press, 1960).

18 "The mining industry," argues Alan H. Jeeves, "was brought into close association with government not because it was strong, united and able to impose its will but because it was divided in its councils and (at frequent intervals) crippled by destructive competition. For the Randlords, the relationship was rather one of dependence than of domination." "The Administration and Control of Migratory

Labour on the South African Gold-Mines: Capitalism and the State in the Era of Kruger and Milner," in P. L. Bonner (ed.), *Working Papers in Southern African Studies* (Johannesburg: University of the Witwatersrand Press, 1977), pp. 162–3.

19 Thompson, *Unification*, pp. 316–17.

20 In arguing that the abolition of the Cape color franchise was insignificant, Martin Legassick in my view overstates his case that the main lines of segregation had been laid down by the early 1920s. "The Making of South African 'Native Policy', 1903–1923: The Origins of 'Segregation,' " unpublished seminar paper, Institute of Commonwealth Studies, University of London, 1973.

21 See Stanley Trapido's seminal article, "South Africa in a Comparative Study of Industrialization," *Journal of Development Studies* 7 (1971):309–20.

22 See Martin Chanock, *Britain, Rhodesia and South Africa, 1900–45: The Unconsummated Union* (London: Cass, 1977); Ronald Hyam, *The Failure of South African Expansion, 1908–1948* (London: Macmillan, 1972).

23 For recent accounts of South African political history see D. W. Krüger, *The Making of a Nation: A History of the Union of South Africa, 1910–1961* (Johannesburg: Macmillan, 1969); René de Villiers, "Afrikaner Nationalism," in Monica Wilson and Leonard Thompson (eds.), *The Oxford History of South Africa,* 2 vols. (New York: Oxford University Press, 1969–71), 2:365–423; and B. J. Liebenberg, "The Union of South Africa up to the Statute of Westminster, 1910–1931," and "From the Statute of Westminster to the Republic of South Africa, 1931–1961," in C. F. J. Muller, *Five Hundred Years: A History of South Africa* (Pretoria: Academica, 1969), pp. 381–407, 408–39. For an interesting hypothesis about the relationship of Native policy to maturing capitalism after 1948 see Harold Wolpe, "Capitalism and Cheap Labour-Power in South Africa: From Segregation to Apartheid," *Economy and Society* 1 (1972):425–56.

24 On the importance of the unitary model, which enabled northern franchise policies to swamp those of the Cape, see Thompson, *Unification*, pp. 480–3.

25 For standard economic histories see De Kiewiet, *History of South Africa;* D. Hobart Houghton, *The South African Economy,* 4th ed. (Cape Town: Oxford University Press, 1976); and Houghton's "Economic Development, 1865–1965," in Wilson and Thompson (eds.), *Oxford History of South Africa,* 2:1–48.

26 On the origins of the closed-compound system see particularly

Charles van Onselen, *Chibaro: Mine Labour in Southern Rhodesia, 1900–1923* (London: Pluto Press, 1976).

27 "Is the colour bar the greatest stumbling block to the mines being worked profitably?" the manager of the East Rand Proprietary Company was asked by the Low Grade Mines Commission. "No, it is not the greatest stumbling block, but it is the only thing over which we have any control which will enable the mines to continue working. The greatest stumbling block is the poverty of the ore." Quoted by Frederick Johnstone, *Class, Race and Gold: A Study of Class Relations and Racial Discrimination in South Africa* (London: Routledge & Kegan Paul, 1976), p. 125.

28 Francis Wilson, *Labour in the South African Gold Mines, 1911–1969* (Cambridge: Cambridge University Press, 1972), pp. 46–8 and passim.

29 Johnstone, *Class, Race and Gold*, pp. 26–49. See also the standard work by Sheila T. Van der Horst, *Native Labour in South Africa* (London: Oxford University Press, 1942).

30 Johnstone, *Class, Race and Gold*, p. 145.

31 Ibid., p. 182.

32 "The proper course to adopt," insisted Frederick Cresswell of the Labour Party, "was to allow natural causes to operate, and if [South Africa's] natives were not sufficiently enterprising to seek work at the mines, then let the white man's labour be employed." 5 March 1912, Union of South Africa, Parliamentary Debates (collected from *Cape Times*).

33 Great Britain, Parliamentary Papers, 1904 [Cd. 1896], 39:119–36.

34 Johnstone, *Class, Race and Gold*, pp. 49–75. "In fact," concluded the Low Grade Mines Commission of 1920, "as recent incidents in the United States of America have proved – race passion in respect to black and white is so deeply rooted in the human breast that any attempt to prematurely promote the native worker to a position of equality, economically or otherwise with the white worker, is bound to rouse passions." The Commission was presumably referring to the race riot in East St. Louis, Illinois, of 1919.

35 Sheila Patterson, *The Last Trek* (London: Routledge & Kegan Paul, 1957).

36 W. M. Macmillan, *The South African Agrarian Problem and Its Historical Development* (1919; reprint ed., Pretoria: State Library, 1974) and *The Land, the Native, and Unemployment* (Johannesburg: Council of Education, 1924).

37 Carnegie Commission on the Poor Whites, 5 vols. (Stellenbosch: Pro ecclesia-duckkery, 1932); Report of Native Economic Commis-

sion, South African Sessional Papers, U.G. 22 (1932). The Tomlinson Commission of the 1950s urged massive investment; otherwise separate development was doomed. See Summary of the Report of the Commission for the Socio-Economic Development of the Bantu Areas within the Union of South Africa, U.G. 61 (1955).

38 See Henry Slater, "Land, Labour and Capital in Natal: The Natal Land and Colonisation Company, 1860–1948," *Journal of African History* 16 (1975):257–83, and "The Changing Pattern of Economic Relationships in Rural Natal, 1838–1914," in Marks and Atmore (eds.), *Economy and Society,* pp. 148–70.

39 "I am inclined to think," J. W. Sauer of the Cape advised the South African Native Affairs Commission, "that the Natives make rather more out of [the land] than do whites . . . if for no other reason than that the land is divided up into small allotments and a man can easily cultivate the whole of his allotment and it is in his interest to do so, and so the whole becomes cultivated." Quoted by Colin J. Bundy, *The Rise and Fall of the South African Peasantry* (Berkeley: University of California Press, 1979), p. 113. See Robin Palmer and Neil Parsons (eds.), *The Roots of Rural Poverty in Central Africa* (Berkeley: University of California Press, 1977), and Frederick Cooper, "Peasants, Capitalists, and Historians: A Review Article," *Journal of Southern African Studies* 7 (1981):284–314.

40 See Jeffrey Butler, Robert I. Rotberg, and John Adams, *The Black Homelands of South Africa: The Political and Economic Development of Bophuthatswana and KwaZulu* (Berkeley: University of California Press, 1977).

41 Bundy, *South African Peasantry;* Wilson and Thompson (eds.), *Oxford History of South Africa,* 2:49–103, 104–71.

42 Godfrey and Monica Wilson, *The Analysis of Social Change* (Cambridge University Press, 1945).

43 Bundy, *South African Peasantry.*

44 In 1911, for instance, the president of the Transvaal Chamber of Mines explained that "the tendency of the native is to be an agriculturalist, who reluctantly offers himself or one of his family as an industrial worker for just so long as the hut tax can be earned, and expects the industrial demand to expand to give him work when his crops are bad. He cares nothing if industries pine for want of labour when his crops and home-brewed drink are plentiful." He therefore advocated "a policy that would establish that outside of special reserves, the ownership of land must be in the hands of the white race, and that the surplus of young men, instead of squatting on the land in idleness . . . must earn their living by working for a wage . . ."

The government should "do everything to encourage the native to be a wage-earner by extending the policy of splitting into family holdings land now held in the native reserves under tribal tenure." Quoted by Johnstone, *Class, Race and Gold*, p. 127. The Natives Land Act of 1913 would fill this prescription precisely.

45 Bundy, *South African Peasantry*, ch. 7.

46 Ibid.; Francis Wilson, "Farming, 1866–1966," in Wilson and Thompson (eds.), *Oxford History of South Africa*, 2:127–8.

47 "Awakening on Friday morning, June 20, 1913, the South African Native found himself, not actually a slave, but a pariah in the land of his birth." Solomon T. Plaatje, *Native Life in South Africa*, 3rd ed. (New York: The Crisis, [1916]).

48 De Kiewiet, *History of South Africa*, p. 13.

49 See Robin Palmer and Neil Parsons (eds.), *The Roots of Rural Poverty in Central and South Africa* (Berkeley: University of California Press, 1977).

50 The reserves, noted Howard Pim for the Royal Commission on Natural Resources of 1914, were "a sanitorium where they [Natives] can recuperate; if they are disabled they remain there. Their own tribal system keeps them under discipline, and if they become criminals there is not the slightest difficulty in bringing them to justice. All this absolutely without expense to the white community." Quoted by Bundy, *South African Peasantry*, p. 126.

4. THE ORIGINS OF SEGREGATION IN THE AMERICAN SOUTH

1 For the historiography of the Woodward thesis see Joel Williamson (ed.), *The Origins of Segregation* (Lexington, Mass.: Heath, 1968); and C. Vann Woodward, "The Strange Career of a Historical Controversy," *American Counterpoint: Slavery and Racism in the North–South Dialogue* (Boston: Little, Brown, 1964), pp. 234–60.

2 C. Vann Woodward, *The Strange Career of Jim Crow*, 3rd ed. (1955; New York: Oxford University Press, 1974), p. 12. On paternalism see W. E. B. Du Bois, *The Souls of Black Folk* (1903; reprint ed. Greenwich, Conn.: Fawcett, 1961), p. 205, and more generally Eugene D. Genovese's *The Political Economy of Slavery* (New York: Pantheon Books, 1965) and *Roll, Jordan, Roll: The World the Slaves Made* (New York: Pantheon Books, 1974).

3 Charles B. Dew's bibliographical essay in the second edition of C. Vann Woodward, *Origins of the New South, 1877–1913* (Baton Rouge:

Louisiana State University Press, 1971) shows how much of Southern economic history remains virtually uncharted territory. See also Harold D. Woodman's review article, "Sequel to Slavery: The New History Views the Post-Bellum South," *Journal of Southern History* 43 (1977):523–54.

4 Woodward, *American Counterpoint,* pp. 253–4.

5 See Lawrence Goodwyn, *Democratic Promise: The Populist Movement in America* (New York: Oxford University Press, 1976).

6 C. Vann Woodward, *Tom Watson: Agrarian Radical* (New York: Macmillan, 1938).

7 Helen Edmunds, *The Negro and Fusion Politics in North Carolina, 1894–1901* (Chapel Hill: University of North Carolina Press, 1951).

8 American blacks "were fundamentally struggling for integration into American society, for the elimination of segregation of any sort," writes August Meier. "Yet in creating a racial equal rights organization, which many deemed necessary for effective action for these rights and for uplifting Negroes economically and socially, they appeared to be creating a segregated movement in itself, to be fostering the very thing they were attacking." *Negro Thought in America, 1880–1915: Racial Ideologies in the Age of Booker T. Washington* (Ann Arbor: University of Michigan Press, 1963), p. 7.

9 For example, John Blassingame, *The Negro in Black New Orleans, 1860–1880* (Chicago: University of Chicago Press, 1973); August Meier and Elliot Rudwick, "A Strange Chapter in the Career of 'Jim Crow,' " in Meier and Rudwick (eds.), *The Making of Black America,* 2 vols. (New York: Atheneum, 1971), 2:14–19.

10 It is true, argues Williamson, that "material changes in post-Reconstruction Southern society pushed the trenches into areas which had not existed before. This often gave the illusion of basic change, of a breakthrough by the dominant whites in the war of races, whereas, actually, it merely represented the extension of the old attitudinal conflict onto new ground . . . Viewed in relation to the total geography of race relations, the frontier hardly changed." Joel Williamson, *After Slavery: The Negro in South Carolina during Reconstruction, 1861–1877* (Chapel Hill: University of North Carolina Press, 1965), p. 298.

11 Woodward, *Strange Career,* p. 15.

12 See Donald G. Mathews, *Religion in the Old South* (Chicago: University of Chicago Press, 1977).

13 See Howard Rabinowitz, *Race Relations in the Urban South, 1865–1890* (New York: Oxford University Press, 1978).

14 C. Vann Woodward, *Reunion and Reaction: The Compromise of 1877 and the End of Reconstruction* (Boston: Little, Brown, 1951).

15 Woodward, *American Counterpoint,* pp. 258–9.

16 See Chapter 5, this volume.

17 Woodward, *Origins of the New South,* pp. 140–1.

18 On the English industrial revolution see particularly David Landes, "Technological Change and Development in Western Europe, 1750–1914," *Cambridge Economic History of Europe,* 2nd ed. (Cambridge: Cambridge University Press, 1967–), 6 (pt. 1), and *The Unbound Prometheus: Technological Change and Industrial Development in Western Europe from 1750 to the Present* (Cambridge: Cambridge University Press, 1969); Ronald M. Hartwell, *The Industrial Revolution and Economic Growth* (London: Methuen, 1971), and Hartwell (ed.), *The Causes of the Industrial Revolution in England* (New York: Barnes & Noble Books, 1967); and Eric J. Hobsbawm, *The Age of Revolution, 1789–1848* (New York: New American Library, 1962).

19 Edward P. Thompson, *The Making of the English Working Class* (New York: Pantheon Books, 1964), pp. 9–11 and passim.

20 On the language of industrialization see Raymond Williams, *Culture and Society, 1780–1950* (London: Chatto & Windus, 1958).

21 On the ideology of industrialism in England see Harold J. Perkin, *The Origins of Modern English Society, 1780–1880* (London: Routledge & Kegan Paul, 1969), and R. S. Neale, *Class and Ideology in the Nineteenth Century* (London: Routledge & Kegan Paul, 1972).

22 Thomas L. Hodgkin, *Nationalism in Colonial Africa* (London: Muller, 1956).

23 For the huge literature on the economic impact of the Civil War see Woodman, "Sequel to Slavery"; Robert Higgs, *The Transformation of the American Economy, 1865–1914* (New York: Wiley, 1971); and Stanley L. Engerman, "The Economic Impact of the Civil War," in Robert W. Fogel and Engerman (eds.), *The Reinterpretation of American Economic History* (New York: Harper & Row, 1971), pp. 369–79.

24 Robert W. Fogel, *Railroads and American Economic Growth* (Baltimore: Johns Hopkins University Press, 1964).

25 Paul M. Gaston, *The New South Creed: A Study in Southern Mythmaking* (New York: Knopf, 1970).

5. THE SOUTH MAKES SEGREGATION: THE ECONOMIC INTERPRETATION

1 Immanuel Wallerstein, *The Modern World-System: Capitalist Agriculture and the Origins of the European World-Economy in the Sixteenth Century* (New York: Academic Press, 1974).

2 The debate concerning Robert W. Fogel and Stanley L. Engerman, *Time on the Cross*, 2 vols. (Boston: Little, Brown, 1974), has centered mainly on the authors' contentions that slavery was benign. See particularly Herbert Gutman, *Slavery and the Numbers Game: A Critique of Time on the Cross* (Urbana: University of Illinois Press, 1975), and Paul A. David (ed.), *Reckoning with Slavery: A Critical Study in the Quantitative History of American Negro Slavery* (New York: Oxford University Press, 1976). The question of profitability appears to have been conceded.

3 See James H. Street, *The New Revolution in the Cotton Economy: Mechanization and its Consequences* (Chapel Hill: University of North Carolina Press, 1957), and Jay R. Mandle, *The Roots of Black Poverty: The Southern Plantation Economy after the Civil War* (Durham: Duke University Press, 1978).

4 Membership in the planter elite had never been constant, and rates of persistence in the sixties and seventies were much the same as those before the war. Jonathan M. Wiener, *Social Origins of the New South: Alabama, 1860–1885* (Baton Rouge: Louisiana State University Press, 1978), p. 5.

5 For the long debate on the rise of the gentry see Lawrence Stone (ed.), *Social Change and Revolution in England, 1540–1640* (London: Longman, 1965).

6 These paragraphs on credit and marketing are based on an excellent book by Harold D. Woodman, *King Cotton & His Retainers: Financing & Marketing the Cotton Crop of the South, 1800–1925* (Lexington: University of Kentucky Press, 1968).

7 The extensive literature is critically and masterfully surveyed by Harold D. Woodman, "Sequel to Slavery: The New History Views the Post-Bellum South," *Journal of Southern History* 43 (1977):523–54. The optimists are represented by Robert Higgs, *Competition and Coercion: Blacks in the American Economy, 1865–1914* (Cambridge: Cambridge University Press, 1977); Stephen J. DeCanio, *Agriculture in the Postbellum South: The Economics of Production and Supply* (Cambridge, Mass.: MIT Press, 1974); and Joseph D. Reid, who has written several articles, including "Sharecropping as an Understandable Market Response: The Post-Bellum South," *Journal of Economic History* 33 (1973):106–30. See also Steven N. Cheung, *The Theory of Share Tenancy with Special Application to Asian Agriculture and the First Phase of Taiwan Land Reform* (Chicago: University of Chicago Press, 1969). The pessimists include Roger L. Ransom and Richard Sutch, *One Kind of Freedom: The Economic Consequences of Emancipation* (Cambridge: Cambridge University Press, 1977), and

"Sharecropping: Market Response or Mechanism of Race Control?" in David G. Sansing (ed.), *What Was Freedom's Price?* (Jackson: University of Mississippi Press, 1978), pp. 51–92; Mandle, *Roots of Black Poverty;* Gavin Wright, *The Political Economy of the Cotton South: Households, Markets, and Wealth in the Nineteenth Century* (New York: Norton, 1978).

8 See the extensive evidence of hard bargaining in Leon Litwack, *Been in the Storm So Long: The Aftermath of Slavery* (New York: Knopf, 1979), pp. 336 ff.

9 C. Vann Woodward, *Origins of the New South, 1877–1913,* 2nd ed. (1951; Baton Rouge: Louisiana State University Press, 1971), p. 180. "The merchant," he adds, "was only a bucket on an endless chain by which the agricultural well of a tributary region was drained of its flow."

10 Higgs, an optimist, makes this point, but does not draw the pessimistic conclusion. *Competition and Coercion,* pp. 68–9.

11 Charles L. Flynn, "White Land, Black Labor: Property, Ideology and the Political Economy of Late Nineteenth-Century Georgia," unpublished Ph.D. dissertation, Duke University, 1980.

12 The concept was used by earlier writers, such as Charles S. Johnson, *Shadow of the Plantation* (Chicago: University of Chicago Press, 1934), and Arthur F. Raper, *Preface to Peasantry: A Tale of Two Black Belt Counties* (Chapel Hill: University of North Carolina Press, 1936), but it has not been employed in recent debates on sharecropping or populism.

13 See particularly Eric R. Wolf, *Peasants* (Englewood Cliffs, N.J.: Prentice-Hall, 1966), and Teodor Shanin (ed.), *Peasant and Peasant Societies* (Harmondsworth: Penguin Books, 1971).

14 LaWanda Cox, "Tenancy in the United States, 1865–1890: A Consideration of the Validity of the Agricultural Ladder Hypothesis," *Agricultural History* 18 (1944):97–105.

15 See J. Carlyle Sitterson, *Sugar Country: The Cane Sugar Industry in the South, 1753–1950* (Lexington: University of Kentucky Press, 1953).

16 The shift away from the plantation economy began during the 1920s, speeded up in the 1930s, and then accelerated dramatically during and after World War II. The number of tractors per thousand acres of cropland harvested increased in Alabama, for example, from 0.1 in 1920, to 1.1 in 1940, to 8.0 by 1950. The state's black population grew only slightly (from 945,000 to 983,000) between 1930 and 1940, and actually declined (to 980,000) by 1950. Alabama's total rural population rose between 1930 and 1940 from 1.4 million to 1.97

million but then declined to 1.8 million by 1950. See Street, *New Revolution in the Cotton Economy,* and Mandle, *Roots of Black Poverty.*

17 Quoted by Sterling D. Spero and Abram L. Harris, *The Black Worker: The Negro and the Labor Movement* (New York: Columbia University Press, 1931), p. 5.

18 Vernon L. Wharton, *The Negro in Mississippi, 1865–1890* (Chapel Hill: University of North Carolina Press, 1947), p. 121.

19 This is briefly suggested by Theodore Rosengarten (ed.), *All God's Dangers: The Life of Nate Shaw* (New York: Knopf, 1974), p. xvii. I have not been able to find a systematic study.

20 Quoted by Woodward, *Origins,* p. 257.

21 Eugene D. Genovese, *Roll, Jordan, Roll: The World the Slaves Made* (New York: Pantheon Books, 1974), and *In Red and Black: Marxian Explorations in Southern and Afro-American History* (New York: Pantheon Books, 1968).

22 Lawrence Goodwyn, *The Populist Moment: A Short History of the Agrarian Revolt in America* (New York: Oxford University Press, 1978), p. 285; Robert C. McMath, *Populist Vanguard: A History of the Southern Farmers' Alliance* (Chapel Hill: University of North Carolina Press, 1975).

23 See Melton A. McLaurin, *The Knights of Labor in the South* (Westport, Conn.: Greenwood Press, 1978); the important essay by Herbert G. Gutman, "The Negro and the United Mine Workers of America: The Career and Letters of Richard L. Davis and Something of their Meaning, 1890–1900," in Gutman, *Work, Culture, and Society in Industrializing America: Essays in American Working-Class and Social History* (New York: Knopf, 1976), pp. 121–208; and the older but valuable study by Spero and Harris, *Black Worker.*

24 See Sheldon Hackney's interesting article, "Southern Violence," *American Historical Review* 74 (1969):906–25.

25 The standard work on American racism in this period is George M. Fredrickson, *The Black Image in the White Mind: The Debate on Afro-American Character and Destiny, 1871–1914* (New York: Harper & Row, 1971).

26 Woodward, *Origins,* p. 211.

27 J. Fred Rippy (ed.), *F. M. Simmons, Statesman of the New South: Memoirs and Addresses* (Durham: Duke University Press, 1936), pp. 90–1.

28 *The Shaping of Southern Politics: Suffrage Restrictions and the Establishment of the One-Party South, 1880–1910* (New Haven: Yale University Press, 1974), p. 238.

29 On the tobacco industry see Nannie M. Tilley, *The Bright-Tobacco*

Industry, 1860–1929 (Chapel Hill: University of North Carolina Press, 1948), and Robert F. Durden, *The Dukes of Durham, 1865–1929* (Durham: Duke University Press, 1975), pp. 26–55.

30 On differentiation see Neil J. Smelser, *Social Change in the Industrial Revolution: An Application of Theory to the British Cotton Industry* (Chicago: University of Chicago Press, 1959).

31 See Robert D. Ward and William W. Rogers, *Labor Revolt in Alabama: The Great Strike of 1894* (University: University of Alabama Press, 1965).

32 "One of the chief reasons which first induced the company to take up the system," explained a director of the Tennessee Coal, Iron, and Railroad Company, "was the great chance which it seemed to present for overcoming strikes." Quoted by Woodward, *Origins,* p. 4, who also quotes Fletcher Green's assessment that the convict-lease system has "parallel only in the persecution of the Middle Ages or in the prison camps of Nazi Germany." *Origins,* pp. 214–15. Or, one might add, it has a parallel in South Africa, where it still flourishes.

33 Wiener, *Social Origins of the New South,* pp. 162–85.

34 Paul B. Worthman, "Working Class Mobility in Birmingham, Alabama, 1880–1914," in Tamara K. Hareven (ed.), *Anonymous Americans: Explorations in Nineteenth-Century Social History* (Englewood Cliffs, N.J.: Prentice-Hall, 1971). See also Carl V. Harris, *Political Power in Birmingham, 1871–1921* (Knoxville: University of Tennessee Press, 1977).

35 John W. DuBose (ed.), *The Mineral Wealth of Alabama and Birmingham Illustrated* (Birmingham: Green, 1886), pp. 109–15.

36 As of 1918 the Census Bureau listed less than 7,000 black workers in cotton mills throughout the country, out of a total of 359,000. The best recent study is Melton A. McLaurin, *Paternalism and Protest: Southern Cotton Mill Workers and Organized Labor, 1875–1905* (Westport, Conn.: Greenwood Press, 1971). See also Robert S. Smith, *Mill on the Dan: A History of the Dan River Mills, 1882–1950* (Durham: Duke University Press, 1960).

37 Daniel A. Tompkins, *Cotton Mill, Commercial Features: A Textbook for the Use of Textile Schools and Investors* (Charlotte: Privately printed, 1899), p. 37.

38 For example, the Cape moderate, John Merriman, saw in the South's informal job-reservation system a more effective means of maintaining white supremacy than the elimination of the Native franchise. Otherwise, Africans would be "the workers and history tells us that the future is to the workers." This drew from General Smuts

the famous statement that he felt "inclined to shift the intolerable burden of solving that sphinx problem [the Native franchise] to the ampler shoulders and stronger brains of the future." Letters of 4 and 13 March 1906, in W. K. Hancock and Jean van der Poel (eds.), *Selections from the Smuts Papers,* 7 vols. (Cambridge: Cambridge University Press, 1966–73), 2:236–7, 242–3. See also the report of the Transvaal Indigency Commission, 1906–8, TG (1908).

39 When shares were sold in Salisbury, North Carolina, a preacher from Tennessee came and gave "a moral drudging which made the people feel their responsibilities as they had not before, and made them do something for these [poor white] folks." Interview quoted by Broadus Mitchell, *The Rise of Cotton Mills in the South,* Johns Hopkins University Studies in Historical and Political Science, ser. 39, no. 2 (Baltimore, 1921), p. 135.

40 Interviews quoted in ibid., pp. 217–18.

41 See Allen E. Burgess, "Tar Heel Blacks and the New South Dream: The Coleman Manufacturing Company, 1896–1904," unpublished Ph.D. dissertation, Duke University, 1977.

42 Tompkins, *Cotton Mill,* p. 110.

43 McLaurin, *Paternalism and Protest.*

6. THE SOUTH MAKES SEGREGATION: THE SOCIAL INTERPRETATION

1 Most of the literature on the black middle class is negative, in my view unjustifiably so. See particularly E. Franklin Frazier, *Black Bourgeoisie* (New York: Free Press, 1957), and Harold Cruse, *The Crisis of the Negro Intellectual* (New York: Morrow, 1975). How black bourgeoisie are to avoid being bourgeois has never been entirely clear.

2 Richard Wade, *Slavery in the Cities: The South, 1820–1860* (New York: Oxford University Press, 1964). Claudia Goldin questions Wade's incompatibility thesis, on the ground that prices in the city rose relative to those in rural areas, reflecting the high value of urban artisans. She does not question the argument that urban slaves were more difficult to control. See "Urbanization and Slavery: The Issue of Compatibility," in Leo F. Schnore (ed.), *The New Urban History: Quantitative Explorations by American Historians* (Princeton: Princeton University Press, 1975), pp. 231–46. See also the editors' introduction to Blaine A. Brownell and David R. Goldfield (eds.), *The*

City in Southern History: The Growth of Urban Civilization in the South (Port Washington, New York: Kennikat Press, 1977), pp. 5–23.

3 C. Vann Woodward, *The Strange Career of Jim Crow*, 3rd ed. (1955; New York: Oxford University Press, 1974), pp. 12–17.

4 In Alabama, for instance, the percentages of blacks in urban areas (defined as population 2,500 or above) declined from 48.1% in 1890 to 46.5% in 1900, to 40.4% in 1910; in Georgia from 48.1% to 46.5% to 41.7%. U.S. Census Bureau, *Negro Population, 1790–1915* (Washington, D.C.: Government Printing Office, 1918), p. 90.

5 Howard N. Rabinowitz, *Race Relations in the Urban South, 1865–1890* (New York: Oxford University Press, 1978).

6 The classic work that will be familiar to American readers is Nathan Glazer and Daniel P. Moynihan, *Beyond the Melting Pot: The Negroes, Puerto Ricans, Jews, Italians and Irish of New York City* (Cambridge, Mass.: MIT Press, 1963). My own limited exposure has been primarily to the African literature. See for example Peter C. Lloyd, *Africa in Social Change* (Harmondsworth: Penguin Books, 1967), pp. 288–303; Lloyd et al. (eds.), *The City of Ibadan* (Cambridge: Cambridge University Press, 1967); and Phillip H. Gulliver (ed.), *Tradition and Transition in East Africa* (Berkeley: University of California Press, 1969).

7 Woodward, *Strange Career*, pp. 68–9.

8 Paul B. Worthman, "Working Class Mobility in Birmingham, Alabama, 1880–1914," in Tamara K. Hareven (ed.), *Anonymous Americans: Explorations in Nineteenth-Century Social History* (Englewood Cliffs, N.J.: Prentice-Hall, 1971), pp. 172–214. "Because Birmingham was a totally new city in the post–Civil War period," Worthman writes, "with no older stock of rundown shacks and Negro quarters along its alleys, a different pattern of housing arose." It was that of the large ghetto usually associated with Northern cities.

9 Gary Becker, *The Economics of Discrimination*, 2nd ed. (1957; Chicago: University of Chicago Press, 1977); Herbert J. Gans, "The Positive Functions of Poverty," *American Journal of Sociology* 78 (1972):275–89, and *More Equality* (New York: Pantheon Books, 1973).

10 Robert Higgs, *Competition and Coercion: Blacks in the American Economy, 1865–1914* (Cambridge: Cambridge University Press, 1977).

11 Robert Higgs, "Race and Economy in the South, 1890–1950," in Robert Haws (ed.), *The Age of Segregation: Race Relations in the South, 1890–1945* (Jackson: University of Mississippi Press, 1978), p. 99.

12 I was particularly struck by the considerable differences between

contiguous counties examined in Helen P. Wiley, "From Slave to Sharecropper: Changes in Labor Organization in Nash and Edgecombe Counties, North Carolina, 1865–1890," unpublished B.A. thesis, Duke University, 1981.

13 Edward P. Thompson, *The Making of the English Working Class* (New York: Pantheon Books, 1964), p. 211.

14 Harry Boyt, "The Textile Industry: Keel of Southern Industrialization," *Radical America* 6 (1972):4–49.

15 See David C. McClelland, *The Achieving Society* (Princeton: Van Nostrand, 1961).

16 Herbert Blumer, "Industrialisation and Race Relations," in Guy Hunter (ed.), *Industrialisation and Race Relations: A Symposium* (London: Oxford University Press, 1965), pp. 220–53.

17 George B. Tindall, "The Cost of Segregation," in Haws (ed.), *Age of Segregation,* pp. 130–1.

18 C. Vann Woodward, *Origins of the New South, 1877–1913,* (1951; 2nd ed. Baton Rouge: Louisiana State University Press, 1971), p. 317.

19 C. Vann Woodward, *Reunion and Reaction: The Compromise of 1877 and the End of Reconstruction* (Boston: Little, Brown, 1951); see William Gillette, *Retreat from Reconstruction, 1869–1879* (Baton Rouge: Louisiana State University Press, 1979).

20 Paul M. Gaston, *The New South Creed: A Study in Southern Mythmaking* (New York: Knopf, 1970).

21 Woodward, *Origins,* p. 211.

22 See William J. Cooper, *The Conservative Regime: South Carolina, 1877–1890* (Baltimore: Johns Hopkins University Press, 1968).

23 Woodward, *Origins,* p. viii.

24 J. Morgan Kousser, *The Shaping of Southern Politics: Suffrage Restrictions and the Establishment of the One-Party South, 1880–1910* (New Haven: Yale University Press, 1974).

25 Moore and Genovese have also been extremely influential in shaping the perspective of the South African neo-Marxists. See Barrington Moore, *Social Origins of Dictatorship and Democracy: Lord and Peasant in the Making of the Modern World* (Harmondsworth: Penguin Books, 1973); Eugene D. Genovese, *The Political Economy of Slavery* (New York: Pantheon Books, 1965); idem, *The World the Slaveholders Made* (New York: Pantheon Books, 1969); idem, *In Red and Black: Marxian Explorations in Southern and Afro-American History* (New York: Pantheon Books, 1971); and idem, *Roll, Jordan, Roll: The World the Slaves Made* (New York: Random House/Vintage Books, 1976).

26 Jonathan M. Wiener, *Social Origins of the New South: Alabama, 1860–1885* (Baton Rouge: Louisiana State University Press, 1978), ch. 1.

27 J. Carlyle Sitterson, *Sugar Country: The Cane Sugar Industry in the South* (Lexington: University of Kentucky Press, 1953).

28 Dwight B. Billings, *Planters and the Making of a 'New South': Class, Politics, and Development in North Carolina, 1865–1890* (Chapel Hill: University of North Carolina Press, 1979).

29 Lester M. Salamon, "Protest, Politics, and Modernization in the American South: Mississippi as a 'Developing Society,' " unpublished Ph.D. dissertation, Harvard University, 1972.

30 Wiener, *Social Origins of the New South*, ch. 3.

31 J. Carlyle Sitterson, "Business Leaders in post–Civil War North Carolina, 1865–1890," in Sitterson (ed.), *Studies in Southern History* (Chapel Hill: University of North Carolina Press, 1957).

32 See E. Merton Coulter, *George Walton Williams: The Life of a Southern Merchant and Banker, 1820–1903* (Athens, Ga.: Hibriten Press, 1976).

33 Billings, *Planters and the Making of a New South*.

34 Immanuel Wallerstein, *The Modern World-System: Capitalist Agriculture and the Origins of the European World-Economy in the Sixteenth Century* (New York: Academic Press, 1974), esp. ch. 5.

35 See Schlomo Avineri (ed.), *Karl Marx on Colonialism and Modernization* (New York: Doubleday/Anchor Books, 1969), especially pp. 132–9: "The Future Results of British Rule in India," written in 1853.

7. A NOTE ON SOUTHERN MODERATES AND SEGREGATION

1 For this identification of segregation with extreme racism see particularly Idus A. Newby, *Jim Crow's Defense* (Baton Rouge: Louisiana State University Press, 1965), and his useful edited volume, *The Development of Segregationist Thought* (Homewood, Ill.: Dorsey, 1968).

2 John Higham, *Strangers in the Land: Patterns of American Nativism, 1860–1915* (New York: Atheneum, 1970).

3 Ronald Robinson and John Gallagher, *Africa and the Victorians: The Climax of Imperialism in the Dark Continent* (New York: St. Martins Press, 1961), p. 470.

4 Jacques Barzun, *Darwin, Marx, Wagner: Critique of a Heritage* (Boston: Little, Brown, 1941), p. 100. See Richard Hofstadter, *Social*

Darwinism in American Thought, 1860–1915 (Philadelphia: University of Pennsylvania Press, 1944).

5 Gordon A. Craig, *Europe since 1815* (New York: Holt, Rinehart & Winston, 1961), p. 488.

6 On American imperialism see Walter LaFeber, *The New Empire: An Interpretation of American Expansion, 1860–1898* (Ithaca: Cornell University Press, 1963), and Walter A. Williams, *The Roots of the Modern American Empire: A Study of the Growth and Shaping of a Social Consciousness in a Marketplace Society* (New York: Random House, 1969).

7 Speech of Theodore Roosevelt, 1899, quoted in Brian Tierney et al. (eds.), *Great Issues in Western Civilization,* 3rd ed., 2 vols. (New York: Random House, 1976) 2:329. See Bonifacio S. Salamanca, *The Filipino Reaction to American Rule, 1901–1913* (Hamden, Conn.: Shoe String Press, 1969); Peter W. W. Stanley, *A Nation in the Making: The Philippines and the United States, 1899–1921* (Cambridge, Mass.: Harvard University Press, 1974); Willard B. Gatewood, *Black Americans and the White Man's Burden, 1898–1903* (Urbana: University of Illinois Press, 1975); Richard E. Welch, *Response to Imperialism: The United States and the Philippine–American War, 1899–1902* (Chapel Hill: University of North Carolina Press, 1979).

8 On the Turner thesis see Ray A. Billington, *Frederick Jackson Turner* (New York: Oxford University Press, 1973), and *The Genesis of the Frontier Thesis: A Study in Historical Creativity* (San Marino: Huntington Library, 1971); George R. Taylor (ed.), *The Turner Thesis Concerning the Role of the Frontier in American History* (Boston: Heath, 1949).

9 See, for instance, Washington's Address before the Brooklyn Institute of Arts and Sciences, 22 February 1903, in Louis Harlan (ed.), *The Booker T. Washington Papers* (Urbana: University of Illinois Press, 1972–), 7:85–97. On the American Indians see particularly Ruth M. Underhill, *Red Man's America: A History of Indians in the United States* (Chicago: University of Chicago Press, 1971); Wilcomb E. Washburn (comp.), *The American Indian and the United States,* 4 vols. (New York: Random House, 1973); and Virgil J. Vogel (ed.), *This Country Was Ours: A Documentary History of the American Indian* (New York: Harper & Row, 1972).

10 "Normal men do not know that everything is possible." Quoted from David Rousset by Hannah Arendt, *The Origins of Totalitarianism* (New York: Harcourt, Brace, 1951), p. 299.

11 Howard N. Rabinowitz, *Race Relations in the Urban South, 1865–1890* (New York: Oxford University Press, 1978).

12 See *Official Proceedings of the Constitutional Convention of the State of Alabama, 1901,* 4 vols. (Wetumpka: State Printer, 1940). Here I found plenty of vigorous racism, a fair bit of paternalism, and occasionally a forthright statement in favor of equality, but not much of the language of segregation or separate development. The best analysis of this convention is Sheldon Hackney, *Populism to Progressivism in Alabama* (Princeton: Princeton University Press, 1969).

13 R. D. W. Connor and Clarence Poe (eds.), *The Life and Speeches of Charles Brantley Aycock* (New York: Doubleday, Page, 1912), pp. 248–50.

14 The standard work is George M. Fredrickson, *The Black Image in the White Mind: The Debate on the Afro-American Character and Destiny, 1817–1914* (New York: Harper & Row, 1971).

15 Quoted by Joseph F. Steelman, "The Progressive Era in North Carolina," unpublished Ph.D. dissertation, University of North Carolina, Chapel Hill, 1955, pp. 187–8.

16 Edgar Gardner Murphy, *The Basis of Ascendancy* (New York: Longman, 1910), pp. 29–30.

17 Paul M. Gaston, *The New South Creed: A Study in Southern Mythmaking* (New York: Knopf, 1970). On the functionality of liberals see Morton Sosna, *In Search of the Silent South: Southern Liberals and the Race Issue* (New York: Columbia University Press, 1977), and Jack T. Kirby, *Darkness at the Dawning: Race and Reform in the Progressive South* (Philadelphia: Lippincott, 1972).

18 Gaston, *New South Creed,* pp. 148–9. See Henry Grady, *The New South: Writings and Speeches* (Savannah, Ga.: Beehive Press, 1971), and Grady et al., *The South* (Charlotte: Observer, 1910).

19 See Walter H. Page, *The Rebuilding of Old Commonwealths* (New York: Doubleday, Page, 1902).

20 Gaston, *New South Creed,* pp. 219–20.

21 Leon F. Litwack, *Been in the Storm So Long: The Aftermath of Slavery* (New York: Knopf, 1979), ch. 9.

22 See Ronald M. Hartwell, *The Industrial Revolution and Economic Growth* (London: Methuen, 1971); E. G. West, *Education and the Industrial Revolution* (London: Batsford, 1975); John F. C. Harrison, *Learning and Living: A Study in the History of the English Adult Education Movement* (Toronto: University of Toronto Press, 1961).

23 See particularly Jack Greenberg, *Race Relations and American Law* (New York: Columbia University Press, 1959); Robert J. Harris, *The Quest for Equality: The Constitution, Congress, and the Supreme Court* (Baton Rouge: Louisiana State University Press, 1960); Mary

F. Berry, *Black Resistance, White Law: A History of Constitutional Racism in America* (New York: Appleton-Century-Crofts, 1971).

24 See Eric D. Anderson, "Race and Politics in North Carolina, 1872–1901: The 'Black Second' Congressional District," unpublished Ph.D. dissertation, University of Chicago, 1978.

25 Murphy, *Basis of Ascendancy,* pp. 17, 26.

26 Louis Harlan, *Separate and Unequal: Public School Campaigns and Racism in the Southern Seaboard States, 1901–1915* (Chapel Hill: University of North Carolina Press, 1958), pp. 79–80.

27 William E. B. Du Bois, *The Souls of Black Folk* (New York: New American Library, 1969), pp. 79–95.

28 See Kenneth J. King, *Pan-Africanism and Education: A Study of Race Philanthropy and Education in the Southern States of America and East Africa* (Oxford: Oxford University Press/Clarendon Press, 1971), which deals with Jones and the Phelps-Stokes Commission and their attempts to promote industrial education in Africa.

29 *Race Problems of the South* (Richmond: Southern Society, 1900).

8. SOUTH AFRICA MAKES SEGREGATION

1 W. K. Hancock, *Smuts,* 2 vols. (Cambridge: Cambridge University Press, 1962–8), 1:47–51, 253. "Do we want a Constitution which will lead to civil wars as the American Constitution led to," asked Smuts rhetorically? "No, we prefer to follow a different type – that of the British Constitution . . . We must not be prevented in far-off years, from going forward because we have an agreement which cannot be altered. What we want is a supreme national authority to give expression to the national will of South Africa, and the rest is subordinate."

2 Peter Walshe, *The Rise of African Nationalism in South Africa: The African National Congress, 1912–1952* (London: Hurst, 1970), pp. 12–15, 339–40.

3 Quoted by Sarah G. Millin, *The South Africans* (London: Clay, 1926), p. 320.

4 J. H. Oldham and others believed, for example, that an increase in the African population was the only possible long-term solution to the chronic labor shortage in Kenya. See my *By Kenya Possessed: The Correspondence of Norman Leys and J. H. Oldham, 1918–1926* (Chicago: University of Chicago Press, 1976). Kenya now has one of the highest growth rates in the world.

5 South African Native Affairs Commission (1903–5). The report,

without the voluminous proceedings, is published in Great Britain, Parliamentary Papers, 1905 [Cd. 2399].

6 Transvaal Labour Commission, Parliamentary Papers, 1903 [Cd. 1896].

7 On Rhodes's Glen Grey Act (1894) see Colin J. Bundy, *The Rise and Fall of the South African Peasantry* (Berkeley: University of California Press, 1979), pp. 134 ff.

8 See E. J. Berg, "Backward Sloping Labour Supply Functions in Dual Economies – the Africa Case," *Quarterly Journal of Economics* 75 (1961):615–34, and the convincing demolition of the concept by G. Arrighi, "Labour Supplies in Historical Perspective: A Study of the Proletarianization of the African Peasantry in Rhodesia," *Journal of Development Studies* 6 (1970):197–234.

9 On the general problem see Talal Asad (ed.), *Anthropology and the Colonial Encounter* (Atlantic Highlands, N.J.: Humanities Press, 1975). Early South African anthropologists were amateurs, often administrators or missionaries. See for instance Dudley Kidd, *The Essential Kaffir* (London: Black, 1904), and *Kaffir Socialism* (London: Black, 1908). But they were very few. Early South African learned periodicals (e.g., *The South African Journal of Science* and *The South African Quarterly*) contain almost nothing on the Native, although of course South Africans contributed to English periodicals (e.g., *Man, African Affairs, Africa,* and the *International Review of Missions*). Only in the early 1920s, with the appointment of A. R. Radcliffe-Brown to the new chair of anthropology at the University of Cape Town and the establishment of the journal *Bantu Studies* by J. D. Rheinallt Jones did academic anthropologists become established, the most notable being Monica (Hunter) Wilson and Isaac Shapera. Their official patron, improbably enough in view of his distinct lack of interest in Africans, was General Smuts! See his Introduction, for example, to Monica Wilson's classic *Reaction to Conquest: Effects of Contact with Europeans on the Pondo of South Africa* (London: Milford, 1936). The question of the relationship of anthropology to Native policy in South Africa still needs more investigation, but see Martin Legassick, "Race, Industrialization and Social Change in South Africa: The Case of R. F. A. Hoernle," *African Affairs* 75 (1976):224–39.

10 On the frozen proletariat in South Africa see Stanley Trapido, "South Africa in a Comparative Study of Industrialization," *Journal of Development* 7 (1971):309–20. See also Bernard M. Magubane, *The Political Economy of Race and Class in South Africa* (New York: Monthly Review Press, 1979). The excellent book by Marian La-

300 Notes to pp. 205–213

cey, *Working for Boroko: Origins of a Coercive Labour System in South Africa* (Johannesburg: Ravan Press, 1981), which is based on extensive research in previously unused materials gathered by government commissions during the 1920s and 1930s, and which would have enabled me to analyze the making of segregation policy in that period with much more precision, reached me too late to be used.

11 For well-founded theoretical objections to the concept of the tribe, which has been applied indiscriminately to all kinds of political systems and to peoples ranging from a few hundred to the millions, see Elizabeth Colson, "African Society at the Time of the Scramble," in Lewis Gann and Peter Duignan (eds.), *Colonialism in Africa,* 5 vols. (Cambridge: Cambridge University Press, 1969–), 1:27–65.

12 On Mosheshoe see Leonard M. Thompson, *Survival in Two Worlds: Mosheshoe of Lesotho, 1786–1870* (Oxford: Oxford University Press/Clarendon Press, 1975), and Peter Sanders, *Mosheshoe, Chief of the Sotho* (London: Heinemann, 1975).

13 On the role of segregation in British policy in the early twentieth century see Ronald Hyam, *Elgin and Churchill at the Colonial Office, 1905–1908: The Watershed of the Commonwealth* (London: Macmillan, 1968), pp. 588 ff. For recent critical analyses of indirect rule see I. F. Nicolson, *The Administration of Nigeria, 1900–1960* (Oxford: Oxford University Press/Clarendon Press, 1969); John E. Flint, "Nigeria: The Colonial Experience, 1880–1914," in Gann and Duignan, *Colonialism in Africa,* 1:220–60, and "Frederick Lugard: The Making of an Autocrat (1858–1943)," in Gann and Duignan (eds.), *African Proconsuls: European Governors in Africa* (New York: Free Press, 1978), pp. 290–312.

14 South African Native Affairs Commission, Parliamentary Papers, 1905 [Cd. 2399].

15 David Welsh, *The Roots of Segregation: Native Policy in Natal, 1845–1914* (Cape Town: Oxford University Press, 1971), pp. 318 ff.

16 See Martin Legassick's unpublished but widely distributed papers, "The Making of South African 'Native Policy' " and "The Rise of Modern South African Liberalism: Its Assumptions and its Social Base," 1972–3, Institute of Commonwealth Studies, University of London; Paul Rich, "The Agrarian Counter-Revolution in the Transvaal and the Origins of Segregation, 1902–1913," in P. L. Bonner (ed.), *Working Papers in Southern African Studies* (Johannesburg: University of Witwatersrand, 1977), pp. 55–122.

17 On the origins and passage of the Natives Land Act of 1913 see Bundy, *South African Peasantry,* pp. 134–45, 213–16, and Francis Wilson, "Farming, 1866–1966," in Monica Wilson and Leonard

Thompson (eds.), *The Oxford History of South Africa*, 2 vols. (New York: Oxford University Press, 1969–71); 2:127–31. See Stanley Trapido, " 'The Friends of the Natives': Merchants, Peasants and the Political and Ideological Structure of Liberalism in the Cape, 1854–1910," in Shula Marks and Anthony Atmore (eds.), *Economy and Society in Pre-Industrial South Africa* (London: Longman, 1980), pp. 247–74.

18 Legassick, "Modern South African Liberalism."

19 Brookes, Loram, and Pim all initially greeted Hertzog's Native policy with enthusiasm. See Edgar Brookes, *The Political Future of South Africa* (Pretoria: van Schalls, 1927); Howard Pim, "General Hertzog's Smithfield Proposals," *South African Quarterly* 7 (1925–26): 3–6. To some extent their views were based on the understandable though mistaken presumption that, if it were given power and responsibility, insurgent Afrikaner nationalism might mellow. In Loram's view, Hertzog might at least be no worse than Smuts, a judgment that must be seen in the context of the 1920s (notably the Bulhoek and Bondelswarts massacres) rather than that of the 1940s, and that in any case remains open. See Loram to J. H. Oldham, 18 November 1925, Oldham Papers, Edinburgh House, London, Box 1229. The Negrophiles soon became disillusioned with Hertzog, especially during the racist election of 1929. And Dr. D. D. T. Jabavu's *The Segregationist Fallacy and other Papers* (Lovedale: Lovedale Press, 1928) helped turn the tide, for he above all was the "right type of Native." In his Phelps-Stokes lectures, *The Colour Problems of South Africa* (Lovedale: Lovedale Press, 1934), Brookes made a frank recantation. His courageous career speaks for itself.

20 On Afrikaner nationalism see particularly T. Dunbar Moodie, *The Rise of Afrikanerdom: Power, Apartheid, and the Afrikaner Civil Religion* (Berkeley: University of California Press, 1975); Hermann Giliomee, "The Growth of Afrikaner Identity," in Heribert Adam and Giliomee, *Ethnic Power Mobilized: Can South Africa Change?* (New Haven: Yale University Press, 1979), pp. 83–127; René de Villiers, "Afrikaner Nationalism," in Wilson and Thompson (eds.), *Oxford History of South Africa,* 2:365–423; and B. J. Liebenberg, "The Union of South Africa up to the Statute of Westminster, 1910–1931" and "From the Statute of Westminster to the Republic of South Africa, 1931–1961," in C. F. J. Muller (ed.), *Five Hundred Years: A History of South Africa* (Pretoria: Academica, 1969), pp. 381–407, 408–39.

21 See the report of the interview of the African delegation protesting the Land Act with Lewis Harcourt in 1913, in Solomon T. Plaatje, *Native Life in South Africa* (London: King [1916]), pp. 194–5.

22 See Ronald Hyam, *The Failure of South African Expansion, 1908–1948* (London: Macmillan, 1972), and Martin Chanock, *Unconsummated Union: Britain, Rhodesia, and South Africa, 1900–1945* (Manchester: Manchester University Press, 1977).

23 See my Introduction to *By Kenya Possessed*.

24 William Roger Louis, *Great Britain and Germany's Lost Colonies, 1914–1919* (Oxford: Oxford University Press/Clarendon Press, 1967).

25 William Roger Louis, "Colonial Appeasement, 1936–1938," *Revue belge de philologie et d'histoire* 49 (1971):1175–91.

26 Hancock, *Smuts,* 1:211–13; 2:120–1, 207.

27 Arthur S. Cripps, *An Africa for the Africans: A Plea on Behalf of Territorial Segregation Areas and of their Freedom in a South African Colony* (London: Longman, 1927). See also James Henderson (principal of Lovedale), *The Position of the Native in the Social System of South Africa* (Johannesburg: Argus, 1919); Walter Cotton, *Racial Segregation in South Africa: An Appeal* (London: Sheldon Press, 1931); Peter Nielsen, *The Black Man's Place in South Africa* (1922; reprint ed., Westport, Conn.: Negro Universities Press, 1970).

28 Cf. Heribert Adam's aphorism that South Africa has evolved toward "racialism without racism." "The South African Power-Elite," in Adam (ed.), *South Africa: Sociological Perspectives* (London: Oxford University Press, 1971), p. 79.

29 Leys to J. H. Oldham, 14 November 1921, in Cell, *By Kenya Possessed,* p. 204.

30 H. Alan C. Cairns, *Prelude to Imperialism: British Reactions to Central African Society, 1840–1890* (London: Routledge & Kegan Paul, 1965).

31 Shula Marks, "Natal, the Zulu Royal Family and the Ideology of Segregation," *Journal of Southern African Studies* 4 (1978):172–94.

32 Colson, "African Society."

33 Asad, *Anthropology and the Colonial Encounter.*

34 "The White Man's Task," in Jan C. Smuts, *War-Time Speeches* (London: Hodder & Stoughton, 1917), pp. 79–94. Smuts developed the same theme in his Rhodes lectures of 1929 at Oxford: *Africa and Some World Problems* (Oxford: Oxford University Press/Clarendon Press, 1930). Smuts's blind spot is explored succinctly in the review of Hancock's biography of Smuts by Roland Oliver, "Blinkered Genius," *Journal of African History* 9 (1968):491–4.

35 Quoted by Bundy, *South African Peasantry,* p. 242.

36 H. M. Robertson, "150 Years of Economic Contact between Black and White," *South African Journal of Economics* 2 (1934):403–15; 3 (1935):3–25. See Cornelius W. De Kiewiet, *A History of South Africa: Social & Economic* (Oxford: Oxford University Press/Clarendon

Press, 1941), and William Keith Hancock, *Survey of British Common-wealth Affairs,* 2 vols. (London: Oxford University Press, 1937–41), 2(pt. 2). The basic point about an economically unified society had already been made by W. M. Macmillan, *Complex South Africa* (London: Faber & Faber, 1930).

37 For a recent formulation see D. Hobart Houghton, "Economic Development, 1865–1965," Oxford History of South Africa, 2:1–42.

38 Legassick, "Modern South African Liberalism."

39 Hancock, *Survey,* 2(pt. 2):15.

9. CONCLUSION: REACTIONS TO SEGREGATION

1 See Heribert Adam, *Modernizing Racial Domination: South Africa's Political Dynamics* (Berkeley: University of California Press, 1971).

2 John Merriman to Jan C. Smuts, 4 March 1906, in W. K. Hancock and Jean van der Poel (eds.), *Selections from the Smuts Papers,* 7 vols. (Cambridge: Cambridge University Press, 1966–73), 2:236–7.

3 Stanley M. Elkins, *Slavery: A Problem in American Institutional Life,* 3rd ed. (1959; Chicago: University of Chicago Press, 1976); Ann J. Lane (ed.), *The Debate over Slavery: Stanley Elkins and His Critics* (Urbana: University of Illinois Press, 1971).

4 See Abram Kardiner and Lionel Ovesry, *The Mark of Oppression: A Psychological Study of the American Negro* (New York: Mentor, 1951).

5 Eugene Genovese, *Roll, Jordan, Roll: The World the Slaves Made* (New York: Random House/Vintage Books, 1976); John W. Blassingame, *The Slave Community: Plantation Life in the Antebellum South* (New York: Oxford University Press, 1972).

6 Thomas Alexander and Samuel Sillen, *Racism and Psychiatry* (New York: Brunner/Mazel, 1972), p. 89. See Jacqueline J. Jackson, "Black Women in a Racist Society," in Charles V. Willie et al. (eds.), *Racism and Mental Health* (Pittsburgh: University of Pittsburgh Press, 1973), pp. 185–268, and Gerda Lerner (ed.), *Black Women in White America: A Documentary History* (New York: Pantheon Books, 1972).

7 Leon F. Litwack, *Been in the Storm So Long: The Aftermath of Slavery* (New York: Knopf, 1979), pp. 229–47 and passim.

8 See Herbert G. Gutman, *The Black Family in Slavery and Freedom, 1750–1925* (New York: Pantheon Books, 1976). Jacqueline J. Jackson, "Black Women in a Racist Society," points out that the single-parent, mother-dominated family was only one of the types recognized by E. Frazier's classic *The Negro Family in the United States* (Chicago: University of Chicago Press, 1939). On slave revolts see particularly Herbert Aptheker, *American Negro Slave Revolts* (New

York: Columbia University Press, 1943), and Eugene Genovese, *From Rebellion to Revolution: Afro-American Slave Revolts in the Making of the Modern World* (Baton Rouge: Louisiana State University Press, 1979).

9 Benjamin E. Mays, *Born to Rebel* (New York: Scribner, 1971), p. 1.

10 Walter White, *A Man Called White: The Autobiography of Walter White* (Bloomington: Indiana University Press, 1948), ch. 1.

11 Ellen Tarry, *The Third Door: The Autobiography of an Amrican Negro Woman* (New York: McKay, 1955), p. 62.

12 Mays, *Born to Rebel*, p. 22.

13 Robert Coles, *Children of Crisis*, 5 vols. (Boston: Little, Brown, 1964–), 1:66–7.

14 Mays, *Born to Rebel*, pp. 25–6.

15 Coles, *Children of Crisis*, 1.

16 Mays, *Born to Rebel*, pp. 25–6.

17 *Ibid.*, p. 67.

18 Zora Neale Hurston, *Dust Tracks on a Road: An Autobiography* (Philadelphia: Lippincott, 1942), p. 102.

19 Richard Wright, *Black Boy: A Record of Childhood and Youth* (New York: Harper, 1937), and *American Hunger* (New York: Harper & Row, 1977).

20 Eugene Brody, "Social Conflict and Schizophrenic Behavior in Young Adult Negro Males," *Psychiatry* 24 (1961):337–46; Morton Kramer, Beatrice M. Rosen, and Ernest M. Willie, "Definitions and Distributions of Mental Disorders in a Racist Society," in Willie et al. (eds.), *Racism and Mental Health*, pp. 423–6. See also Herbert Hendin, *Black Suicide* (New York: Basic Books, 1969).

21 I owe this point to discussions with Sherman James of the School of Public Health, University of North Carolina, Chapel Hill, who pointed out to me that the subject of racism and epidemiology is a minefield.

22 Kenneth B. Clark, *Dark Ghetto: Dilemmas of Social Power* (New York: Harper & Row, 1965), p. 81.

23 Among autobiographies see particularly Albert Luthuli, *Let My People Go* (New York: McGraw-Hill, 1962); Ezekiel Mphahlele, *Down Second Avenue* (London: Faber & Faber, 1959); Bloke Modisane, *Blame Me On History* (Southampton: Thames & Hudson, 1963); Lewis Nkosi, *Home and Exile* (London: Longman, 1965); Naboth Mokgatle, *The Autobiography of an Unknown South African* (Berkeley: University of California Press, 1971). See also Carol Hermer (ed.), *The Diary of Maria Tholo* (Johannesburg: Ravan Press, 1980),

a fascinating insight into the mind and life of an urban middle-class African woman during the children's revolt of 1976.

24 See Henry Lever, *South African Society* (Johannesburg: Bell, 1978), ch. 9 and 10; S. P. Cilliers, *The Coloureds of South Africa: A Factual Survey* (Cape Town: Banier, 1963); James Midgley et al., *Crime and Punishment in South Africa* (Johannesburg: McGraw-Hill, 1975).

25 Peter Lambley, *The Psychology of Apartheid* (London: Secker & Warburg, 1980). See I. D. Macrone, "Psychological Factors Affecting the Attitudes of White to Black in South Africa," in Henry Lever (ed.), *Readings in South African Society* (Johannesburg: Ball, 1978), pp. 74–80; Stanley J. Morse and Christopher Orpen (eds.), *Contemporary South Africa: Social Psychological Perspectives* (Cape Town: Juta, 1975). For recent reviews of the literature of mental health in South Africa see E. Toher, "Mental Illness in the White and Bantu Populations of South Africa," *American Journal of Psychiatry* 123 (1966): 55–65; and Silvano Ariete and Gerard Chrzanowski (eds.), *New Dimensions in Psychiatry: A World View*, 2 vols. (New York: Wiley, 1977), 1:409–27, 2:179–92.

26 Noel C. Manganyi, *Being-Black-in-the-World* (Johannesburg: SPRO-CAS/RAVAN, 1973); *Alienation and the Body in Racist Society: A Study of the Society that Invented Soweto* (New York: NOK, 1977).

27 Fanon's most relevant work is *Black Skin, White Mask* (New York: Grove Press, 1967).

28 Lambley, *Psychology of Apartheid*. See also David Mechanic, "Apartheid Medicine," *Society* 10 (1973):36–44.

29 For a recent survey see Bruce P. and Barbara Snell Dohrenwend, "Social and Cultural Influences on Psychopathology," *Annual Review of Psychology* 25 (1974):417–52. See also W. Z. Conco, "The African Bantu Traditional Practice of Medicine: Some Preliminary Observations," Z. A. Ademuwagun et al. (eds.), *African Therapeutic Systems* (Waltham, Mass.: African Studies Association, 1979). See also Michel Foucault, *Madness and Civilization: A History of Insanity in the Age of Reason* (New York: Pantheon Books, 1965).

30 M. J. Field, *Search for Security: An Ethno-psychiatric Study of Rural Ghana* (Evanston: Northwestern University Press, 1960).

31 Edward P. Thompson, *The Making of the English Working Class* (New York: Pantheon Books, 1964); Eugene Genovese, *Roll, Jordan, Roll;* Barrington Moore, *Injustice: The Social Basis of Obedience and Revolt* (White Plains: Sharpe, 1978).

32 Moore, *Injustice,* pp. 438 and passim.

33 Richard Wright, *Native Son* (New York: Harper, 1940), p. 330.

34 See Joel Williamson, *New People: Miscegenation and Mulattoes in the United States* (New York: Free Press, 1980).

35 Leonard M. Thompson, *The Unification of South Africa, 1902–1910* (Oxford: Oxford University Press/Clarendon Press, 1960).

36 Gunnar Myrdal, *An American Dilemma: The Negro Problem and American Democracy* (New York: Harper, 1944).

37 *Malcolm X Speaks* (New York: Grove Press, 1965), p. 33.

38 Donald Woods, *Biko* (New York: Paddington, 1978).

39 See particularly C. Crane Brinton, *The Anatomy of Revolution* (New York: Norton, 1938), and Chalmers A. Johnson, *Revolution and the Social System* (Stanford: Hoover Institution, 1964).

40 Moore, *Injustice*, p. 464.

41 The literature on African resistance is voluminous. See particularly Robert I. Rotberg and Ali Mazrui (eds.), *Protest and Power in Black Africa* (New York: Oxford University Press, 1970), and Terence O. Ranger, "African Resistance to the Imposition of Colonial Rule in East and Central Africa," in Lewis Gann and Peter Duignan (eds.), *Colonialism in Africa,* 5 vols. (Cambridge: Cambridge University Press, 1969–), 1:293–324.

42 Charles W. Chesnutt, *The Marrow of Tradition* (1901; Ann Arbor: University of Michigan Press, 1969), pp. 281–4.

43 See George S. Mwase, *Strike a Blow and Die: A Narrative of Race Relations in Central Africa,* ed. Robert I. Rotberg (Cambridge, Mass.: Harvard University Press, 1967); George Shepperson and Thomas Price, *Independent African: John Chilembwe and the Origins, Setting, and Significance of the Nyasaland Native Rising of 1915* (Edinburgh: Edinburgh University Press, 1958).

44 On Gandhi in South Africa see the brilliant chapter in W. K. Hancock, *Smuts,* 2 vols. (Cambridge: Cambridge University Press, 1966–8), 1:309–47. Mohandas K. Gandhi's relevant writings are *An Autobiography: The Story of My Experiments with Truth* (Boston: Beacon Press, 1957), and *Satyagraha in South Africa* (Madras: Ganesan, 1928). See also Robert A. Huttenback, *Gandhi in South Africa: British Imperialism and the Indian Question, 1860–1914* (Ithaca, N.Y.: Cornell University Press, 1971). Very helpful on the Indian period in Gandhi's life are Erik H. Erikson, *Gandhi's Truth on the Origins of Militant Non-Violence* (New York: Norton, 1969); Ravinder Kumar (ed.), *Essays on Gandhian Politics: The Rowlatt Satyagraha of 1919* (Oxford: Oxford University Press/Clarendon Press, 1971); and two books by Judith M. Brown, *Gandhi's Rise to Power: Indian Politics, 1915–1922* (Cambridge: Cambridge University Press, 1972), and *Gandhi and*

Civil Disobedience: The Mahatma in Indian Politics, 1928–1934 (Cambridge: Cambridge University Press, 1977).

45 Hancock, *Smuts,* 1:329.

46 Ibid., 1:337–8.

47 See August Meier, *Negro Thought in America, 1880–1915: Racial Ideologies in the Age of Booker T. Washington* (Ann Arbor: University of Michigan Press, 1963); Earl E. Thorp, *The Mind of the Negro: An Intellectual History of Afro-Americans* (Westport, Conn.: Negro Universities Press, 1970.

48 Louis R. Harlan, *Booker T. Washington: The Making of a Black Leader, 1856–1901* (New York: Oxford University Press, 1972); Harlan (ed.), *The Booker T. Washington Papers* (Urbana: University of Illinois Press, 1972–).

49 Stokely Carmichael and Charles V. Hamilton, *Black Power: The Politics of Liberation in America* (New York: Random House, 1967).

50 Biographies include Francis L. Broderick, *W. E. B. Du Bois: Negro Leader in a Time of Crisis* (Stanford: Stanford University Press, 1959), and Elliott M. Rudwick, *W. E. B. Du Bois: Propagandist of the Negro Protest* (New York: Atheneum, 1968). The essays and autobiographical writings are the best guide. See *Souls of Black Folk* (1903; reprint ed., Greenwich: Fawcett, 1961). *Darkwater* (New York: Harcourt, Brace, 1920); *Dusk of Dawn* (1940; reprint ed., New York: Schocken, 1968); and *Autobiography* (New York: International Publishers, 1968). Compared with the Booker T. Washington project, the Du Bois *Correspondence,* ed. Herbert Aptheker, 3 vols. (Amherst: University of Massachusetts Press, 1973–) is underfinanced and disappointingly thin.

51 Amy Jacques-Garvey (ed.), *Philosophy and Opinions of Marcus* Garvey (1923; reprint ed., London: Cass, 1957); Edmund Cronon, *Black Moses: The Story of Marcus Garvey and the Universal Negro Improvement Association* (Madison: University of Wisconsin Press, 1969); Tony Martin, *Race First: The Ideological and Organizational Struggles of Marcus Garvey and the Universal Negro Improvement Association* (Westport, Conn.: Greenwood Press, 1976).

52 Du Bois, *Dusk of Dawn,* pp. 277–8.

53 Joseph W. Holley, *You Can't Build a Chimney from the Top: The South through the Eyes of a Negro Educator* (New York: William-Frederick, 1948), pp. 60, 87–8.

54 William J. Edwards, *Twenty-Five Years in the Black Belt* (Boston: Cornhill, 1918), pp. 40–1. See Theodore Rosengarten (ed.), *All God's Dangers: The Life of Nate Shaw* (New York: Avon Books, 1974).

55 Thomas L. Hodgkin, *Nationalism in Colonial Africa* (London: Muller, 1956).

56 Norman Crockett, *The Black Towns* (Lawrence: Regents Press of Kansas, 1979).

57 On the period of conquest see Leonard M. Thompson, "The Subjection of the African Chiefdoms, 1870–1898," in Monica Wilson and Leonard M. Thompson (eds.), *The Oxford History of South Africa*, 2 vols. (New York: Oxford University Press, 1969–71), 2:245–88; Donald R. Morris, *The Washing of the Spears* (New York: Simon & Schuster, 1965).

58 See Leo Kuper, *An African Bourgeoisie: Race, Class, and Politics in South Africa* (New Haven: Yale University Press, 1965), and Mia Brandel-Syrier, *Reeftown Elite: A Study of Social Mobility in a Modern African Community on the Reef* (London: Routledge & Kegan Paul, 1971).

59 For the West African comparison see John E. Flint, "Nigeria: the Colonial Experience from 1880–1914," in Gann and Duignan, *Colonialism in Africa*, 1:220–60.

60 "Questions Affecting the Natives and Coloured Peoples Resident in British South Africa," in Thomas Karis and Gwendolen Carter (eds.), *From Protest to Challenge: A Documentary History of African Politics in South Africa, 1882–1964*, 4 vols. (Stanford: Hoover Institution Press, 1972–7) 1:18–29.

61 The standard accounts are Peter Walshe, *The Rise of African Nationalism in South Africa: The African National Congress, 1912–1952* (London: Hurst, 1970); Leo Kuper, "African Nationalism in South Africa, 1910–1964," in Wilson and Thompson (eds.), *Oxford History of South Africa*, 2:424–76; and Gail M. Gerhart, *Black Power in South Africa: The Evolution of an Ideology* (Berkeley: University of California Press, 1978). See Mary Benson, *South Africa: The Struggle for a Birthright* (Harmondsworth: Penguin Books, 1966), and Edward Roux, *Time Longer than Rope: A History of the Black Man's Struggle for Freedom in South Africa* (1948; reprint ed., Madison: University of Wisconsin Press, 1964).

62 See the extensive transcriptions from police reports in Frederick A. Johnstone, *Class, Race, and Gold: A Study of Class Relations and Racial Discrimination in South Africa* (London: Routledge & Kegan Paul, 1976), ch. 4.

63 See Clements Kadalie, *My Life and the ICU: The Autobiography of a Black Trade Unionist in South Africa,* ed. Stanley Trapido (London: Frank Cass, 1970).

64 Report of Proceedings of Annual Conference of African National

Congress, January 1926, in Karis and Carter, *Protest to Challenge,* 1:299–302.

65 Jan C. Smuts, *The Basis of Trusteeship in African Native Policy* (Cape Town: Institute of Race Relations, 1942).

66 See Shula Marks, "The Ambiguities of Dependence: John L. Dube of Natal," *Journal of Southern African Studies* 1 (1975):162–80.

67 Karis and Carter, *Protest to Challenge,* 1:84–5.

68 D. D. T. Jabavu, *The Segregationist Fallacy and other Papers* (Lovedale: Lovedale Institution Press, 1928).

69 Quoted from *Cape Times,* July 1933, by Walshe, *Rise of African Nationalism,* p. 234.

70 For the later period see Leo Kuper, *Passive Resistance in South Africa* (London: Cape, 1956); Gerhart, *Black Power;* and Karis and Carter, *Protest to Challenge.*

71 Du Bois, *Dusk of Dawn,* ch. 7. See Joel Williamson, "W. E. B. Du Bois as a Hegelian," in David G. Sansing (ed.), *What Was Freedom's Price?* (Jackson: University of Mississippi Press, 1978), pp. 21–49.

72 Aptheker, ed., *Correspondence,* 1:153.

Index

311